THE LIVING GOD
AND THE FULLNESS
OF LIFE

Jürgen Moltmann

THE LIVING GOD
AND THE FULLNESS
OF LIFE

Translated by Margaret Kohl

WESTMINSTER
JOHN KNOX PRESS
LOUISVILLE • KENTUCKY

Translated by Margaret Kohl from the German *Der lebendige Gott und die Fülle des Lebens*, published by Gütersloher Verlagshaus in 2014.

English translation published 2015 by World Council of Churches, Geneva. Published in North America by Westminster John Knox Press.

16 17 18 19 20 21 22 23 24—10 9 8 7 6 5 4 3 2

Unless otherwise indicated, Scripture quotations are from the New Revised Standard Version Bible, © copyright 1989 by the Division of Christian Education of the National Council of the Churches of Christ in the USA. Used by permission.

Book design and typesetting: Michelle Cook / 4 Seasons Book Design
Cover design by Marc Whitaker / MTWdesign.net

Library of Congress Cataloging-in-Publication Data

Names: Moltmann, Jürgen.
Title: The living God and the fullness of life / Jürgen Moltmann ; translated by Margaret Kohl.
Other titles: Lebendige Gott und die Fülle des Lebens. English
Description: Louisville, KY : Westminster John Knox Press, 2015. | Includes bibliographical references.
Identifiers: LCCN 2015033890 | ISBN 9780664261610 (alk. paper)
Subjects: LCSH: Theological anthropology. | Christian life. | God (Christianity)
Classification: LCC BT701.3 .M6513 2015 | DDC 233--dc23 LC record available at http://lccn.loc.gov/2015033890

♾ The paper used in this publication meets the minimum requirements of the American National Standard for Information Sciences—Permanence of Paper for Printed Library Materials, ANSI Z39.48-1992.

Most Westminster John Knox Press books are available at special quantity discounts when purchased in bulk by corporations, organizations, and special-interest groups. For more information, please e-mail SpecialSales@wjkbooks.com.

Contents

Preface

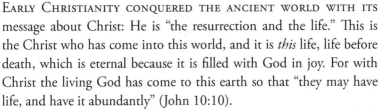

EARLY CHRISTIANITY CONQUERED THE ANCIENT WORLD WITH ITS message about Christ: He is "the resurrection and the life." This is the Christ who has come into this world, and it is *this* life, life before death, which is eternal because it is filled with God in joy. For with Christ the living God has come to this earth so that "they may have life, and have it abundantly" (John 10:10).

This book is meant to be a reminder of the living force that the message of Christ as "the resurrection and the life" set free among the early Christians, the force that enabled the new beginnings and the change that allowed men and women to create what had hitherto been unknown. I believe that this force can unfold in the modern world, too, and that it holds within itself the fullness of life for which many people today are yearning. The modern world takes its bearings from humanistic and materialistic concepts of life. And what men and women experience there is a diminished life. A life that has forgotten God is a life without transcendence, a life without any light shed from above. There is so much unlived, unloved, even sick life that has failed and is lived without any point. Believers, lovers, and the hopeful take their bearings from the living God and, in their closeness to God, experience life in its fullness.

A short time ago my Italian publisher and friend P. Rosino Gibellini introduced me as a theologian "who loves life." I believe that all Christians, and especially the theologians among them, love life, "this one, eternal glowing life," as Friedrich Hölderlin described it in his *Hyperion*. But at the same time I know what Gibellini meant.

From early on, my spirituality took its stamp from Dietrich Bonhoeffer and his perception of Christianity's "profound this-worldliness," in which "the awareness of death and resurrection is always present."[1] Bonhoeffer's letters from prison first appeared in 1951, and for years were for me something like a devotional handbook.

My personal life was also deeply marked by Christoph Blumhardt, his hope for the kingdom of God, and his love for the earth. Blumhardt's addresses, sermons, speeches, and letters are for me something like a breviary for the soul and a treasury for the searching theological mind.

During the last 29 years, a "theology of life" has been sought by many people and from very different sides. Latin American liberation theology expanded into a kingdom-of-God theology (Gustavo Gutiérrez); in Geneva the World Council of Churches put forward a programme for the theology of life; in Korea, Presbyterian Christians founded an institute for the theology of life; in Rome, in his encyclical *Dominum et vivificantem* of 18 May 1986, Pope John Paul II called for a spirituality embracing body and soul. Today the oldest and the youngest churches, the Orthodox and the Pentecostal ones, are coming to meet each other in the passionate sanctification of earthly life. The theological approaches are as varied as life itself, but fundamentally they all come down to the same thing, the same impulse: Christ's resurrection from the dead and the appearance of the divine life in him. If it were not for this experience on the part of the women and the disciples, we would know nothing about Jesus, and there would be no Christian faith. But with Christ's resurrection, the horizon of the future, which is otherwise darkened today by terrorism, nuclear threat, or environmental catastrophe, becomes light. With that, a new light is cast on the past and the fields of the dead. With that, a life enters the present, which cannot be sufficiently loved and enjoyed. "This life was revealed and we have seen and testify to it, and declare to you the eternal life that was with the Father and was revealed to us" (1 John 1:2). What I wish to do is to present a transcendence that does not suppress and alienate our present life but that liberates and gives life a transcendence from which we do not need to turn away, but that fills us with the joy of life.

With this contribution to a theology of life, I am continuing what I began in 1991 with *The Spirit of Life* (ET 1992) and supplemented in 1997 with *The Source of Life: The Holy Spirit and the Theology of Life* (ET 1997). I have taken up ideas that I already expressed earlier and have developed them further. I have gathered together previous experiences and insights about the fullness of life, and am setting them in the new context of this book.

Part One is therefore concerned to understand what the Bible means by "the living God" and to free the God of Israel and Jesus Christ from the imprisonment of metaphysical definitions, which are due to Greek philosophy and the religious Enlightenment. Can God neither move nor be moved, and be therefore *immutable*? Is God unable to suffer, so is apathetic and *impassible*? Is God "the all-determining reality," and hence "the Almighty"? Or does God have power over Godself, and thereby also can withdraw in order to concede freedom to those whom God has created? Is God "one" God, or is the application of numbers such as one or three in itself a desanctification of God's name?

Part Two has to do with the unfolding of human life in the life of God. How does human life flourish in God's wide spaces and future times? My aim is to show this flourishing from the development of human life in the joy of God, in the love of God, in the broad space of God's freedom, in the spirituality of the senses, and in the productive imaginative power of thinking that crosses frontiers. The vista at the end is based on a saying of the great Athanasius that I first came across in the context of the Taizé community: "The risen Christ makes of life a never-ending festival." That is also the place where, with the young Ernst Bloch, we can discover "truth as prayer," and where we may end with the praise and adoration of the saints.

With regard to the style: this is not a technical book nor an article in an encyclopedia, but neither is it a handbook. I have tried to write comprehensibly for theologians and nontheologians and had in view both those who enjoy thinking theologically and those who have not yet tried to do so.

Introduction

The Diminished Life
of the Modern World

THE MODERN WORLD TAKES ITS BEARINGS FROM HUMANISTIC AND naturalistic concepts of life, and in so doing, what it experiences is a diminished life. Christian life takes its bearings from "the living God," and in doing so, it experiences the fullness of life. But:

> What is life?
> What is fulfilled life?
> What is eternal life?

Modern life proceeded not from religion, but from the criticism of religion. In all criticism of religion not only is something won, but something is lost as well. In Western criticism of religion, what was gained was the new value given to life in this world; what were lost were the transcendent spaces in which this life moves. But in every criticism of religion, the religion criticized remains as the negative pole. We shall look at this fact as it emerges in the different modern worlds. We then shall first describe the religiously "self-sufficient" humanist (whom Gotthold Ephraim Lessing put forward as being the enlightened contemporary in the modern world), and, second, the atheistically "reduced" Ludwig Feuerbach, as well as the naturalistic and economic reductionism that followed, our aim being to bring out, in contrast, the riches of a life lived in God here and now.

The Many Modern Worlds

The modern world is not a single unified entity, because its origins are very varied—in France and Europe's Catholic countries, in the English-speaking countries, in Germany, and in the Scandinavian counties. It is superficial and levels these differences down to talk about "the secular world" or about a general "secularization" in the modern world of what had earlier been religious. The word *secularization* originally meant the secularization of the church's property. But this never took place at all in England, the United States, or Scandinavia. So, from the religious point of view I shall distinguish between "laicizing" modernity, "free-church" modernity, and "secularized" modernity.

Laicizing modernity

Laicizing modernity originated in the French Revolution.[1] Its negative image of religion was a reaction to the feudal and clerical dominance of the Roman Catholic Church in French politics and public life. Cardinals Richelieu and Mazarin were the creators of French absolutism. After the 1685 abolition of the toleration granted under the 1598 Edict of Nantes, the Protestant Huguenots were banished and a unified Catholic state was established: *une foi—un loi—un roi* ("one faith, one law, one king").

Consequently, the democratic principles of the bourgeois revolution—*liberté, egalité, fraternité*— could only be established by way of anticlerical laicism. The clergy belonging to the Roman Catholic Church had to be excluded from politics and public life. Theology had no place among the disciplines taught at the state universities. There was no longer any state religion. In this way religious liberty was achieved, though in a negative sense. But laicism also stabilized clericalism in the Roman Catholic Church and replaced the absolute centralism that had obtained in France.

"Free-church" modernity

"Free-church" modernity grew out of the revolutions in the English-speaking countries.[2] Its negative image was Henry VIII's state church in England. But there it was not the church that dominated the state; it was the state that laid down what the church had to believe. It was against this that the free-church resistance of the "dissenters" came into being, the resistance of the Quakers and Baptists. They were repressed, and emigrated to the New England colonies so that they could live out their faith without state tutelage.[3] Here what was definitive was "soul liberty"—Roger Williams's motto from 1638 onwards in the first Baptist church in America, in Providence, Rhode Island. The state has to keep out of the churches, because it understands nothing about religion. It has to dispense with a state religion so that, as a covenant of free citizens, it can regulate the common good in accordance with the U.S. Constitution and the human rights laid down in the Declaration of Independence of 1776. Here the reason given for the thesis that "there is no state church" was not laicism; it was based on the freedom of the churches themselves. The modern Protestant world was shaped by religious liberty in its positive, not its negative, sense. Theology was not excluded from the scholarly community. The divinity schools became, rather, the nuclei of private universities independent of the state. But the beginnings of a civil religion were, nevertheless, continually part of the political ideology of the United States, because the United States was linked from its beginnings with the messianic vision of a "new world order": *novus ordo seclorum* are words that appear on every U.S. one-dollar note.

Secularized modernity

In the German-speaking countries, the French Revolution and the new Napoleonic order led to a juridical "secularization," that is, to the state's appropriation of church property. Ever since, Germany has been characterized by a "secularized modernity." This was also a humanistic response on the part of the Enlightenment to the horrors of the Thirty Years' War, which was interpreted as a war between the religions. In 1648 the Peace of Westphalia ensured the peace of the German states on the basis of the principle *cuius regio, eius religio*— the religion of the people had to conform to the religion of the ruler. Only the right to emigrate was left open. The German states were ruled as small units: one ruling prince, one state religion, one state university, one state law, and often one state currency as well. The Protestant churches were state churches but not church states, like the Roman Catholic ones. Consequently, they were not much affected by modern "secularization." "Secularization" seems to be mainly a Roman Catholic problem. Secularization presupposes the distinction between church and state. Consequently, in the Scandinavian state churches it never existed at all. The state had already appropriated church property during the Reformation period. But when in 1815 the king of Württemberg acquired Catholic Upper Swabia in addition to Protestant Württemberg, he established a Catholic theological faculty at his own University of Tübingen, in order to meet adequately the religious needs of his subjects. Today the government in Baden-Württemberg has established an Islamic theological institute in Tübingen in addition to the two faculties for Christian theology, in order to meet adequately the new religious conditions of a religiously plural population. That is a modern form of the old state religion in the shape of institutional religious liberty as the freedom of religious communities. It is true that ever since the Weimar Constitution (Art. 137) there has no longer been any state church in Germany; but the privileges of the traditional Christian churches have still been retained and are laid down between the churches and the state in agreements and concordats. That is why in Germany there are theological faculties at state universities. A Catholic laicism has no more gained a footing in Germany than have the "free" churches of the English-speaking countries.

Secularized modernity is the German contribution to the modern world. The Basic Law (or constitution) of the German Federal Republic guarantees religious freedom—both individual and institutional— "in responsibility before God," as it says in the preamble. That may sound paradoxical, but it is not in fact a paradox at all; it is the religious guarantee of religious liberty, whether positive or negative.

In the wake of European integration, Catholic laicizing modernism is becoming noticeable in Germany, too, and is pushing the churches and theology out of public awareness. This makes the situation in the European union contradictory. European cultural politics are dominated by French laicism, whereas in Eastern Europe, after the disappearance of Soviet atheism, the theological faculties that had been pushed onto the fringe returned to the universities, and the German modernity model has come to prevail.

In the course of the discussion, the term *secularization* has come to be used not just for the legal transference of church into state property, but also increasingly to describe the general modern "secularization" of what was formerly religious.[4] The result of this transformation of the church into the state, of the religious into the secular, of transcendence into immanence, is that the secular world, and not merely the secular state, as Wolfgang Bockenförde said, is living from presuppositions that it did not itself create. What is religious is still inherent in the secular world, as something transformed. That can easily be seen in the secular ideologies that were developed as substitutes for religion. The belief in progress and the striving for dominance over nature betray their religious origins. Yet the transformation process of secularization declares religion to be a thing of the past, and secularization to be the watchword of the future. With that, the process becomes irreversible and can hardly be held back by Christian programmes for "desecularization," such as Pope Benedict XVI demanded. Nevertheless, neither the term *secularization* nor the term *desecularization* are adequate descriptions of the transformation processes of the religious in the modern world.

Lessing and the Religiously "Self-Sufficient" Humanist

In his dramatic poem *Nathan the Wise* (1779), Gotthold Ephraim Lessing[5] presents the three world religions of Judaism, Christianity, and Islam—the ones we today describe as the Abrahamic religions—and in his ring parable treats them by way of the figures of Nathan, the Templar, and Saladin, depicting each as being of equal value and contemporaneous. The mysterious ring that was the possession of "a man from the East" has the secret power to make someone pleasing to God and human beings, At his death, this man leaves his three sons three rings, with the condition:

Let each of you compete
in proving now the virtue of the stone in his own ring,
aiding its power through courtesy and warm good will,
with inner resignation then to God.[6]

The person who has inherited the true ring will prove himself as such through his humane morality, for the true ring can be ascertained in no other way—it is "almost as unprovable as it is for us to prove which of the faiths is true." In this way the symbolic relation to the three modes of faith is established. The power to be well pleasing to God and human beings—that must decide. By this he means love for God and one's neighbour. But if everyone loves only oneself most, then "you are all deceived deceivers"!

For none of your three rings is now the true one.
We must suppose the true one has been lost.[7]

This "as if" faith is supposed to motivate the wearer of the ring to the better life. Another Judge, before whom Jews, Christians, and Muslims will have to render an account, will one day decide. The standard against which Lessing tests these three forms of faith is the "universal ethic" of general humanity. He does not enter into the Jewish Torah, the Christian Sermon on the Mount, or the Muslim Sharia. With his lofty humanity ideal, Lessing relativizes the three modes of faith, and by doing so gives them equal validity—or, equally, none.

In its application to the three world religions, the ring parable has a long, interesting pre-history. Lessing took it over from the third novelle of Boccaccio's *Decameron*, but it actually goes back to the medieval *De tribus impostoribus* ("The Treatise of the Three Impostors"), which was printed in 1598[8] and was condemned and suppressed equally by all three religious groups. Whereas Lessing leaves the question about the true religion open and judges the religious groups according to the standards of humanistic tolerance, the early cynical story denounces all three religious founders—Moses, Jesus, and Mohammed—as being "deceivers of humanity." Some historians suppose that an earlier version made the rounds at the table of the emperor Frederick II

(1194–1250) in Sicily. Pope Gregory IX brought an accusation against him on the grounds of this writing, but it was not taken any further. Others have supposed that the tale originated in the Islamic world. In the Baghdad schools the comparison of the three religions was already linked with a ring parable as early as the 10th century.[9] A saying of the Qarmatian general Abu Tahir, who conquered Mecca in 912–924, has been passed down, which reads:

> *In this world there are three who have deceived men:*
> *a shepherd, a physician, and a camel-driver,*
> *and the camel-driver is surely the worst of the three.*[10]

The ambivalence of the three religious founders or deceivers of men and women has also found its way into the ring parable. Lessing also mentions the "deceived deceivers."

Ever since the Enlightenment, the intention of a comparison between the religions, and the aim of today's interreligious discussion in institutions and at conferences, is overtly the positive tolerance by way of which the three world religions are supposed to be enabled to live peaceably with one another. But although this is undoubtedly honestly meant, in the background this stance—unintentionally—ministers to the negative religious indifference that conduces to make the religions dispensable. Especially if these religions are treated as "monotheism" or as "monotheistic modes of belief," their unique characters and differences are ironed out and their irrelevance for modern life is documented. Modern, secularized Europeans feel themselves to be "religiously unmusical," to cite a much-quoted saying of the sociologist of religion Max Weber. They assume that a feeling for the religious dimension of life is an aptitude which some people have but which many are without and do not miss, and they thereby fail to be aware of life's transcendent realms. It is certainly possible to live without music, but life is richer with it. It is certainly possible to live without religion, but with religion life is broader and more festive.

Lessing uses the ring parable in a postreligious sense. Universal humanity has to take the place of particularist religious identities, and the human family must replace the families of the different religious confessions. Lessing puts the key statement for his "dramatic poem" into the mouth of the Nathan he reveres, the Nathan he calls "the Wise":

> *Are Jews and Christians rather such than men?*
> *Oh, if in you I could have found another yet*
> *For whom it was enough to be a man![11]*

For the person "for whom it is enough to be a man," these three world religions will be a matter of indifference. They should live in peace with one another and leave the other in peace, for even without the religions he or she is content with him- or herself and with the world. For that person, the universal standards of humanity suffice. He or she has become, religiously speaking, "a sufficient" person.

In his reflections on "The Education of the Human Race" (*Die Erziehung des Menschengeschlechts*, 1770), Lessing lent support to his postreligious view of humanity by way of his "messianic doctrine of the three ages." He took this over from Joachim of Fiore and secularized it:

> *It will most surely come,*
> *the time of the eternal gospel*
> *. . .*
> *promised to us even in the primal books of the New Covenant.*
> *(§86)*

> *It will come, it will most surely come,*
> *the time of fulfillment when he [i.e., the human being]*
> *will do the good just because it is the good,*
> *and not for the sake of some promised arbitrary reward. (§85)*

Lessing turned Joachim's "Third Age of the Spirit" into the Age of the Truths of Reason, which are comprehensible to everyone. He makes of Joachim's ages of the Father, the Son, and the Holy Spirit, which interlace in a trinitarian sense, an "Education of the Human Race through the Providence of God" in three separate and succeeding ages. The eschatological era of "the eternal gospel" becomes in him "the age of perfecting," and for Lessing this age is already dawning in his own time. He therefore interprets himself and his Enlightenment era messianically. The time has come *now* to make the transition from Christianity to the universal experience of the spirit: the time has come *now* to advance from the particularist faith of the church to the universal faith in reason: "The development of revealed truths into the general truths of reason is simply necessary if the human race is thereby to be helped. When they were revealed they were indeed not yet truths of reason; but they were revealed in order that they might become them" (§76). It was this transference of the trinitarian separation of God's history with the world into the three ages of world history that gave rise to the German division into the ancient world, the Middle Ages, and modern times. "Modern times" means the final era of the world, since after this there can be no other new time. It is pointless to declare "the end of the modern world," as Romano Guardini tried to do after the Second World War.[12] What has to be called in question is the division as such. What German calls the *Neuzeit* (literally: "the new time") cannot be translated into English or French. It is not identical with "modern times" or with "*le monde moderne.*" But it is typical for the messianic, millenarian spirit of the German Enlightenment. Because nothing at all can follow it, the *Neuzeit* is simultaneously the "end time." The *Neuzeit* is typical of the 19th-century's faith in progress. The *Endzeit* ("the end-time") is typical of the contemporaneous spirit of German Romanticism. The time of completion is always simultaneously the time of the end. There *telos* and *finis* coincide. In English, "the end of history" is equally ambivalent: it can be history's goal and also history's end. In the Christian expectation of the end, apocalyptic is always the reverse side of millenarianism.

Ludwig Feuerbach and the Atheistically "Reduced" Life

Ludwig Feuerbach (1804–1872) counts as a "left-wing" (or revolutionary) Hegelian materialist and philosopher belonging to the prelude leading to the bourgeois revolution of 1848. His theory about religion as an illusion brought to an end what Kant had criticized about

Anselm's ontological proof of God, namely that it takes "mere self-creations of thought as being the immediately true essence of reality": "All the paths which one may strike out with this intention begin either from that one particular experience, advancing from that according to the laws of causality to the supreme cause external to the world, or they abstract in finite terms from all experience and deduce, entirely a priori from mere concepts, the existence of a supreme cause."[13] Feuerbach also turned the logic of his teacher Hegel on its head. Hegel had written that "The human being only knows about God insofar as God in the human being knows himself," because for him the infinite is only infinite when it absorbs the finite into itself and becomes a differentiated unit both of itself and the finite. Feuerbach simplifies this when he maintains that when "God thinks Godself in the human being" this "is nothing other" than that "the human being is thinking oneself in God." This reversal, as such, is indistinguishable. Hegel preserves the difference between the infinite and the finite, which is crossed from the side of the infinite. Feuerbach abolishes this differentiation: God and the human being are a single being. Consequently, he could no longer differentiate between the two.

Feuerbach began as a theologian and ended up as a naturalist: "God was my first thought, reason my second, the human being my third and final thought"—that was the way he described the path he had taken.[14] He "discovered," as he proudly put it, that anthropology is "the secret" of theology: in actual fact the human being is the criterion for God, and is him- or herself the absolute being—the being of God.[15]

- That means for Feuerbach, first, that religion is the expression of a divided and alienated humanity. In their misery, human beings project into God what they themselves have to dispense with, yet wish for. They project into heaven what they are missing on earth. If life here is "a vale of tears," then human beings know that they are only "guests on earth," heaven being their home. It is only in human misery that God is born. Yet religion also projects into the world beyond what it takes from this one. It is not merely the expression of the human being's self-alienation; religion is itself this alienation.

- It means, second, that the new anthropology explains the religious alienation of human beings by exposing their pictures of God as being merely "the self-creations of human reason." That is the anthropological criticism of religion.

- It means, third, that the enlightened human being takes religion back into him- or herself and becomes a "whole human being." The illusory heaven returns to earth, and the world becomes an undivided universe. The consequence of denying a life beyond this one is the affirmation of life in the present. Feuerbach's criticism of religion was not a-religious. What he wanted, in contrast to the atheists of his time, was "a new religion"—the religion of life:

Life is God.
The enjoyment of life is the enjoyment of God.
A true love of life is the true religion.[16]

All the positive attributes of God are retained; it is only the subject of these predicates that changes: the human being takes the place of God. All the predicates of a transcendent heaven are retained; only their subject alters, their place being taken by the earth and by this life here and now. That means that the human and the divine are indistinguishable, the heavenly and the earthly become one. Life itself is divine and the earth is heavenly. *By turning theology into anthropology, Feuerbach turns anthropology into theology*: "The new philosophy is essentially speaking philosophy for human beings. . . . It takes the place of religion, it holds within itself the essence of religion, it is, in very truth, itself religion."[17]

What does this look like in detail? Feuerbach condemns Johann Gottlieb Fichte's "I" philosophy and the subjectivity theories of German Idealism:

Loneliness is finitude and limitation.
Sociality is freedom and infinity.
Man with man—the unity of I and Thou is God.[18]

And: "The true dialectic is not a monologue between the solitary thinker and himself; it is a dialogue between I and Thou."[19] With this, Feuerbach anticipates Martin Buber's "dialogical principle" and 20th-century personalism.

Furthermore, he succeeds in arriving at another important recognition: the significance of pain for thinking. "Thinking is preceded by suffering."[20] "Pain is the source of poetry." Feuerbach is talking about pure pain without any religious, otherworldly consolation—inconsolable pain. "Faith in a world beyond makes of every pain a figment, an untruth."[21] And yet: "Only what can suffer deserves to exist. Only the being who knows pain to the full is a divine being. A being without suffering is a being without a being, but a being that does not suffer is nothing other than a being without feeling, without substance."[22] With this he has reached a limit where the divine, or what theology ascribes to God, cannot be transferred to the person who is enlightened in the sense of being critical of religion: God's inability to suffer. He writes, "The religious feeling, the heart, says, for example, that 'God suffers.' Theology, on the other hand, says that God does not suffer. That is to say, the heart denies the difference between God and human being while theology maintains it."[23] Feuerbach considers that every human being who is able to suffer is greater than a God incapable of suffering. But in this way he is unable to transfer into anthropology the divine attributes that rest on the negation of human ones, such as the inability to suffer and unalterability—and that also benefits his "new philosophy for human beings."

At the end of his lectures on "The Essence of Religion" (*Das Wesen der Religion*, 1845), he describes his intention as follows: "To turn them from being friends of God into friends of human beings, from believers into thinkers, from those who pray into those who work, from candidates for the world beyond into students of this one, from Christians who according to their own belief and admission are 'half beast and half angel' into human beings, *whole* human beings."[24]

Theological criticism has for the most part fallen on Feuerbach's optimism about life, accusing him of overlooking evil, suffering, and death. What he says about pain shows that this is not correct. But what is true is that what comes into being is a "God complex" on the part of the modern human being, once he or she no longer distinguishes between what is human and what is divine, and exalts him- or herself into a "God-human being." Then the human being becomes an unhappy God because he or she is a mortal one.

What is also true is that by explaining the human origins of the ideas of God and the images of God, what those ideas and images are aiming at do not cease to exist. If religious ideas are "projections," what then is the "white wall" that they reflect? asked Paul Tillich. At that point Ernst Bloch assumed that this was "an ante-room of the future" for human projects, because he believed the messianic to be the true religion.

Anthropological criticism will cling fast to the human being's reflexive, eccentric position. As life is lived, reflexivity and spontaneity are in tension with one another. Anyone who, going along with Feuerbach, becomes a "whole"—that is to say, an undivided—person, may suffice for him- or herself, but he or she will also be totally unknown, because he or she is no longer capable of knowing him- or herself. Feuerbach compensates for this in the relationship between I and Thou, but this is not just a "unity," as he maintains; it is also a difference that cannot be set aside. The reversal of his thesis about the divine life can be considered true:

- Where God is, there is life, for God is the living God.

- The enjoyment of God (*fruitio Dei*) is the enjoyment of life, and God is experienced through the affirmation of life, not through its denial.

- Religion, in Christianity especially, is true joy in life, because Christ makes of life "a festival without end."

Not least, Feuerbach's reduction of "the world in heaven beyond our grave" to "the world beyond our grave on earth"[25]—that is to say, the reduction of the heaven of eternity to the historical future of humanity—is a substitute for a qualitative transcendence by way of a quantitative transcending. This reduction is certainly typical for the capitalist and Marxist belief in progress, but it leads in the wrong direction, because belief in a future, better life loses its momentum as time goes on unless it is nourished from the source of a qualitative transcendence, that is to say, from the eternity of heaven. Human self-transcendence in God is the origin and power for the historical overstepping of every present in the direction of a better future. In other words, the restlessness of the heart that only finds its rest in God makes the human being restless in every present time, urging on the future, "seeking a future city" in a "classless society" as well—and even in capitalist society.[26] Feuerbach's reduction is not an enrichment of this world at the expense of the next; it is an impoverishment of this world through the loss of the world to come.

Basically speaking, Feuerbach surrenders God's qualitatively different world beyond this one because he follows the epistemological principle that "like is only known by like." God is known only by God, and the human being is known only by the human being. With this, the surmounting of the qualitative frontier between God and human being disappears. God and human being must be a single entity. As a result, anything that crosses the frontier, such as God's incarnation into human life, and the self-transcendence of human life in God, can no longer be understood, for the principle that governs this surmounting of frontiers is that "only the unlike know each other. For what is the same, whatever is no different is a matter of indifference."[27] To transcend means to cross frontiers. Feuerbach's merely immanent human beings who have been robbed of transcendence remain confined within their limitations. They have surrendered the religious adventure and prefer to remain at home.

Ideological reductionism

Feuerbach's reductionist rhetoric can be seen in the revealing phrase ". . . is nothing other than . . ." It is like the transformation brought about by a conjuring trick. It can be extended at will: theology is "nothing other" than anthropology; anthropology is "nothing other" than economy; economy is "nothing other" than biology; biology is "nothing other" than neurology; neurology is "nothing other" than system theory; and so forth. The consequences can be briefly described:

- In the logic of ideological reductionism a further "exposure" follows. What is the "secret" of anthropology? Being determines consciousness, says materialism. And what determines the being of the human being? The economy! That is the world of capitalism, in which everything human becomes merely a commodity for sale. The human being is what he or she produces and what he or she consumes. Life is the ability to work and the capacity for enjoyment. The material life is the only true life. Everything else, such as culture and religion, are epiphenomena—they are secondary and can be explained by material conditions. That is reduced life.

- In the logic of reductionism a further "exposure" follows: the "secret" of the human being is "nothing other" than biology; life is a "struggle for existence" and what is at stake is "survival." The meaning of the struggle is "the survival of the fittest," and that means not just the strongest but also the most adaptable. But it is the law of life's evolution, say the naturalists, who were earlier called "social Darwinists." If the biological "struggle for existence " is the true life, then everything else has a point only inasmuch as it can be utilized in this struggle. The politics that have adopted this ideology of the struggle for existence have hence made all its purposes conform to it in a totalitarian sense. That is reduced life.

- Today economic materialism and the naturalism of evolution-biology are being replaced by the mechanistic world of "*l'homme machine*." That means the adaptation of human beings to the computer world they themselves have created, the world of the mainframes, the drones, and the robots. The drones pursue their wars, the robots produce their commodities, the mainframes in the banks regulate their finances, and the computers simulate their thinking with artificial intelligence. Modern human beings are then modern when they "function well." It is true that they no longer fully grasp their virtual world, and that it is also presented to them as being without an alternative. They are imprisoned in the electronic shell of their own products and are monitored by them. These products have long since become "trans-human." This can be a life of luxury and a perpetual party, but it is a reduced life without liberty, without transcendence, without future.

• The naturalistic interpretation of modern research into the brain declares that modern human beings are without guilt, and are not responsible for their wrongdoing, which thus turns them into machinery that is part of the modern world. This, to put it bluntly, means the final abolition of human beings as we have hitherto known them. They are then "antiquated"[28] figures in their own, modern world. That is a paradoxical situation.

If atheism is victorious and theism disappears, what then happens to atheism? What becomes of the negation when the positive is no longer there? Then atheism disappears, too, and what comes into being is the post-atheistic type of human being—what Jürgen Habermas calls "the post-secular human being," who has left behind these ancient antitheses and conflicts. The denial of a world beyond by no means has as its consequence an affirmation of this present one. If there is no longer any world beyond, then there is no longer "this world here," either. Suffering is divested of its complaint, and pain of its protest against God. Why am I suffering? This question is unanswerable in an atheistic sense. If there is a God, why is there suffering and evil in the world? These questions then become meaningless: if there is no God, then things are simply as they are. Suffering is then no longer a question, and evil is "so-called evil" and is quite natural. In one of Ingmar Bergman's films, two characters are walking along the beach. One of them says: "Without God, everything would be O.K.," which provokes the other to the indignant contradiction: "But with God, nothing is O.K." With God, suffering is called in question and there is a protest against evil, for God is the inexhaustible protest against injustice and violence. A much-quoted saying by Theodor Adorno maintains that "there is no true life in a life that is false." That is not convincing because it is illogical. How can a "false life" be recognized except in contrast to a "true life"? If there is no true life, there is no false life either. It is only over against true life that the false life proves itself to be false.

Are We Living in the Era of the Enlightenment?

(*a*) Yes, one might think so, for it was in the era of the Enlightenment (which has also been called the scientific age) that the "secular world" came into being. In 1899, at the turn of the century, the famous German naturalist Ernst Haeckel published his book *Die Welträtsel* ("The Riddles of the World") and in 1904, as its complement, *Die Lebenswunder* ("The Wonders of Life").[29] Both books were published in popular editions at a very modest price. They were sold all over the world in many editions, and disseminated the popular interpretation of the German Enlightenment. The riddles of the world were solved by way of empirical research into nature; the wonders of life were cleared up through experience and human thought. By about 1900 many people were looking back proudly to the glorious progress that had been made in the natural and life sciences, and promised to the world the completion of the scientific and technological age. And it came about just as they had promised: nuclear physics has elucidated the components of the atomic nucleus to such a degree that today not much more is left to discover. Genetic research has deciphered the human genome to such a degree that the genetic code of human beings can be read. Brain research, in its investigations into the central human organ, has left very little mystery about the human being to be taken into account.

The method of explaining the riddles of the world and the wonders of life is always the same reductionism: the unknown is reduced to the known, the complex is reduced to the simple, the new to the old, the spiritual to the material, the transcendent to the immanent, the religious to the human, and so forth. What does the result look like? What comes into being is a world without mystery, a world devoid of surprises, a calculable world, a controlled world, and a world without any surprises, as in Hermann Hesse's novel *The Glass Bead Game*.

Every five years the quantity of knowledge in the natural and life sciences and in sociology is said to be doubled, and is made accessible on the Internet. The result is a transhuman world of knowledge that no one is now able to grasp. Computers think more quickly than the human brain. Once programmed, they regulate the financial markets.

Major technical plants, such as nuclear power plants, seem technologically reliable. But because human beings are not reliable, but are fallible and represent a technological risk, nuclear power plants are unreliable, too, as the Chernobyl and Fukushima catastrophes have proved. They are "error-intolerant."[30] It may be that at some time or other it will be possible to breed infallible human beings by way of genetic engineering—human beings who react just as they have been programmed to do. Then the technology functions, but the development of humanity stops at the same time. Human beings make mistakes, and learn from their mistakes if they are wise. Once bitten, twice shy, as the saying goes—always provided that one survives the first bite. If mistakes are no longer permissible, learning stops and, technologically speaking, "the end of history" has been reached.

Modern high-power technology produces major experiments that are unable to contribute to human wisdom, because we cannot retrieve the radiation issuing from the nuclear power plants that have been destroyed any more than we can retrieve the genes we have modified or the viruses we have bred once they have ceased to be under our control. No wisdom can be acquired through a worldwide war fought with weapons of mass destruction, because it is improbable that anyone would be able to survive. No one will become wise through the major-project "modern world," which goes hand in hand with the population explosion and the urbanization of men and women, and in which the climate balance of the earth is changed, because we cannot retrieve things once they become dangerous. In the Enlightenment age, humanity became involved in a major project with an uncertain outcome. What began naïvely as the elucidation of the riddles of the world and as the stripping away of life's wonders has become a danger for the world with a universal risk to life. The world without mysteries has itself become the mystery.

(b) Yet: "What is Enlightenment?" In 1783 Immanuel Kant provided an answer to this question of questions: "Enlightenment is the human being's departure from his self-imposed infancy. Infancy is the incapacity to use one's understanding without drawing on the guidance of someone else. *Sapere aude!* Have the courage to use your own understanding." In the world of that time, with its absolute rulers and obedient subjects, this was just as revolutionary as the French Revolution, which Kant admired. It is revolutionary in the world of today as well, for we do not exist in the age of Enlightenment or in a "world that has come of age,"[31] but—if we accept Kant's definition of enlightenment—in times of self-imposed infancy.

- It was self-imposed infancy when the German people chose the Nazi dictatorship of the "Führer" Hitler, and people stopped using their own understanding.

- It was self-imposed infancy when the socialist peoples submitted to Stalin's dictatorship, and people only used their own understanding under the guidance of the party.[32]

- It is self-imposed infancy when today people all over the world allow themselves to be reduced to their economic utility for the market and, as market-conforming "egoists," lose the courage to use their own understanding,[33] but surrender to the secret seducers of the total market.

To think independently, or to think at all, was extremely dangerous in the German army, and was punished, for "orders are orders" was the mindless motto of a total intellectual infancy. The Führer's commands had to be obeyed without reflection. In the Nazi dictatorship, the "Eichmanns" were happy to surrender their own thinking, and not to be compelled to have a conscience.[34] Their infancy was self-imposed, which was Kant's reproach to the submissive subjects of his time. In doing so they surrendered their humanity and on command were prepared for every inhuman act. The victims of the dictatorships were degraded into a subhuman race so that they could be eliminated, like weeds or pests, while the mass murderers willingly allowed themselves to be made inhuman.

The 20th century saw in Germany the deadly consequences of a "self-imposed infancy." Russian Stalinism was the model for totalitarian rule, not only for East Germany (the GDR) but for Mao's China and Pol Pot's Cambodia, too. The courage to use one's own understanding found as little place in Nazi atheism as it did in Stalin's. There is no room for reason in any authoritarian faith.

In place of "enlightened" reductionism, Kant maintained that the *departure* from infancy in the direction of independent freedom was the Enlightenment's anthropological method. With this he picks up the old biblical motif of the exodus from slavery into the land of freedom and, applying it to humanity's human era, invokes the courage for self-esteem: *sapere aude!* Have the courage to use your own understanding without any guidance or assumption of responsibility by authoritarian "powers that be." This is the demand not just for autonomy but for responsibility, too. To be aware of one's own understanding is also an expression for the conscience that human beings make out of what they do. The refusal to surrender oneself and one's own thinking, and willingly to accept tutelage as a relief—that costs courage, and in dictatorships often one's own life. For that reason the courage to be oneself and not to be turned aside finds a better place in the religion of the exodus and the resurrection than in atheism.

PART ONE

The Living God

Chapter 1

The Living God

My soul thirsts *for God,*
for the living God. (Ps. 42:2)

My heart and flesh sing for joy
to the living God. (Ps. 84:2)

Evidently, the spiritual longing of the soul for God is not enough, so in Psalm 42 the physical "thirst" for "the living God" is added. That becomes understandable once we realize that the Hebrew word *näfäsch* means the vital power that was thought to have its seat in a human being's throat. That is why here the human being's vital power thirsts in the same way as the thirsty deer cries out for living water. It thirsts for the source of life, for its wellspring. That wellspring is the living God, who is not only living in Godself but who makes everything that comes into proximity with the divine alive, too. Life thirsts for life; life becomes a living force through other life; vitality is enlivening in its effects. In human beings, knowledge of the "living God" awakens a thirst and hunger for life. It makes them dissatisfied with what they are, and impels them to look for a future in which more life will enter the lives they already have.

This vitality makes the living God very attractive. God draws to the divine self the people who are hungry for life. But the living God is also capable of community, and is communicative. God's living power goes out of Godself and seeks the thirsty souls of men and women. This is a sign of movement: through the hunger and thirst the living God evokes in them, God puts them on the move and, in so doing, makes them live. God is on the move in a different way in order to satisfy their hunger for life. That is why "their hearts and souls rejoice *in* the living God," that is to say, in God's presence—not God's presence in heaven or general omnipresence in creation, but God's special "indwelling" in God's people, in God's temple, in God's Spirit. It is God's *Shekinah* that interpenetrates body and soul: the joy of body and soul is also the joy of God *in* the human body and soul. In the Christian mystical tradition everything in us falls silent when God is experienced as being present. This is brought out in Gerhard Tersteegen's familiar hymn "*Gott ist gegenwärtig*":

> *Lo! God is here. Let us adore.*
> . . .
> *Let all within us feel his power,*
> *and silent bow before his face.*

Israel's experience is different: if God is far off, the people cry out and thirst for God. When God comes, God's people lift up their gates and the ancient doors are lifted up so "that the King of glory may come in" (Ps. 24:7). If God is present, the people sing and dance and are carried away by joy. They eat and drink and celebrate the festival of life.

How Can God Be Both Living and Eternal?

According to our experience of life between birth and death, health and sickness, happiness and suffering, the eternal God cannot be living and the living God cannot be eternal. So how can we conceive the vitality of God if God is the eternal God? And how are we to understand God's eternity if God is the living One?

What is life? We can begin with a biological concept of life that is derived from simple forms of life, but this is already inapplicable where more complex living things are concerned. If "living" means something that can reproduce itself, that certainly applies to all living things on earth, but it is not sufficient to let us grasp the "humanness" of human life. It is not even enough to let us understand the vitality of the earth, which produces all living things but does not reproduce itself. So we shall start with the philosophical definition of life that Plato put forward for the universe: "What is alive is endowed with automobility"—that is, it can move of its own volition.[1] The principle of life is movement and, moreover, self-movement. That also accords with the primitive experience of life; what moves by itself is alive, what is no longer able to move, or is incapable of movement in general, is dead or was never alive.

Plato solved the problem of the movement into life and out of it—that is to say, the problem of birth and death—by conceiving the soul to be not the force of life but a higher, immortal being, and by ascribing birth and death to the temporal body. But this raised the question about the life of the soul: if the soul is immortal it will not be born either, for it is what is eternal, permanent, unchangeable—what always remains the same, over against the continual changes of the mortal body. If this is so, the soul is immovable and cannot, for its own part, move anything else. Plato left behind him two problems:

1. Can life and immobility be united?

2. Is there a unity of life and death, a unity between coming into being and passing away, between being and nonbeing, finitude and infinity, time and eternity?

Plato's pupil Aristotle arrived at a brilliant solution with his image of "the unmoved Mover": How can what is unmoved, since it is divine, "move" the universe? The divine (*theion*) is itself eternal, perfect, and unmoved, but through its perfection, its goodness and beauty, it moves all other things by way of the enraptured eros.[2] As the "beloved" of all imperfect, temporal things, it everywhere provokes the movement of eros without itself moving. The good, the true, and the beautiful of what is divine moves through attraction, as a magnet attracts iron filings. That presupposes a firm correlation between *eros* and *eidos*. Love and the beautiful are necessarily related to one another. If the divine is absolute beauty, then the whole universe is erotically moved, and the yearning for the divine drives everything beyond itself.

The "unmoved Mover" became definitive for Christian metaphysics and, down to the present day, puts its stamp on what are considered to be the attributes of God's divinity, such as God's immutability and impasssibility. If God's divinity is understood in this sense, is it then identical with "the living God" of the Old and New Testaments? No, "the living God" is not in love with Godself. On the contrary, God goes out of Godself and loves the beings God has created. God's love for those God has created is the first thing; the love for God by the beings whom God has created is the second. As used to be said, "The God who loves human beings makes human beings who love God." The biblical experience of God would correspond to a "self-moved Mover" rather than to an "unmoved Mover."

For the second problem Plotinus offered an initial dialectical solution. He viewed the self-movement within the divine and the movement out of which the universe emerges and to which it reverts as being a single, great divine movement: the divine is the endlessness that wells up eternally, a never-self-exhausting being "which in itself, as it were, overflows with life."[3] It is a self-moving eternity that separates from itself time as the measure of the movements of the universe and brings it back again.

How does the transition take place? The One brings the other: eternity brings time, the infinite brings forth finitude. The One is the origin, and the whole is the goal of the universal movements of life. Everything proceeds from the One, and returns to the All-One. Thus, the great divine life embraces the little temporal life. The life that is eternal presents itself in the birth and death of the temporal life. The rigid dualism of the immortal soul and the mortal body is replaced by the moved dialectic of eternal life that encompasses temporal life and temporal death in its own movements. Eternal life, which presents itself in mortal life in the form of total and universal life, is the whole and the universal life. Plotinus thinks of the unity in difference in the image of emanation; it is like the water, which, in a Roman fountain, flows down from basis to basin, from a single source. This image makes it easy to see the continuity and the discontinuity.

With regard to the divine self-movement, life and eternity are not contrasted and do not have to be defined over against one another by way of reciprocal exclusion. The living eternity of overflowing life, and the subsuming of temporal life in the movements of the life that is eternal are complementary. It is true that the neo-Platonic concept of emanation is incompatible with the biblical idea of creation, but with regard to the divine Spirit, the giver of life, "outpouring" is the metaphor which is continually used, and that is the language of emanation.

The Eternal God

Let us continue with another little meditation:

> LORD, you have been our dwelling place
> in all generations.
> Before the mountains were brought forth,
> or ever you had formed the earth and the world,
> from everlasting to everlasting you are God. (Ps. 90:1-2)

The astonishing phrase "from everlasting to everlasting" can be explained by its origin in the Hebrew *olam*, which means a long time. The God who is the subject addressed as *you* is the one who was already there before the creation of the world. Psalm 90 stresses as emphatically as Plato the essential difference between what is nontransitory and what is transitory. Human beings belong to the transitory sphere:

> You sweep them away; they are like a dream,
> like grass that is renewed in the morning;
> in the morning it flourishes and is renewed;
> in the evening it fades and withers. (Ps. 90:5-6)

Yet in this fathomless difference God is our refuge, our dwelling place. God is present in the midst of transitory time and is an open space of safe-keeping in which human beings can remain. In God's presence the difference between eternity and time is not unbridgeable. The protecting God is what abides in the river of time.

But just because God is present as refuge, the river of time and the transience of all things, their withering and dying, are not viewed as something quite natural. They are experienced as a sphere of human misdeeds and God's wrath. God has created human beings for eternal life, so temporal life is experienced as remoteness from God.

Grief over the transience of all present experiences is countered by the yearning for redemption. This redemption is expected to be the outcome of a change of direction on God's part: God's "wrath" goes together with God's turning away from the men and women who have forsaken God. This is "*hester panim*," the face of God that is turned away and darkened—the eclipse of God.

> *Turn, O LORD! How long?*
> *Have compassion on your servants! (Ps. 90:13)*

In turning back, God shows human beings "the light of [God's] countenance" (v. 8). Divine grace and divine blessing radiate to human beings from God's face, which shines for joy, and they will remain in the eternal God even when they die. Nothing goes missing in the river of time, for in God everything is caught up and preserved.

In this section we shall approach the concept of eternity from the aspect of life's experience so as to understand the living God as the God who is eternal. For this, our starting point is that it is this life which is the eternal life. Ludwig Feuerbach reduced God's eternity to "the enjoyment of life." Friedrich Nietzsche chose the opposite direction, and brought the dimension of eternity into this life, which, after all, is both temporal and mortal. How it that possible?

It is not enough for human life to be lived; the human being must affirm life as well, for it can also be denied. The dimension of eternity holds within itself the affirmation of life:

Highest constellation of Being!
which no wish attains,
which no denial sullies,
eternal Yea of being, I am your Yea for ever:
For I love thee, O eternity.[4]

In affirming life we chime in with the divine Creator's great *yes,* the *yes* of the Creator who desires life to exist and that it should be lived and loved. This assurance is certainly prerational, but through its wisdom it sheds light on the understanding.

For you love all things that exist . . . ,
for your immortal spirit is in all things. (Wisd. 11:24, 12:1)

The supreme form of life's affirmation is the joy in living. The longing for life and the enjoyment of life make life live from within. Nietzsche thought that what is essential is "eternal vitality." Consequently, he saw the dimension of eternity in life's joy, not in its suffering.[5]

"The eternal pleasure in creating" is the joy in life that gives life. It does not just make things alive but eternal, too, for it is the reflection and radiance emanating from the living God. "In the beginning God created . . . ," so as God's earthly image the human being will effect beginnings through the creation of something new. Every human being who is born is a new beginning of life. The joy in life that yearns to be eternal is directed toward the birth of life, not toward death. Birth is superior to death, for without birth there would be no death. So the joy that longs for eternity is superior to the suffering over the past. Pain wants the suffering to have an end, pleasure wants the joy to be eternal. To say that is certainly in contradiction to general religiosity, complaint, and grief and the groanings of the creation that is in bondage; but they are closer to "the living God." General wisdom tells us that all life bears death within itself. Living faith says that what all life bears within itself is resurrection.

If we measure eternity over against the concept of life, not death, then we come upon the definition of eternity put forward by the Latin philosopher Boethius: "*aeternitas est interminabilis vitae tota simul et perfecta possessio*":[6] eternity is the unlimited, whole, simultaneous, and perfect possession—or, I would say, enjoyment—of life.

If this is applied to God, then God's eternity means God's eternal life, God's blissful vitality, and God's inexhaustibly creative fullness of life. Applied to human beings, it means that this life itself is already eternal life, because it is affirmed through God's YES and is loved with God's creative love. It is affirmed and loved and enjoyed in the living God.

Of course, these are temporal concepts of eternity, when we start from the life that we experience. To put it more exactly, they are temporal attempts to grasp God's eternity. Are there other temporal experiences of eternity?

- God's Spirit is present with us in "the darkness of the lived moment."[7] The phrase is Ernst Bloch's, and at the beginning he also talks about "the darkness of the lived God." In saying this he was taking up the experience of the indescribable mystical moment, the *nunc aeternum*, and applying it in the context of the life that is wholly lived here and now. Søren Kierkegaard called this unique moment between the times "an atom of eternity."[8] We can experience it at any time, but if we are asked to describe it, the experience of it eludes us. It is within us, we are within it, but we cannot make an object of this moment of eternity. If we try to hold on to it, to possess it, it disappears. "O tarry a while, thou art so fair," to echo Geothe's *Faust*—that is our wish; but we know that it cannot tarry, since we ourselves cannot tarry either.

- Another temporal concept of eternity can be found in the "immediacy to God of every epoch," as the historian Leopold von Ranke put it.[9] His purpose was to treat all the different epochs as being of equal value and not to devaluate any of them as mere preliminary steps leading to the next, as the 19th-century faith in progress did, with the intention of declaring its own epoch to be the spearhead of progress. If all epochs are immediate to God, then their meaning is also to be found in them themselves, and not in some other historical epoch. But if history's relationship to transcendence is directed toward "the God of hope" of the Bible's prophets and apostles, and is aligned toward the coming of God "on earth as in heaven," then they point at the same time to God's coming "on earth as in heaven" and are hence aligned toward "the fullness of the times." The historical epochs have to be read as anticipations of "the end of history" and of the beginning of the new everlasting creation. All historical epochs are then not merely immediate to God; they are also "past future," as Reinhard Koselleck puts it, following Ernst Bloch.[10]

- Finally, reflections of transcendent eternity can be found in nature as well, in the circulation of the days and years. The circle, which has no beginning or end, has been seen since ancient times as being a reflection of eternity. In Peking, the Temple of Heaven has three circular roofs, which symbolize heaven. It stands on a square that symbolizes the earth. The endlessness of the circles corresponds to the eternal unendingness. Cyclical time is permanent time, and in this sense eternal time.

When we distinguish God's essential eternity from the created eternity of heaven, and use the Latin word *aevum* for the eternity of heaven, eternity and time in creation are related to each other like heaven and earth, the invisible and the visible world. When it is understood as creation, the world is not a unified universe; it is a duality of heaven and earth, world and "anti-world." Eternity and time are therefore as transparent for one another as are heaven and earth, the invisible and the visible world. That brings us to the conclusion that, as temporal life, our life is simultaneously eternal life.

The Living God

Our temporal life can only be eternal life if the death of life is taken up into life. But that is only possible if finite life is elevated into eternal life or, to put it more exactly, if the endless life appears in finite life, and can be lived within it. Finite life is distinguished from infinite life through birth and death. Consequently, infinite life can only appear in finite life if it is born and dies, in this way proving itself to be unending life. The movements from infinite life to finite life and from finite to infinite life are the supreme forms of vitality.

We find traces of this kind of dialectical thinking in Plotinus. The self-moved Mover of the universe does not merely set everything on the move; through its emanations the overflowing source of Being also calls into life the multifarious forms of finite being. That is not a quantitative movement from one place to another; it is a qualitative movement from infinite being to finite being, from the one to its other.

In Hegel and Hölderlin we find this dialectic in completed form, accentuated by the biblical belief in creation through the God "who . . . calls into existence the things that do not exist" (Rom. 4:17). The fluid transitions found in Plotinus are replaced by the union between contrasts and the reconciliations of what has been divided.

Life in supreme vitality consists in its restoration out of profoundest separation. Nonbeing is united with Being and what emerges is Becoming. Finite life is gathered into infinite life and what comes to be is eternal life. This eternal life is a dialectical process of contradiction and the ending of contradiction, of dying and resurrection. As Hegel wrote in his *Phenomenology of Spirit* (1807),[11]

> The life of the spirit is not the life that is afraid of death and keeps itself untouched by devastation, but the life that endures death and maintains itself in it. It attains its truth only when, in utter dismemberment, it finds itself. It finds this power, not as something positive which turns away from the negative, as when we say of something that it is nothing or is false, and then, being finished and done with it, leave it and pass on to something else; on the contrary, spirit is this power only by looking the negative in the face and lingering over it. This lingering over it is the magic power that converts the negative into being.

Friedrich Hölderlin. the friend of Hegel's youth at the time when he was in the Theologische Stift in Tübingen, casts back to Hegel's early writings, in which the primal form of dialectic is love, which unites and divides. At the end of his *Hyperion* he writes, unforgettably:

> The dissonances of the world are like lovers' quarrels.
> In the midst of the strife is reconciliation,
> and all that is separated finds back to itself.
> The blood divides and joins again in the heart,
> and what remains is a *single, eternal, and glowing* life.[12]

Chapter 2

God's Attributes

The Living God and the Attributes of Divinity

Greek metaphysics developed out of the religiously enlightened view of the Greek hierarchy of the gods and remained associated with it in a critical sense. The Greek gods required no special revelation, since they were present in all happenings and evident in the cosmos: "Everything is full of gods." When Heraclitus was warming his hands at the kitchen fire, and visitors did not have the temerity to draw closer, he said: "Come in. The gods are here, too."

Greek metaphysics reduced the many gods of Olympia to a single divine Being. The *theion* is an impersonal divine substance. Aristotle connected it with the universe by way of its universal monarchy in the sense that a pyramid's apex is connected with the pyramid as a whole.

When Christian theology came into being on the foundation of Hellenistic culture, this Greek metaphysics became fused with the biblical testimony to the living God. But since YHWH, the God of Israel, is neither related to nor identical with Zeus, the divine universal father of all according to Greek thinking, this gave rise to the theological tensions in the Christian doctrine of God that have remained unresolved down to the present day. What has "the Father of Jesus Christ" to do with Jupiter, the father of the Roman gods, in whose name Christ was crucified?

I encountered this unresolved tension in Karl Rahner's criticism of my book *The Crucified God*. In the last interview he gave before his death, he said: "God is in a true and consoling sense for me the *Deus impassibilis*, the *Deus immutabilis*, and so forth. In Moltmann and others I think I can sense a theology of the absolute paradox and of a patripassionism about which I would say, first of all, what do we know so exactly about God? And would ask, secondly, how would this serve me as consolation in the truest sense of the word?"[1]

It is easy to respond to the first question with a second: How, then, can we know so exactly what God cannot do when we assert that "God cannot alter" and that "God cannot suffer"? In reply to the second question, we can reply: "If God is unalterable, why do I pray? If God is impassible—if God is incapable of suffering—why is what happens to me of concern to God? Is a *Deus impassibilis et immutabilis* an apathetic and inaccessible God? What do these attributes say, and what don't they say?

Is God Immovable?

"Immutability" is a statement of comparison: what is divine is not subject to change in the course of time, or to change brought about by force, like earthly phenomena. It is independent of these things. It has its foundation in itself, not in anything else. Immutability is an attribute of the *theion*, the divine substance; it cannot be applied to the divine subject without destroying its freedom and autonomous movement. If we take it literally, there is no such thing as a *deus immutabilis*—an immutable God—but merely a *divinitas immutabilis*, an immutable divinity. If we were to see immutability as an attribute of the divine subject, we should deprive it of its vitality for, in the world of our experience, unchangeableness and immovability are only manifested in what was never alive or is no longer so. It is impossible to consider God as being unchangeable and immovable without declaring God to be dead.

But the living God is free to move and to change. God can creatively go out of Godself and arrive at God's Sabbath rest. God is not a "movable God" in the general sense that God can be moved by alien forces or by God's own moods, like the Greek gods. God is a God who moves of God's own volition.[2] Does that mean that God is an arbitrary God?

If we understand the living God as subject, then the divine *immutabilis* of ancient physics is replaced by God's *faithfulness*, a faithfulness on which we can rely. According to Israel's experience of God, God is not essentially bound to God's faithfulness, for God can also "repent." God' s "repentance" is in contradiction to God's immutability, but it does not contradict God's faithfulness and constancy, for it awakens ever-new human astonishment over God's grace. "If we are faithless, he remains faithful—for he cannot deny himself" (2 Tim. 2:13). Compared with God's repentance, God's faithfulness is so overwhelming that truth, *emuna*, is even viewed as God's faithfulness to Godself. When human wickedness acquired the upper hand on earth, God "repented" of having created human beings. God let them perish in the flood but made a new covenant with Noah and his descendents, as well as with the living things that accompanied them, promising enduring faithfulness (Gen. 8:21-22; 9:9-11). In Genesis 6:6 God's repentance is also called "the pain of God."[3]

Is the living God merely a sovereign, autonomously moving God, or can God also be "moved" to something by human beings? Israel's familiar exodus out of its captivity in Egypt is preceded by a happening in God:

I have seen the affliction of my people, . . .
and have heard their cry.
I know their sufferings,
and I have come down *to deliver them . . . (Exod. 3:7-8, RSV)*

God's *descent* for the purpose of God's people's liberation is motivated—moved—by God's compassion, and God is moved to compassion by the people's suffering. From God's standpoint, the story of the people's exodus is a *Shekinah* story.

But the prayers in the Psalms also urge God toward a change of direction: "Turn, O Lᴏʀᴅ! How long? Have compassion on your servants!" (Ps. 90:13). God is even woken up by the cry of abandonment, "Awake!" (90:24), and is urged to rise up (44:26) on their behalf.

As subject, God is free. God can be present—God can be absent. God's nearness and absence are Israelite and Christian experiences. God can let the light of God's countenance "shine" on those God knows, and bless them; God can also hide God's face and "forget" the afflicted and the oppressed (Ps. 44:24). God can love and be moved to anger out of wounded love. God is the living God.

Anyone who rejects all these actions and sufferings on God's part on the ground that they are anthropomorphisms fails to take seriously the human subject's likeness to God. Immutability is a nonhuman metaphor. In the sense in which we used it at the beginning, what it says is very limited. What it intends to say is that God is God, and not part of the changeable world. But by merely negating the world's attributes, what we arrive at is not the divine but merely—nothingness.

Is God Impassible?

If we ask Greek philosophy in this way what is "apppropriate" for God (*theoprepes*), difference, manifoldnesss, movement, and suffering all have to be ruled out from the nature of the Deity. The divine substance is incapable of suffering; otherwise it would not be divine. Immovable and incapable of suffering, the Godhead confronts the moved and suffering world of life. The divine substance is the sustaining principle (*hypokeimenon*) and the eternally abiding factor for this world of fleeting phenomena, so it cannot itself be subject to this world's destiny. It was out of this insight that Aristotle formulated the apathy axiom in Book 12 of his *Metaphysics: Theos apathes* (XII,1073 a.11).[4]

At that time *apatheia* meant unalterability in the physical sense, "unfeelingness" in the psychic sense, and, in the ethical sense, freedom. What is divine has no needs, and is subject to no lower drives (*pathe*). What is divine knows neither hate nor love, neither anger nor compassion. Its likeness to God consists of its unshakeableness (*ataraxia*). It is without needs and without passion (*apatheia*). It is always sovereign. To be without pride in good fortune, to endure suffering without complaint, to bear with dignity what must be borne: these are the virtues inculcated by our grandparents. In striving for virtue the wise acquire similarity with that which the deity possesses by nature. But nowadays apathy is a symptom of illness; it means a dulling down of the senses, a lack of participation of heart, and of interest spiritually. Today apathy is a preliminary stage on the road to dying.

If we inquire about the proclamation of God in Christian tradition, we find at its centre the story of Christ's passion. The gospel tells us about Christ's suffering and dying. The self-giving of God's Son for the reconciliation of the world with God is communicated to us in the eucharist in the form of bread and wine. By making present the passion of Christ in word and sacrament, the faith is evoked which believes in God for Christ's sake: the God of Jesus Christ, whom we call Abba, dear Father.

The history of Christ's passion is the history of God's passion, too. If that were not the case it would be impossible for it to radiate any reconciling and redeeming efficacy. Simply as the story about the sufferings of the good man from Nazareth, it would long since have been forgotten, lost in the general history of humanity's sufferings. "When sin brought forth suffering, God's pain found its full human expression through the Holy Spirit in the crucified Christ. Here we have a paradoxical mystery of love: in Christ God suffers." So wrote John Paul II in his encyclical *Dominum et vivificantem.*[5] But that means that Christian theology must discover God in Christ's passion, and must think of Christ's passion in God.

There have been numerous attempts to bring together the metaphysical concept of the inability of the deity to suffer with the suffering of the living God in Christ. But they all end up in a sum of contradictions, as can be seen from the title of Bertrand Brasnett's book, *The Suffering of the Impassible God* (London: SPCK, 1928). Bernard of Clairvaux's saying, which Benedict XVI praises and cites affirmatively, sounds no better: *Impassibilis est Deus sed non incompassibilis*—"God cannot suffer but God can co-suffer." But how is it possible to feel sympathy without suffering oneself? Here Benedict XVI writes: "Man is worth so much to God that he himself became man in order to suffer with man in an utterly real way—in flesh and blood—as is revealed to us in the account of Jesus' passion. Here in all human suffering we are joined by One who experiences and carries that suffering with us—hence consolation is present in all suffering, the consolation of God's suffering love—and so the star of hope rises."[6]

In my view it is theologically better, and corresponds to the biblical experiences of the living God, to depart from the Aristotelian apathy axiom and to start with Abraham Heschel's axiom of *God's pathos*, so as to understand God's suffering from the initial point of God's passion for God's people and God's creation.[7] The prophets were not animated by a metaphysical notion about the world. Their starting point was the people's specific situation with regard to God. Heschel calls this situation "God's pathos." What he means is not an attribute of the divine, but God's passionate relationship to God's people, a relationship that in Amos is called "righteousness," and in Hosea "love."

Because Israel's God loves God's people, God suffers from Israel's disobedience, and seeks for divine justice and divine joy in the people of God's choice. God takes God's people, every single one of them, so seriously that God is hurt by what they do, and suffers from it. God's anger is God's injured love. The opposite of divine love is not divine wrath but the loss of divine concern—God's apathy or indifference.

In God's *Shekinah*, God's "indwelling" in the people of God's choice, Israel's God becomes the people's companion on their way as well as their fellow sufferer. So, in this sense Israel's sufferings are God's sufferings, too. Israel's exile is also the exile of God's *Shekinah*. Consequently, Israel's redemption will mean the redemption of God's *Shekinah* as well, and Israel's joy will at the same time be God's joy.

In the sphere of the divine *apatheia*, the wise human being will become an unshakeable and untouchable sovereign soul. In the sphere of God's pathos, the human being will become a *homo sympatheticus*, a loving person capable of suffering, a life-affirming person capable of participation. Christian theology is, at its depths, a theology of the cross. It sees Christ's suffering and dying as a revelation of God's passion.

"Only the suffering God can help," wrote Dietrich Bonhoeffer in his prison cell in 1944.[8] Here the word *passion* has the double meaning of overwhelming emotion and suffering. Christian faith lives from the suffering of Christ's great passion, and is itself a passion for life, which is prepared for suffering. "Christians stand beside God in God's suffering."

Often no differentiation is made between God's "pain" (Kitamori), God's "suffering" (Bonhoeffer), or God's "sorrow" (G. A. Studdert Kennedy). If by this we mean God's situation on Golgotha, we have to make a trinitarian distinction. Jesus, God's Son, suffers his dying from Gethsemane to Golgotha in abandonment by God. God, on whom he called in the Gethsemane night as Abba, dear Father, suffers the death of God's Son, for God has to survive it. Our own experience of death is similar. At the end we die, but we do not suffer our death because on earth we do not experience it. But we do experience death in the people we love and who are our whole happinesss; for with their death we have to live. As Mascha Kaléko wrote after the death of her only son,

Remember, our own death we merely die,
but with the death of others we must live.

Mediaeval painters depicted this pain of God the Father over the death of his "beloved Son" (Mark 1:11) in the image of the dead Jesus in God's arms. It is also reflected in the familiar form of the Pietà, where Mary cradles her dead son in her lap.

What is manifested here in the suffering of the Son and the passion of the Spirit is the inner-divine mystery of God's self-giving for the redemption of the world. A famous picture of the Trinity derived from the Western church is known as "the throne of grace."[9] With evident pain, God the Father holds in God's hands the cross-beam of the cross on which God's Son hangs. The Holy Spirit in the form of a dove descends from the face of the Father on to the crucified Jesus. What divine situation is depicted here? It is the breathtaking situation of Holy Saturday, following the death of the Son and before his resurrection from the dead—a kind of mystical stillness between cross and resurrection. On this day Johann Rist's hymn is sung, the hymn Hegel quoted for his dialectic of the Spirit:

O great distress,
Godself is dead,
he died upon the cross.

If one has a liking for abstract formulas, one can call this patri-compassionism. But if terms themselves need explanation, then they no longer explain anything. What is more important is the consolation that radiates from God's passion, a consolation aptly expressed in a Methodist hymn:

And when human hearts are breaking
under sorrow's iron rod,
then there is the self-same aching
deep within the heart of God.

The living God cannot be a God who is unable to suffer, because God is not a God without relationships. All that the apathy axiom says is that God is not passively delivered over to the finite world's fate of suffering and death. But beyond this suffering that fate imposes, and beyond any essential incapacity for suffering, there is also the freely accepted suffering of love. People who are able to love are also prepared to suffer, for they lay themselves open to the experience of others. The apathy axiom says merely that God is not delivered over to God's drives and needs like human beings. The Deity is sovereign—consequently, God is a–pathetic. But freedom is not "untouchability," nor is it merely sovereignty; it is love as well. If God were in every respect "apathetic," then God would be a God without relationships, and absolute in the sense of being detached from everything. For us, a being of this kind would be a matter of indifference, because it could not enter into relationship with us.

The living God is a being rich in relationships. In God's relationships to the world of those God has created and to their lives, God is experienced as living and as life-giving.[10] In God's relationships to men and women, the living God is experienced both actively and passively. God speaks and God listens. God acts and God suffers. If the relationships are loving ones, then they are liberating; and in spite of all the qualitative differences between God and human beings, they are reciprocal relationships. If this were not the case, prayers would be pointless. Human beings also make positive or negative impressions on God. God is not a heavenly substance incapable of suffering;

God is a subject of unending divine love. This love is not supreme power; it is compassion and is therefore patient and able to suffer. God's freedom is not arbitrary and devoid of reason, nor is it a crushing superpower. It is a communicative freedom in the interests of love. It manifests itself not just in creating but in its bearing of what it has created, and in its interest in creation's life and well-being.

The "absolute God" is set apart from the world of the living through negations of worldly characteristics, such as alterability and the capacity for suffering.

The "living God" is experienced in God's active and passive relationships in the world of the living.

Is God Almighty?

Now that we have described God as subject in God's freedom and in God's relationships, we have to look at the most familiar attributes of the Deity. The Deity is said to be essentially almighty, omnipresent, and omniscient.

Is the living God the Almighty, the Omnipresent, and the Omniscient One?

"The Almighty"?

If we see the Deity as the all-determining summit of universal monarchy, then it must be the "all-determining reality." But its relation to this world is then that of its ruling principle, so that we can deduce its primal cause and its *primum movens* (its moving principle) from the universal order. There is a necessary connection between the worldly order and its monarch. The "all-determining reality" is perceived from the "absolute dependence" of everything. The Deity must be the almighty power in the universe, and the Almighty must have supreme power in everything that happens in the history of the world.

In 1925 Rudolf Bultmann began his essay "*Welchen Sinn hat es von Gott zu reden?*" ("What is the point of talking about God?") by maintaining that whenever the idea of God is thought, it means that God is the Almighty, that is, the all-determining reality.[11] But he did not mean "everything," in the sense of the totality of what was, is, and will be, but reduced his own thesis immediately to "the reality that determines our existence," for "God's activity cannot be thought of as a general happening." But what is "our existence"? For Bultmann, it is our relation to ourselves—in traditional terms, our soul. And that does not belong to the objective world. It follows from this that if we ask how it is possible to talk about God, the answer has to be: only as a way of talking about ourselves.

Power is divine—that is why human beings find it so fascinating. The powerful feel superior and free, the powerless feel inferior and unfree. The powerful know that the Almighty is on their side—the weak feel forsaken by the Almighty God. Power is life. Weakness is death. That is why the Almighty was invoked for preference as the God of battles, to "inscribe victory on our banners"—by Hitler, too. In this perspective we can find an idolatry of power in world history, and an ideology of the struggle for power. But let us return to "almighty" as one of God's predicates.

Is the Almighty free? No, for God has to be "the all-determining reality." For God there is no alternative to rule over the world. In this way God is tied down to this Almighty role. Is the Almighty a subject? Yes, but a "fixed" subject. Is the Almighty a God in relationship? Yes, but only in the single relationship of determining everything. Has the Almighty power over Godself? No, God can do nothing other than rule over everything. So, in fact, the Almighty is powerless and a prisoner of the universe. The one who determines everything is also responsible for everything, so the Almighty is also the acccused in the theodicy question. The almighty God has no power over Godself. God has to rule; God cannot withdraw Godself. The almighty God is not the living God, for the living God has power over Godself first of all. God determines Godself before determining others. Is that speculation? No, it is decisive for the Israelite and Christian experience of God, for it is only in this way that the love of God can be understood.

God's self-limitations

Kierkegaard ascribed God's withdrawal of Godself to God's omnipotence:

> Only almighty power can withdraw by giving itself and it is this relationship which constitutes the independence of the recipient. So God's almighty power is his goodness. For it is goodness to give oneself utterly but in such a way that in almighty power one withdraws, thus making the recipient independent. All finite power creates dependence. Only what is almighty can create independence, bringing out of nothingness what receives its inner existence because the almighty power withdraws itself.[12]

Here Kierkegaard makes no distinction between power over the universe and God's power over Godself. When in God's power over Godself—which is God's freedom—God "withdraws" God's power over the universe, God makes the universe free and independent and does not keep it captive in "complete dependence," as Schleiermacher maintained, thereby merely translating objective almighty power into subjective dependence. Power is a relational concept and links a dominating subject with a dominated object. If the dominated object becomes free and an independent subject in this relationship, the dominating subject must withdraw itself in order to create space and time for the freedom of the dominated object. In what relationship does this relationship come about? In the relationship of love, free spaces for the beloved develop. Even God's creative power already holds within itself "a self-renunciation of unlimited power," as Hans Jonas remarks, for as Creator, God enters into this world and renounces other options.[13] As the Creator of this world, God also respects this world's space, time, and autonomous movements. The limitation of God's unending power is an act of God's power over Godself. Only God can limit God.

Is creation an act of *self-contraction* on God's part? Before God went out of Godself in order to create a nondivine world that would nevertheless conform to the divine, God withdrew into Godself in order to make a space free for that world. That was Isaac Luria's idea, the idea he called "*zimzum*."[14]According to the Jewish Kabbalah, the Infinite One withdrew God's omnipresence in order to concede a space for the limited presence of God's finite creation. There are two remarkable points about this idea. First, before God created heaven and earth God determined Godself to be the creator of this world. That is the reflexive structure of every decision. In German one says, "I decide *myself* to do this or that ("*ich entscheide mich . . .*)." Second, when God withdraws Godself, a God-free space comes into being. This space is the "nothing" of the creation out of nothing (*creatio ex nihilo*), as Gershom Scholem notes.[15]

Is the creation an act of self-humiliation on God's part? Many theologians, from Nicholas of Cusa down to Emil Brunner, have seen it in this way. Self-limitation, self-restriction, self-withdrawal are only different words for God's self-humiliation, God's kenosis. In Brunner's words: "But that means that God does not occupy the space of his being alone; he wishes to make room for other being too. By so doing he restricts himself. . . . The kenosis which arrives at its supreme point in Christ's cross already begins with the creation of the world."[16]

When God commits Godself to this fragile and corruptible creation, it is the first act in God's commitments to the people of God's choice and God's indwellings, in Israel and in Jesus Christ. God's readiness to suffer begins with God's resolve to create the world, and with the divine love for those God has created on this earth. The power of the living God does not consist in God's keeping everything in "absolute dependence"; it is found in the fact that God "bears" everything in endless patience, thereby creating a space for them and leaving them time to develop in freedom. That is important for an understanding of what creation means.[17]

God's weakness

In the light of his theology of the cross, Paul paradoxically sees God's "almighty power" in world history in God's weakness: "For God's foolishness is wiser than human wisdom, and

God's weakness of is stronger than human strength (1 Cor. 1:25)." By this he means not just Christ's weakness on the cross, but also the weakness of Christ's people in the world: "Consider your call . . . not many were powerful. . . . But God chose . . . what is weak in the world to shame the strong; God chose what is low and despised in the world, things that are not, to reduce to nothing things that are, so that no one might boast in the presence of God" (1 Cor. 1:26ff.).

God is not on the side of the mighty as "the Almighty"—God is on the side of the weak, as the liberator who is in solidarity with them.[18] The living God chooses the weak in the world and rejects the mighty. That is God's "preferential option for the poor," as the Latin American Episcopal conference in Medellin declared in 1968, backed up by biblically supported liberation theology. In Paul, that entirely conforms to the prophet Isaiah's vision, in which all the valleys will be exalted and all the mountains will be brought low so that all flesh "together" can see God's coming glory (Isa. 40:5). In this godless world of violence, God's weakness has a revolutionary effect, as Mary says in the Magnificat:

> *He has brought down the powerful from their thrones*
> *and lifted up the lowly. (Luke 1:52)*

Is God Omnipresent?

Psalm 139 gives a wonderful testimony to God's omnipresence:

> *You hem me in behind and before,*
> *and lay your hand upon me . . .*
> *Where can I go from your spirit?*
> *Or where can I flee from your presence?*
> *If I ascend to heaven, you are there; if I make my bed in Sheol,*
> *   you are there.*
> *If I take the wings of the morning*
> *and settle at the farthest limits of the sea,*
> *even there your hand shall lead me,*
> *and your right hand shall hold me fast.*

A point to be noted is that this God does not crush men and women through God's omnipresence, but surrounds them as if in a "broad place" (Ps. 31:8), so that they can move freely in every direction and are nevertheless still in God's hands. Another remarkable point is that the omnipresent God is addressed in the familiar form— "thou," as we used to say. Omnipresence is not an attribute of the divine substance; it belongs to the divine subject, who desires to be present everywhere to all the beings God has created. This is not pantheism, which equates God with nature.

That became particularly plain in 20th-century mysticism, in Edith Stein and Simone Weill. In the mass dying of that terrible century, that was above all an immersion in the "silence of God" and an inward enduring of "the dark night of the soul." It is a mystical experience of God's absence. The consoled trust in God has been replaced by what Johann Baptist Metz calls "a bitter missing of God."[19]

From early on, Pope John Paul II belonged to the tradition of the Gethsemane prayer. His is an answer to Jesus' question to the disciples in the Garden of Gethsemane, "Could you not watch one hour with me?" Why were the disciples supposed to watch with their Master? Because he was mortally assailed: "In his anguish . . . his sweat became like great drops of blood" (Luke 22:24). "[He] began to be greatly distressed and troubled. And he said to them, 'My soul is very sorrowful, even to death'" (Mark 14:33, 34; cf. Matt. 26:38, RSV). What assailment is this? It is God's silence in response to Jesus' prayer that the cup might pass him by. What cup? The cup of dying in Godforsakenness. On Golgotha Jesus experiences what it is to die in Godforsakenness. The Gethsemane prayer is not really a prayer but a "watching" with the assailed Christ, the Christ surrendered by God the Father for the redemption of the world. "Christians stand beside God in his suffering."[20] In one's own experience of remoteness from God and the dark night of the soul, Christ becomes the sole consolation that sustains life. "The Gethsemane prayer goes on," exorted John Paul II.[21] "Jesus' agony will endure until the end of the world. Until then we may not sleep," as Pascal said.[22]

Following Christ's suffering from God, we have to ask: Where is God not present? If God was in Christ, God was not present in the forces that let Christ suffer and die on the cross. According to Paul and the Deutero-Pauline epistles, that means "all rule, all power and violence." The risen Christ who has been exalted to God will "destroy" them, hopes Paul, together with the powers of death on which their rule is built. "For he must reign until he has put all his enemies under his feet. The last enemy to be destroyed is death" (1 Cor. 15:25-26). According to the epistles to the Ephesians and the Colossians, God "disarmed the principalities and powers, and made a public example of them, triumphing over them in him" (Col. 2:15, RSV). For the exalted Christ is "the head of every ruler and authority" (Col. 2:10). These are the forces of chaos, powers hostile to creation and contemptuous of human beings, as well as the godless forces of destruction. In them God is no more present than God is in the power of sin (Romans 7). According to Paul, they will all be destroyed through the omnipresence of Christ. But for both Paul and the Deutero-Paulines, the power of sin and the violence of death will be excluded from Christ's cosmic rule. After the passion of God in Golgotha, through the exaltation of the crucified One to God, God's omnipresence through Christ will be disseminated, reconciling and life-creating. Because Christ has suffered the hell of separation from God, there is no longer any hell in which God is not present.

Even the darkness is not dark to you,
the night is as bright as the day
for darkness is as light with you. (Ps. 139:12)

Those who perceive in Christ the crucified God can be assured that "neither principalities nor powers" will be able to separate them from "the love of God in Christ Jesus" (Rom. 8:38-39).

Is God omnipresent in the sense that God is present in everything, everywhere, and at all times, in just the same way? No, there are godforsaken spaces and situations, there are godless powers. But in the crucified Jesus, God is present even in godforsaken spaces and situations, and in Jesus Christ, the risen and exalted Lord, the godless powers have lost their power. In Christ God is omnipresent, and through him God will be "all in all" (1 Cor. 15:28).

Is God Omniscient?

Omniscience is accounted to be one of God's attributes, as well as omnipotence and omnipresence. God knows everything, God remembers everything, the eye of God sees everything. Belief in God's good providence belongs to trust in God, in traditional piety. But to see God's providence as predetermination, destiny, fate, or kismet also makes a human being irresponsible and irresolute and lays every cosmic disaster and all human crimes at the door of the Deity. How ought we realistically to understand God's omniscience and God's providence?

a. In creating the world, God concedes to human beings their own space and time, thereby giving them their flexibility and freedom. In discussing God's almighty power, we also said that God's creation is therefore bound up with God's limitation of Godself, and God's withdrawal of God's power. The same may be said about God's omniscience.[23] So, instead of maintaining that God must know and predict everything, because God is the all-determining reality, we now say that the living God does not know everything in advance, because God has no wish to do so. God waits for the response of those God has created, and leaves them time for their response, and creates possibilities for it. God does not only create the realities of this world, God is also the source of its unforseeable potentialities. If God is the source of the potentialities of those God has created, then God does not know in advance how those potentialities will be realized, and therefore is not responsible for their misuse.

b. In the history of this world and of every individual person, what one knows is divided between the remembrance of the past and the pre-vision of the future. The God of history absorbs all time's potentialities into God's eternal memory, and anticipates the potentialities of the future God intends through God's commandments of righteousness and promises of freedom. God does not prevent the perversions of sin and the misfortunes of the created beings who have gone astray. God is responsible for human freedom, but not for human misdemeanours.

But God's memory is not a heavenly video that mechanically records everything that happens. It is the remembering of the living

God. That is why men and women pray, "Remember me according to your great mercy" and "Remember not the sins of my youth." God's memory is a gracious remembrance that puts things right.

God's providence is directed not to future realities but to future possibilities. Providence has nothing to do with predetermination and fate; it originally meant foresight, provision, early insight, and was bound up with the gift of prophecy. In human beings this means the anticipatory awareness of the transcending power of the imagination. In hope, we conjure up that for which we hope, and intervene in the world of negative possibilities, in order to avert them in good time or so as to prepare ourselves for them. The prophets and apocalyptic writers have always worked in this way. They did not examine the entrails of animals, lay out tarot cards, or read palms. They did not foresee realities; they anticipated possibilities. In the context of the living God, providence (*providentia*) is linked with promise (*promissio*): foresight is an advance glance into the possible, and that is God's promise.[24] It indicates God's intention, to which we can trust ourselves, as well as the trends in history, which we are supposed to realize. This is, then, not a one-sided advance knowing; it is a kind of advance knowledge on God's part, realized in dialogue. It is the advance knowledge of the living God intended for a cooperation with those God has created, especially with human beings, God's image, for a shared future.

The Prohibition of Images: The Living God

> You shall not make for yourself a graven image, or any likeness of anything that is in heaven above or that is in the earth beneath, or that is in the water under the earth; you shall not bow down to them or serve them; for I the LORD your God am a jealous God, visiting the iniquity of the fathers upon the children to the third and fourth generation of those who hate me, but showing steadfast love to thousands of those who love me and keep my commandments. (Exod. 20:4-6, RSV)

This is first of all a prohibition of idolatry, directed against the worship of the forces of this world in heaven, on earth, and under the earth. Do not worship them and do not serve them! But for human beings power always has a divine and a demonic fascination. The forces of nature and the political forces are always admired, with the hope that they will be well disposed, and that we may have a share in them. They are worshipped when pictures and likenesses of them are made and when their powerful manifestations are revered and we can visibly participate in them. The power of male procreation is revered in bulls, the power of the sun in the fire, the capacity to bear children in maternal statues, while political power was, in an earlier time, reflected in statues of the pharaohs and, quite recently, in pictures of the Führer, such as we find in fascism and communism. The biblical story behind the prohibition of images is the dance around the golden calf in the absence of Moses and his God. The "calf" was a bull, and the people made for itself this image of the mysterious divine power in the absence of the "LORD"—the God who had led the people out of slavery into freedom.

Underlying this ancient story is a deeper stratum of meanings. What does a picture do? It presents the impression of something in the mind of the observer. It not only says something about what is presented, but also tells something about those that present it. The picture shows not just what the observer sees but also what he or she wants to see or does not want to see, and the way he or she sees it or does not want to see it.

A photo ties a movement down to a moment. What is involved in temporal alteration is fixed, confined to a timeless space. Even the moving pictures in a film "freeze" a movement. They make repeatable what is actually unrepeatable. Why do people today take photos of everything and everyone everywhere? Because they want to possess and hold fast to impressions and moments that in reality they are unable to keep hold of and possess.

In the magical world of ancient times, one robbed people of their mystery if one made a picture of them. One could stab someone to death magically by injuring his or her picture. Today we have the magic of the image. Everyone possesses an aura, the impression one makes on other people. One can cultivate one's image, one can damage the image of other people, but one can never keep one's image for oneself, or identify the image of other people with oneself. The image has a role of its own—in the realm of the imagination.

Why and when do we construct an image of other people? When I am together with my wife, and she is beside me, I have no need to have a picture of her in my hand. If I had a picture of her in my head, instead of enjoying a living give-and-take with her, I should not be really present and she would not be beside me as a living person. Pictures are preconceived ideas and are harmful in our living contacts. But when my wife is absent, I like to look at her picture. Her picture makes present the person who is absent, but it represents her only until she is there again. In our living dealings with one another, pictures are damaging, because they tie an absent person down to a picture of them belonging to the past, and in that way affect the living present. It is love that comes forward to a continual iconoclasm. Love frees us from images with which we pin other people or ourselves down. Love enters with curiosity into the mutual transformations of human beings; indeed, it encourages them because it keeps the future open for the beloved. So in love the beloved feels free. When love disappears, we begin to pin the other person down: "That's you all over. You have always been the same. I don't know what to do with you." In his *Tagebuch 1946–1949*, Max Frisch writes: "Love frees us from every image. That is the exciting thing, the adventure, the truly captivating thing, that we never come to an end of the people we love: because we love them, as long as we love them."[25]

We cannot make any image of the living God without destroying God's living presence with us by setting a distance between us. There are no pictures of God because the living God is closer to us than our main artery, as the Qu'ran says, or than we ourselves can be, as Augustine puts it; and because we "live and move and have our being" in God there are no images of God. We cannot picture God, not because God is so far off in heaven or in the next world, but because God is so close that we cannot find any detachment from God. That is the message of Psalm 139.

What is true of images of God—that they are impossible—is also true of our concepts of God. They stand between us and the God who is present, and destroy our life in the living God. They pin down what cannot be pinned down. "Concepts create idols," said Gregory of Nyssa, rightly; "Only astonishment can grasp anything."[26]

Is the prohibition of images followed by a prohibition of concepts, including the ontological ones?

a. *Is there a God?* ask children, and atheists maintain there is probably no God. The theological answer is that there *is* no God in the way that there "are" many things. God is not one phenomenon among many others. There isn't a God who is there, declared Dietrich Bonhoeffer succinctly.

b. *Does God exist?* asked Hans Küng in his well-known book of 1978, and applied the concept of human existence to God. Anthropologically, existing means ex-isting, being out of oneself. With this, existential philosophy describes the inner self-transcendence of the human spirit. Helmuth Plessner uses it to describe the "excentric positionality" of the human being. So if God "exists," is God then outside Godself, excentric and not resting within Godself? To apply the concept of existence to God presents the same difficulties as does the application of the concept of existing to God. These are human analogies applied in spite of the qualitative difference between God and human being. In another respect it quite well makes sense to talk about the existence of God. God exists when God goes out of Godself and is with human beings, as we see in Exodus 3:8: "I have come down to deliver them," and in John 1:14: "The Word became flesh and dwelt among us" (RSV).

c. *Is there God?* The application of the concept of being is the most general ontological definition of God. God is not no being, but the being of what is. God is being, not this or that existence. As a way of freeing God from this ontotheological metaphysics, Jean-Luc Marion suggested thinking "God without being." God is beyond being.

Every position in affirmative theology is paralled by a position in negative theology. The path of theological perception leads through this dialectic to the point where it began: in fathomless astonishment.

So is there no theology? Yes, there is. There is theology and God's will, with the one presupposition that "the Word became flesh and dwelt among us." The *logos tou theou* is the precondition for theo–logy.

Chapter 3

The Living God in the History of Christ

The One God: What Unity?

There is one metaphysical divine attribute we have not looked at yet: *God's unity*. This attribute seems so obvious that it is seldom treated in theology. Over against the multiplicity of things in the world, and all the different fleeting impressions, it would seem to be a matter of course that the Deity must be a single, self-contained unity, with a continuance and identity of its own. In the history of religion the term *monotheism* has become the word customarily used for this, a term that probably originated with David Hume. But what Hume was referring to was the Persian monarchy under Xerxes. Today it means belief in the One God: Judaism, Christianity, and Islam worship only the One God, other than whom "there can be no other gods": "There is no God but God."

The term *monotheism* excludes polytheism, but it does not imply any further reflection about the meaning of *monas* and *myrias*. Does it mean "one," or "single," or "always one and the same"? If the divine unity is defined only through the exclusion of worldly multiplicity, its own mode of being remains undetermined. Consequently, none of the so-called monotheisms resembles another.[1] Judaism, Christianity, Islam, Hinduism, Echnaton's sun worship, and Ludwig XIV's unifying absolutism—these differ so greatly from one another that they cannot be thrown together under the overriding term "monotheistic world religions." That is due to the fact that God's unity is determined only negatively, through the exclusion of the Many or the Other, but not positively because of the nature of God.

- Ought we to understand the unity numerically as "one"—God is One? Then God would also be applicable as the "one" in the numerical sequence of the Many, but it would have nothing to do with God.

- Should the One be understood as the opposite of the other? Then the One would always imply the other, and the One would be dependent on the other.

- Should God's unity be understood as ultimately nondivisible? Then God would be like an atom or an individual devoid of relationship, and would be unable to "im-part" itself.

- If God's unity, understood as a *monas*, is a "windowless monad" (to use a phrase of Leibniz's), then the One God would also be the solitary God who cannot concern us. God would be imprisoned in a self-contained system that we could know nothing about, because there can be no exchange of energy with closed systems, and thus no communication either.

If, on the other hand, we try to understand God's unity in the light of the living God, then we have to understand it not as a predicate but as a verb: it can mean the *uniting of God* with Godself. God is either always one with Godself, as the Old Testament name "I am who I am" asserts, or God re-establishes the unity with Godself out of God's self-relinquishment in the other. In either case we no longer understand God's unity passively as an exclusion of plurality, but actively as God's activity in relation to the many-faceted world. God's unity, then, has an inviting, unifying power to link the many things in the world with God, and to reconcile with God the wholly other of the godless world. "Everything divided finds its way back to itself . . ." Then God's unity has a soteriological function.

That on which your heart is set

But monotheism is also held to be belief in one God. If we take as our starting point not metaphysics but the subjectivity of faith, "monotheism" becomes highly questionable. "That on which thy heart is set and on which thou dost rely, that is in truth thy God," says Luther's *Large Catechism*, "for the faith of thy heart maketh both God and idol." And according to Luther, the most commonly worshipped God on earth is "mammon." The capitalist who sets his or her heart on money and possessions and "depends" on them alone is a monotheist; the communist for whom the party is always right is a monotheist; the Nazi for whom you are nothing and your people everything is a monotheist; and so on. Subjective monotheistic belief is generally speaking nothing other than idolatry and the worship of false gods. Seen in this light, immanent monotheism is a monomania that destroys the protean richness of life. It is only a plural monotheism that opens men and women for the wealth of life.

Can God be numbered?

Does it make sense to apply numbers to God, whether it be the number one or the number three? No, that is not a sanctification of God's name; it is a trivializing abstraction: God cannot be numbered off, or counted. God's unity is not a numerical unit, and the Tri-unity is not the sum of one plus one plus one equals three, or three times one. The number three equalizes the differences between the Father, the Son, and the Holy Spirit, and reduces their eternal history to three numbers. If we look critically at the numerical sequence from the aspect of the Deity, God is either that than which nothing less can be counted, or that than which nothing greater can be counted. The 0 (nil) stands for Nirvana, the ∞ (infinity) stands for the totality.

The Living Space of the Triune God

Some people think that the Christian doctrine of the Trinity is difficult to understand and is pure speculation, so it is something only for learned theologians—and even for them the Trinity is "a mystery."

None of this is true. The Christian faith has itself a trinitarian structure because it is a trinitarian experience of God. That is easy to understand since every believer lives in this experience of God, and knows it.[2]

a. Christian faith is a life *in community with Christ*. Community with Christ means that Jesus Christ becomes my Lord and my brother, my liberator and my redeemer, and that I trust myself to him in living and in dying. Jesus Christ has found me, and takes me with him on his way to the eternal life of the future world. I find myself accepted into his history, for he lives and dies for me, and I rise with him. Paul takes this to its ultimate point when he professes: "It is no longer I who live, but it is Christ who lives *in* me" (Gal. 2:20). In those who discover for themselves the self-giving of Jesus Christ, Christ lives, too. Christ is not only God's beloved Son (Mark 1:11); he is also "the first-born among within a large family" (Rom. 8:29). So in community with him I experience myself as God's child, or—to be more precise—as God's son or daughter and, being a co-heir with Christ, as an inheritor of eternal life.

b. Jesus, God's Son, called God "Abba, dear Father."[3] So, those who are his also pray in his name and in his spirit, "Abba, dear Father" (Rom. 8:15; Gal. 4:6). In community with Christ, the God of Jesus Christ becomes their God, too. Through Christ they have free access to Christ's God. But that means nothing other than that Christians believe in God for Jesus' sake, and believe in no God other than the God of Jesus Christ. Here "God" is not a general religious term; it is shaped by the form and history of Jesus Christ. We can also express this by saying that God "revealed" Godself in Jesus Christ. When we use God as a general religious term, this does not as yet say anything about the Christian belief in God. In the New Testament, the name of God is primarily used for "the Father of our Lord Jesus Christ" (Rom. 15:6). Logically, that subsumes the Godhead of Jesus, the "Son of God," and of the Holy Spirit.

But what has happened to the intimate "Abba" address? Paul still heard this being used in the congregations in Galatia and Rome, but in the second century it was replaced by the address to "our Father" as was the "*Maranatha!*" cry of imminent expectation. The address "Our Father" was supplemented by the distancing words "in heaven," and the delayed *parousia* joined the imminent expectation. It is only recently, in Taizé and other Christian communities, that the "Abba" prayer has been reintroduced. When we address God as Abba, dear Father, we sense Jesus' closeness to us and his closeness to his God, and we cease to think of the concept of father simply in a family and politically patriarchal context.[4] With the Abba address we practice a nonpatriarchal and nonmonarchical way of addressing God. The bond with Jesus constitutes the difference between the Father of Jesus Christ and Zeus, the father of the gods, and the father god Jupiter. This difference is important for Christian identity.

c. On the other hand, in community with Christ we experience an undreamed-of encouragement to live. We sense powers of healing, we know that we are consoled, and we chime in with God's great yes to this life. That is to say, we receive the *energies of God's Spirit.* That does not make God's Spirit our spirit, and our spirit is not deified. Paul makes the distinction when he writes: "It is that very Spirit bearing witness with our spirit that we are children of God" (Rom. 8:16). But when we receive the divine Spirit in the community of Christ, we accept it as *the Spirit who has become human.* Otherwise, it would overwhelm us though its divinity. We are not told that God's Spirit "became human." What we are told is that the Spirit has been "poured out" and "dwells in us." That is the particular *kenosis* of the divine Spirit, which has to be distinguished from the self-emptying incarnation of Christ (Philippians 2).[5] The Spirit who gives life is "poured into our hearts" (Rom. 5:5). Our body of flesh and blood becomes "a temple of the Holy Spirit" (1 Cor. 6:19). Not least, we experience God's Spirit in the relationships in the community of Christ, where everyone brings their vital energies as *charismata* into the community (1 Corinthians 12). What is the consequence of these experiences of the Spirit in the community of Christ? A new, unthought-of vitality in God's open living-space. "Where the Spirit of the Lord is, there is freedom" (2 Cor. 3:17). These are the daybreak colours of the eternal, divine life, which already shine in our finite human life.

d. We experience these three divine dimensions in the community of Christ. These are the three actors in our history with God: we live in community with Jesus, the Son of God; and with God, the Father of Jesus Christ; and with God, the Spirit of life. So we do not only *believe* in God; we *live* in God, that is to say, in God's trinitarian history with us.

But then where is *God's unity* to be found? This emerges from the inner relationships of God's Son, God the Father, and God's Spirit. When we look at Christ we also find in him the God whom he called "Abba, dear Father," as well as the healing and life-giving Spirit who emanates from him. When we look at God the Father, we also find in him Christ, God's Son, and God's Spirit. In the powers of the Holy Spirit we find God the Father, from whom the Spirit proceeds, and Christ through whom God heals and illuminates us. They are so present with one another that they cannot be separated. A Jesus humanism without God is for Christians as pointless as a Father religion without Jesus, or an esoteric Spirit meditation without God and Jesus.

The three actors in our salvation history are so present in one another that they cannot be separated without destroying the salvation. They are "one" in the sense of a *henosis*, a unity such as the Gospel of John lets Jesus express when he says: "The Father and I are one" (John 10:30). That is not just a unity of will; it is also a mutual personal and interwoven being: ". . . that they may all be *one*. As you, Father, are *in* me and I am *in* you . . . (17:21). These reciprocal "indwellings" represent a unique unity in which the differentiations are presupposed and preserved. The divine Persons of the Father, and of Jesus the Son, and of the Holy Spirit constitute their unity through their mutual opening for the indwelling. They give themselves to each other and receive from one another. Consequently, their unity is not a closed unity, like a circle or a triangle (which are traditional figures for the Tri-unity); it is wide open, so that the disciples—and then all created beings as well—find their space for living within it. "May they also be *in us*" (17:21). Just as the Son is in the Father, and the Father is in the Son, so we human beings are to be in them. The self-giving and openness of the Son and the Father for each other find their correspondence in their shared openness and self-giving toward beloved human beings. Conversely, our life in God corresponds to the inner trinitarian fellowship of like with like, as well to as the fellowship of the unlike: "Those who abide in love abide *in* God and God abides *in* them" (1 John 4:16). This love is the true force that transcends frontiers. Whoever lives in God's Spirit lives in God and God in him or her. That would come close to a deification of the human being if it were not for the inner-trinitarian indwellings of God through nature, and for the divine–human indwellings though grace. The Israelite idea about the *Shekinah*, and the patristic concept of *perichoresis*, are appropriate representations of the mutual indwellings that we expressed in the New Testament language of Paul and John.[6] That is the soteriological function of God's *unity*.

The History of God in Christ

When we think about our own situation with God, we think about our present experience. We shall do that now by passing over from the trinitarian experience of faith to the trinitarian history of Christ. The patristic formula runs:

> *Three hypostases—one being, or*
> *Three Persons—one substance.*

The three *hypostases* or persons signify Father—Son—Holy Spirit. The one substance or one being signifies the one Godhead. If now this one Godhead is defined metaphysically through the exclusion of what is characteristic of earthly and mortal life, it is hardly conceivable that the Father, the Son, and the Spirit could communicate themselves to earthly and temporal life in living relationships of openness and self-giving, and that they are hence related to each other. Nevertheless, this says that God the Father and God the Son and God the Spirit are divine beings and are therefore related to one another. But the human way of accessing knowledge cannot be a speculation about the nature of God in Godself; they have to begin with the Son of God who has become human. The trinitarian ideas are not formed about God in heaven; they are based on the history of Christ on earth: three persons—this one, single history.[7]

The modern understanding of the Trinity replaces the substance of the one Deity by an absolute subject: "God is spirit" (John 4:24). Wolfhart Pannenberg writes, "According to Hegel, God is conceived of as 'Spirit' in that he makes himself the object of himself, the Son, that he then remains in this object through love and is thus identical with himself, goes together with himself in this love of his."[8] However, every self-consciousness has a triadic structure. The "I" makes itself the object of its consciousness and identifies itself with itself.

At the beginning of his *Church Dogmatics*, Karl Barth follows Hegel. He not only proceeds from the absolute subject, but also understands the doctrine of the Trinity as the expression of the absolute sovereignty of God: "God is the Lord" and God's self-revelation has a triadic structure: God reveals Godself through Godself.[9] God is the revealer, the revelation, and the being-revealed. This is God's thrice "repetition" of Godself. So the conditions of the patristic doctrine of the Trinity are turned upside down. It begins with the unity: "One subject—in three modes of being." God is not one, but one and the same who reveals Godself in a threefold way. With this the three divine persons lose their own subjectivity and action; they become modes of appearance of the one personal God. The concept of person is reduced to the concept of relation. At the beginning of his *Church Dogmatics,* Karl Barth reduces the trinitarian persons to the modes of appearance of the One God. That is also consistent if one proceeds from the self-consciousness, the self-revelation, or the self-communication of the One God.

In his new version of the doctrine of the Trinity (1928 and 1932), Karl Barth assumes that the doctrine of the Trinity was intended to secure the subjectivity and sovereignty of God (I/1, 363 [Ger. ed.]). Consequently, he talks there not about three divine "I"s, but about three times the one divine I (370). It is "the one personal God" in the mode of the Father, in the mode of the Son, and in the mode of the Holy Spirit (379). But this one God is three times God in a different way (380). Barth calls this triadic "repetition in God" the *repetitio aeternitatis in eternitate*, meaning by that the "closed circle" of the church's doctrine of the Trinity (400). With this he has accepted the number one. But three times one is not as yet a trinity. Why should the repetition in God stop at three? To put this reason for the doctrine of the Trinity before the "history of Christ" is not to be recommended because in his doctrine of reconciliation Barth himself has tacitly departed from it. Nor has it found any successor.

But why is this self-opening of God found specifically only in the history of Jesus Christ? Barth establishes the connection through God's election, taking up the Calvinist doctrine of decrees. God could have contented himself with himself and his unimpaired glory and the bliss of the divine inner life, but as God's royal throne God chose the cross on Golgotha. In other words, it is so because God wills it to be so. That is arbitrary, fortuitous, and unconvincing. With it he sets the immanent Trinity, *God for Godself*, in contradiction to the Trinity, *God for us*, which belongs to the economy of salvation. The one is self-sufficient, the other culminates in the cross of Christ. Here there is no correspondence. Does that mean that "the history of Jesus of Nazareth" is alien to the "inner-trinitarian being of God?"[10]

The new trinitarian thinking,[11] in contrast, starts from the history of Jesus Christ and develops the doctrine of the Trinity from Jesus' relation as Son to the Father (Pannenberg), or from the interpersonal and communicative happening of the persons who act in the history of Jesus about whom the biblical history of Christ tells (my own proposal). The purpose of the doctrine of the Trinity is not to secure the subjectivity of the Spirit (Hegel) or the sovereignty of God (Barth); its purpose is to interpret the history of Jesus Christ as the *history of God*.[12] The Trinity is not the speculative presupposition for the divine history of Christ; it follows from that because it can be detected there for the first time. The history of Jesus Christ is itself the trinitarian history of God in the co-workings of the Father, the Spirit, and the Son. The being of God does not lie behind the appearance of the history; it is this history-become-human itself. Consequently, we must "tell" the divine history of Jesus Christ if we want to understand the Tri-unity of God.

Jesus the Son of God receives his mission and endowment with the Spirit from the Father in baptism. Jesus' Abba prayer makes God addressable as his Father. The Spirit of truth makes the community of the Son with the Father manifest. In their co-workings in the history of Christ, they form their community with one another and their self-differentiation from one another. This is not three self-revelations of God, but the Son reveals the Father and the Father reveals the Son and the Spirit reveals the Father and the Son.

The trinitarian history of Jesus Christ reaches its decisive point in the Gethsemane night, which precedes his death on the cross on Golgotha. Just as at his baptism, the Father calls Jesus "my beloved Son" (Mark 1:11), so Jesus prays here, "Abba, Father . . . remove this cup from me" (14:36). By "this cup," he means the Godforsakenness and the divine self-giving, for "my soul is very sorrowful even to death" and "he became greatly distressed and troubled" (14:34, 33, RSV), for here the will of the Father and the will of the Son are not the same. They are in conflict. Here God stands over against God, the Son against the Father. It is not God the Father who solves the conflict, but the Son of God, who does so by surmounting himself: "Not my will but yours be done" (14:36, RSV). In this way the unity of the Tri-unity is preserved by the Son, who surrenders himself to his Father's still-hidden will, a will revealed for the first time only on Golgotha.

The scene in Gethsemane is the key to an understanding of what takes place between the Son and the Father on Golgotha in the death of the Son. The death of Jesus Christ on the cross is, in the profoundest sense, a happening between God and God. The Son suffers his dying in forsakenness by the Father, and God the Father suffers the death of his beloved Son. Both of them experience, though in different ways, *the death of God*. By this we understand sin as sickness unto death, and lostnesss in the abyss of annihilation. They experience the apocalyptic downfall of the world—Jesus in "the dark night if the soul." "My soul is very sorrowful, even to death." The God whom he called Abba, dear Father, experiences in the forsakennesss of the beloved Son the "eclipse of God in the world" (cf. Luke 23:44).

The answer of God the Father to the self-surmounting of the Son in Gethsemane and his death in Godforsakenness is the raising of the crucified and dead Son through the Spirit, the life-giver, into the life that overcomes death.[13]

There is no convincing argument to the "why?" question in suffering that does not justify suffering and therefore says "because" as only the new beginning of life—so one could generally say. The Father's answer to the "why?" question with which the Son dies is not an interpretation of his dying, but his raising into the life that triumphs over death—"the eclipse of God in the world" and the dark night of the soul (cf. 1 Cor. 15:55).

The cross and resurrection of Jesus Christ belong together. *There is no sombre theology of the cross without the sun of the resurrection,* which rises behind the cross on Golgotha. There is no perception of the night of Gethsesmane without the daylight colours of Easter day. Without the resurrection, Gethsemane and Golgotha would be only one of the unnumbered tragedies of human life. Without Golgotha, Easter would be no more than a celebration of the spring.

But for Paul the death and resurrection of Jesus Christ do not have the same value:

> *Who is to condemn?*
> *It is Christ Jesus, who died,*
> *yes, who was raised,*
> *who is at the right hand of God,*
> *who indeed intercedes for us. (Rom. 8:34).*

In its significance the resurrection of Christ surpasses his death, just as grace surpasses sin: "But where sin increased, grace abounded all the more" (Rom. 5:20). The whole of the fifth chapter of the epistle to the Romans is stamped by the logic of the "how much more."[14] How much more is God's joy on the day of Christ's resurrection than God's pain on the day of Christ's death! Christ's history does not end with his death but goes further with God. It embraces his rule over the living and the dead, and his struggle against "the principalities and powers" that brought him to his death on the cross. "For he *must* reign *until* [God] puts all his enemies under his feet." After he has "destroyed" those godless lordships and destructive powers Christ will give "the kingdom," which is only then completed, to the Father, so that "God may be all in all" (1 Cor. 15:24-28). The trinitarian history of the Father and of the Son will be completed in the co-efficacy of the two in the Spirit. The Father overcomes Christ's enemies, the Son gives the kingdom over to the Father, thereby completing his Sonship through his own obedience to the One who has subjected everything to him. Then God is *in* everything and all things are *in* God: the new eternal creation, the transfigured world, the God-imbued cosmos. The unity of the triune God that unites the world is then consummated once God is the all-one God.

This trinitarian history of Christ shows the vitality of God among us, but where is God's *eternity*?

One can fall back on philosophical tradition and draw *the trinitarian conclusion*. Because God is what God has revealed God to be (since God remains true to God in what God does), we can deduce God's eternal being from God's acts in history. God is "beforehand in himself," what God has revealed God to us as being (Barth).[15]

But together with the liturgical tradition we can also practice the doxological anticipation.[16] Where do we encounter God's eternal trinity of being? Surely when we praise God, and laud God for God's own sake!

> *Glory be to the Father and to the Son and to the Holy Spirit.*
> *As it was in the beginning, now and ever shall be,*
> *world without end.*

In this way we anticipate in worship what it will be in the universal completion—*In the beginning* God created heaven and earth—and this beginning ends in the eternal kingdom of the triune God.

> *Holy, holy, holy is the LORD of hosts,*
> *the whole earth is full of his glory. (Isa. 6:3; Rev. 4:8)*

And since this is so, the triune God revealed in the history of Christ is God from eternity to eternity.

Let us sum up:

The living God can be none other than the triune God. The triune God lives eternal life in mutual love within God. The history of Christ is his life history for us, among us, and with us. In the history of Christ his eternal life absorbs our finite life into itself. And that being so, this mortal life is then already eternal life. We live in his eternal life even when we die.

PART TWO

The Fullness of Life

Chapter 4

✦

This Eternal Life

THE HUMAN BEING DOES NOT HAVE A REFERENCE SOLELY TO HIM- OR
herself. He or she is to a much greater extent a participatory being, a
being with relationships. He or she is not an individual, but is a social
being. It is only with the participation of others and in others that one
can have a reference to oneself and it is only in community with others
that one becomes a person. A human being is conceived and born out
of a sexual relationship. All human life begins in the female body. It
dies a social death when it has no relationships.

We shall look at this in three dimensions. As an earthly creature,
the human being lives in the community of the earth; as parents and
children, human beings live in the sequence of human generations; as
God's children, they live a divine life.

In the Fellowship of the Divine Life

It is generally said that life here on earth is nothing but a finite and
mortal life. To say this is to allow human life to be dominated by
death. But that is then a reduced life. In fellowship with the living
God, *this* mortal and finite life, here and now, is a life interpenetrated
by God and hence it immediately also becomes a life that is divine
and eternal. In participation in the divine life, *this* human life is the
"one, eternal, glowing life" that Hölderlin extolled. If we cease to
contemplate the temporal end of human life, but look instead at its

eternal beginning, then human life is surrounded and accepted by the divine, and the finite is part of infinity. Eternal life is here and now. This present life, this joyful and painful, loved and suffered, successful and unsuccessful life is eternal life. In the incarnation of Christ, God has accepted this human life and interpenetrated it, reconciled and healed it, and qualified it with immortality. We do not live a merely earthly life, and not only a human life, but simultaneously also live the life that is divine, eternal, and infinite. Eternal life is not endless life but life that is filled with God, life in abundance (John 10:10). Eternity is a divine qualification of human life, not its endless prolongation. To experience a moment of the divine eternity is more than to have survived many years.[1] That is what the Gospel of John means by the presence of eternal life in faith: "Whoever believes has eternal life" (6:47); "Those who believe in me, even though they die, will live" (11:25).

But it is not human faith that acquires eternal life. Eternal life is God-given, and is present in every human life; but it is the believer who perceives it. One recognizes it objectively, and subjectively one absorbs it into one's life as truth. Faith is joy in the divine fullness of life. This participation in the divine life presupposes two movements that cut across frontiers: *God's incarnation* into this human life, and the *transcendence of this human life* in the life that is divine.

> a. "The Word became flesh and lived among us and we beheld his glory" (John 1:14). That is the way John describes the divine mystery Jesus Christ. "In him was life, and the life was the light of all people" (1:4) This does not mean that the eternal creative Word of God has transformed itself into a created being; what it means is that the Word has *taken on* our fragile, corruptible, mortal human life: "the Word became flesh." What is taken over by God is healed of its godlessness and Godforsakenness. God's incarnation in Christ is a universal miracle of healing for humanity, and not for humanity alone. As John Paul II wrote, "The incarnation of God the Son signifies the taking up into unity with God not only human nature but this human nature in the sense *of everything that is 'flesh'*: the whole of humanity,

the entire visible and material world. The Incarnation, then, also has a cosmic significance, a cosmic dimension."[2]

b. "Your body is a temple of the Holy Spirit . . . therefore glorify God in your body" (1 Cor. 6:19, 20). Then, in human beings—in their spirit (Rom. 8:15), in their hearts (Rom. 5:5), and even in their bodies—one finds divine vital power. In their finite, imperfect, and mortal being there dwells what is infinite, perfect, and immortal, which we can call God's Spirit. We can follow Karl Rahner and call this the "self-transcendence" of human existence, which is a consequence of the self-immanence of the divine Spirit in human existence.[3]

With the indwelling of the divine Spirit, God is not "humanized" and the human being is not divinized. The divine and the human nature remain "without confusion and without division," as the Chalcedonian Council of 450 said, but—one must make the positive addition—perichoretically interpenetrated.

How does that come about specifically?

• God *justifies* godless, guilt-ridden human beings, and acquits them, and human beings respond to their liberation with *the beginning of a new life.*

• God *loves* those who are lost, and human beings become *lovely* and respond with overflowing *joy.*

• God *sanctifies* human beings, redeems them, and claims them as God's possession (Isa. 43:1), and human beings respond with fearless *self-confidence.*

We are born into this open, divine life. Even before our birth God's broad space is there for us: "Before I formed you in the womb I knew you" (Jer. 1:5). Before we came into the world we were already loved by God and were God's "children" and "offspring" (Acts 17:28f.). Paul Gerhardt brings this out especially finely in his Christmas hymn:

Ere ever I began to be,
Thou hadst for me appeared
And as Thine own hadst chosen me
Ere Thee I knew or feared.
Before I by Thy hand was made,
Thou hadst the plan in order laid
How Thou Thyself wouldst have me.[4]

This enfolds the birth of every child in a great, transcending safe-keeping, which the Psalms extol because they find it so important:

Yet it was you who took me from the womb;
you kept me safe on my mother's breasts.
On you I was cast from my birth,
And since my mother bore me you have been my God.
(Ps. 22:9-10)

That means that every child is born into God's great yes to his or her life. An affirmation of life is necessary if life is to be affirmed, but it is not a matter of course, because life can also be rejected and denied. Our energy to affirm life varies in good and bad days, in times of stress and times of relief, in times of sickness and times of healing. It gives people a sure stance if they constantly remember that they were born with God's great yes, and have therefore been affirmed—have been "wanted"—from eternity onward. We can also call this a firm assurance about existence, an assurance that can endure doubt and depression because it is stronger than them. How could we deny what God has affirmed ever since we were born?

We shall die into this open, divine life. For us, our death is the end of our mortal life, but for the divine life in which we have lived, loved, and suffered it is a transition from mortality to immortality, and from transience to what is everlasting, as Paul says (1 Cor. 15:42-44, 53-54).

In the Fellowship of the Living and the Dead

As human beings we exist in a community of the living and the dead, even when we are not always aware of it.[5]

In our modern Western society, the individual awareness of being oneself pushes out the collective awareness of living in a sequence of generations. This reduces our fellowship with the dead. The dead are "dead" in the modern sense, that is to say, they no longer exist and have no significance for the living. The living take no account of their ancestors. These neither enrich their lives nor do they have any influence on them. Since they are no longer there, they are simply absent and without any influence.

In traditional societies, the ancestor cult regulates life. It is a sign of the community between people's ancestors and those who succeed them and, conversely, they also depict and celebrate the fellowship of the living with the dead. Those who have died are not "dead." The world of the ancestors is the reverse side of the world of the living, and it is the greater side. Consequently, the life of those who have followed must be integrated into the world of their ancestors, and must be answered for accordingly. If these ancestors have suffered injustice, then they press upon those who have succeeded them and find no peace. At the Chinese New Year festival, the eldest son pays reverence to his ancestors. In the Korean Chosuk festival, the community between the living and the dead is celebrated with a feast of eating and drinking at the graves of those who have died. On Taiwan and Okinawa, the graves are furnished with benches and tables. In Asian families, the present generation lives in awareness of the presence of those who have preceded them. Consequently, the family name is everything and the personal first name is of only secondary importance, whereas in modern America a person is addressed as soon as possible only with his or her first name.

Is reverence for one's ancestors a religious cult or a self-evident part of the reverence for life and human society? Here I am not entering into the dispute between the missionary societies in China, but am assuming that this is a valuable cultural expression of participation in the sequence of human generations. The long genealogies in the Old Testament have their parallels in the ancestral tablets in China and

Korea, in Japan, and on Okinawa. In the countries belonging to the modern Western world, we need a new culture of remembrance so as not to live just for ourselves as individuals, but in order to look beyond ourselves. The person who lives without memories also exists without hope. Our modern individualism has led to our seeing time in very small segments. If we relate time only to ourselves, we soon become pressed for time, for "life is short," as we say, and life is full of possibilities. It is only when we see our own lifespan in the greater complexes of the generations that we acquire time in the remembrance of the past and future in hope for what is to come. For the person who forgets the rights of the dead, the life of whoever comes afterward will also be a matter of indifference. We are born within a particular history and must pass our lives with the inheritance of our fathers and mothers but also with their faults. Through our own lives we determine the life of our children, and our faults are a weight on the lives of those who come after us. The sins of their forebears burden the consciences of those who follow them. The suffering of parents burdens the love of their children. But the blessings of ancestors make the lives of those who come later easy. It is time for even the modern, individualized world to be aware of the community of the living and the dead, and to live it in real terms. That has not yet been attained in public life through the culture of remembering and memorial. It must also be realized in personal life and in the attitudes and practices of families.

Are there Christian reasons for the community of the living and the dead in the sequence of the generations? A transcendence of life and death is required if the living and the dead are to be brought into community with each other. Christian faith sees this community of the dead and the living in the Christ who died a human death and was raised into a divine life. Consequently, the Christian community is a community not only of the living but of the dead as well, not only of brothers and sisters belonging to a single generation, but also of parents and children belonging to different ones.

For to this end Christ died and lived again,
that he might be Lord both of the dead and the living.
(Rom. 14:9)

Since he "descended into the realm of the dead," as the Apostles' Creed puts it, Christ has broken death's power, has destroyed the realm of death, and has taken the dead up into his divine life partnership. That is why the community of Christ includes the community of the dead with the living, and of the living with the dead. The barrier of death that divides the dead from the living has been broken down in Christ's resurrection into eternal life. In the community of Christ, the dead are not "dead" in the modern sense, but are present in a highly primal one. But other than in the Asian cult of ancestors, they are not merely made present through remembrance, and the living are not merely fitted into the sequence of the generations. In community with the One who has been raised, those who have gone before are remembered in the light of the resurrection hope. Christ's resurrection has a significance not just for the living, but for the dead, too, for through his death he became their divine Brother, the Brother who shared their fate.

> *Everything now is filled with light,*
> *heaven and earth*
> *and the realm of death.*

So it stands in the Orthodox liturgy. The prospect of resurrection is the Christian light that is shed on the Asian reverence for ancestors. In the light of this universal hope, Christians in the modern Western world will also turn to their dead and begin to live in their presence.

There is a remarkable passage in the first epistle of Peter (3:16-22; 4:6), which expresses the assurance that Christ descended into "the realm of death" in order to proclaim the gospel to "the spirits in prison" or, as is said later, to "the dead," so that they might have life in God's way, "in the spirit" (4:6). This means, first of all, the dead "who formerly did not obey, when God's patience waited," but then all the dead as well so that they may live in the spirit like God. How it is possible for the dead to "hear" the gospel and "believe" is not said. It is enough to know that death can set no limits to the risen Christ, and that the life-awakening Spirit of God is with the dead, so that they have "life"—that is, the divine, eternal life. For the living, they are dead, but for the risen Christ they are not dead. He can do something for them, and he does do something for them. He raises them up, and takes them with him on his way to the resurrection and to life.

As all *die in Adam,*
so all *will be made alive in Christ. (1 Cor. 15:22)*

In the Fellowship of the Earth

"From the earth were you taken, to the earth you shall return": so we hear at funeral services. "Dust to dust, ashes to ashes . . ." That seems to express the nullity of human life. The human being who as God's image was supposed to "subdue" the earth, in dying returns to the earth again, and once more becomes "earth" him- or herself. What is this earth? The territory, sphere of control of human beings who subdue the world, or "Mother Earth" who takes her human children in her arms again when they die? Because it is embarrassing for many people to carry this "earthly residue" about with them, for many people it is more consoling to know that those they love are in heaven rather than in the earth, because there they are in proximity to God, who, after all, "is" in heaven." But is that a contradiction? Why do we then visit people's graves, as a way of remembering the dead? Or is the return to the earth already a consolation in itself because it is "natural," "for you are dust and to dust you shall return" (Gen. 3:19)? *What is the earth?*[6]

Ever since the beginning of modern times the earth has been viewed as a conglomerate of matter and energy so that its mineral sources could be exploited and its energies put to use. The earth has been viewed as human territory and the spirits and myths that were part of the old world picture have been stripped from it and have lost their magic. The positive result was the construction of the modern global world, the negative ones the climate catastrophes and the spread of the deserts. The more humanity expands, the more uninhabitable wide areas of the earth become. Because the modern world's religion was dominated by the one-sided use of the biblical creation story, the more a theological about-turn at this point is necessary.

a. According to the modern way of reading the story of creation, the human being is "the crown of creation" because it is only the human being who has been created to be God's image, and destined for rule over the earth and all earthly things. According to Psalm 8, God has even given human beings "dominion over the works of your hands; you have put all things under their feet." With the beginning of modern times this led to an anthropocentric worldview.

According to the modern ecological way of reading the same creation story, the human being is God's final created being and, hence, the most dependent living thing. Humans are dependent for their lives on the existence of all other created things—on the earth, the heavens, and the light, and they cannot live at all without the earth's plants and animals. Human beings only exist because of all the other created things and their earthly community. They can all live without human beings, and have done so for millions of years, but human beings cannot live without them. So human beings are only one link in the community of earthly created beings. They are and remain part of nature, as the Earth Charter of 2000 says, even if they exalt themselves to be lord over parts of nature and of the earth. "Subdue the earth," although it is "the mother of all," as Ecclesiasticus says (40:1). This puts its finger on the contradiction of the modern world picture: Can one "subdue" one's mother, exploit her, sell her, and destroy her, as Leonardo Boff rightly asks?

The new ecological worldview starts from the assumption that the earth is our "home": "Humanity is part of a vast evolving universe. Earth, our home, is alive with a unique community of life. . . . The protection of earth's vitality, diversity, and beauty is a sacred trust." (Earth Charter, 2000). That corresponds to the rich biblical traditions about the earth.

According to the first creation account, the earth is not subject to the human being; it is a great, unique, creative being; it brings forth life—plants, trees, and animals of every kind (Gen. 1:24). That is said of nothing else created—not of human beings, either. The earth does not merely offer a home and living space for a variety of living things; it also produces them.

According to the Gaia theory of James Lovelock and others, the earth, our blue planet, is a unique complex system with the capacity for bringing forth life and for creating spaces for living.[7] It is seen in its totality as a "living organism." If one interprets life in its narrow biological sense, then the earth is not living, because it does not reproduce itself. But it must be called more than living, because it brings forth life. It is also more than an organism, because it produces organisms. It is more than intelligent, because it brings forth intelligences. The earth is greater than humanity. It will survive even if humanity puts an end to itself. Human beings are earthly beings. If earth is "our home," then we return to it again, and when we "return to earth" once more we are in safe-keeping.

b. The earth belongs to an alliance with the Creator. Behind the Noahic covenant with human beings and animals there is a special covenant between God and the earth: "I have set my bow in the clouds, and it shall be a sign of the covenant between me and the earth" (Gen. 9:13). There is a bond between God and the earth. There is a covenant between the earth's life and the living God. That is its revered secret.

c. The earth's rights find expression in Israel's sabbath enactments. The earth has a right to sabbath rest so that it can regenerate its vital forces. That is at the same time the religion of the earth: "In the seventh year there shall be a Sabbath of complete rest for the land" (Lev. 25:4) . Whoever disregards the earth's sabbath must leave the country. For the prophet Isaiah the earth holds within it the mystery of salvation: "Let the earth open that salvation may spring up, and let it cause righteousness to spring up also" (Isa. 45:8).

For Christianity the earth's mystery of salvation is the cosmic Christ. God has "reconciled" (Col. 1:20) the universe by uniting all things in Christ, "things in heaven and things on earth" (Eph. 1:10). The risen Christ is also the Christ who has been exalted to the right hand of God, and the exalted Christ is the cosmic Christ. He is already present in all things. The cosmic Christ, finally, is the coming Christ who will fill heaven and earth with his righteousness and justice.

According to the biblical understanding, the earth is by no means a lower form of matter, or merely territory to be ruled by human beings. In the earth Christ is waiting for human beings, so to speak, in order to bring them to salvation together with the earth.

Now in mystic union join
Thine to ours, and ours to thine.

It is true that in the Christian traditions hope is expected to come from heaven. But there is also the mystical tradition, which expects the coming of Christ for the redemption of the world to come from the earth. In the 20th century Christoph Blumhardt witnessed to this tradition. For him, "the kingdom of God stands in a direct relationship to the earth, for it lives with the earth." Christ will appear as "the glory of the earth." Dietrich Bonhoeffer followed him when he said that Christ does not lead men and women into the backwoods of a religious flight from the world, but gives the world back to them as their faithful son.[8] In modern ecofeminism the relationship "new women—new earth" is particularly stressed.[9]

d. So what happens when we "return to the earth"? We return to the community of all earthly creatures with the living, life-bearing earth. The great universal life embraces us. For Christian faith that is not enough: hope is added. The Christ hidden in the earth receives us, and when he "springs from the earth" in order to let the springtime of the new eternal creation come, we shall "spring from the earth" with him. We return to the saving mystery of the earth in order to wake in the joy of the earth when the living God comes. Then we shall join in what Dante called "the laugher of the universe," and the earth "will enjoy God for ever."

The Christian hope for the coming of God has long been crushed by a Gnostic religion of redemption. Children pray, "Take me when I die to heaven." The theologian Helmut Thielicke entitled his autobiography *Zu Gast auf einem schönem Stern* ("A visitor on a lovely planet"). For some people a favourite hymn is Paul Gerhardt's "Ích bin ein Gast auf Erden" ("I am a guest on earth . . ."). If men and women are only guests on earth, then they are not responsible for the guesthouse "earth," for they are only occasionally present in this earthly inn. It is impossible to ignore the inherent contempt for the earth. Even worse is a refusal to be a human being. If human beings are inhabitants of heaven, then they are obviously undisclosed angels. They come from heaven and return to heaven again. That is fantasy. Men and women are earthly creatures, angels are heavenly ones. Personally speaking, when I die I have no wish "to go to heaven"; I expect "the resurrection of the dead and the life of the world to come," to put it in the Christian terms of the Nicene Creed. The "life of the world to come" includes the new creation of all things and the new heavens and the new earth in which God dwells. And there I should like to be present. In Gnostic redemption religion, the divine sparks return from the alienation of the earth into the eternal light of heaven. In Christian thinking this gave rise to the alternative: after the last judgment the good will go to heaven and the wicked will go to hell. And what about all the rest of the living? They will be annihilated in a general conflagration. The hope of going to heaven results according to this expectation in the annihilation of the earthly world. It is, consequently, a vision hostile to life and a destructive spirituality.

Participation in the life of the earth leads to a feeling for universal life. This new earthly spirituality awakens cosmic humility, which takes the place of the modern arrogance of power,[10] and which is reflected in the dominance over nature. Every serious scientist knows this cosmic humility in astonishment over the unexplored mysteries of nature (as long as he or she does not intend to "market" his or her discoveries). Another characteristic is cosmic love, which the Starez Sosima expresses in Dostoevsky's novel, *The Brothers Karamasov* :

Love the whole creation, all of it and every grain of sand. Love every little leaf, every ray of God's light. Love the animals, love the plants, love every single thing. If you love every single thing, then God's mystery in them will be revealed to you. Once it is revealed to you, then you will perceive it more and more every day. And in the end you will love the whole universe with an all-comprehensive love.[11]

This human comprehensive love is a resonance of the universal love of the universe, which has waited for the appearance of the human being. Whether there is a strong or a weak "anthropological principle," we human beings are expected in the nature of the earth, if we are human and natural. Nature is not our "stepmother," as Johann Gottfried Herder complained, nor is the earth the sphere of our dominance. Nature, the nature of the earth, is our hope, for it is waiting for the natural human being.

Chapter 5

Life in the Wide Space of God's Joy

I HAVE ALREADY WRITTEN A "THEOLOGY OF JOY." THAT WAS IN 1971, at the height of the Vietnam War and the worldwide indignation over it, in the middle of the student rebellions, and the liberation movements in the Third World. The English title of my book was *Theology and Joy* (London: SCM Press, 1973). My question then was: How can we laugh and rejoice when so many tears have to be wiped away, and new tears are shed every day? "How can I sing the LORD's song in a strange land?" That is the complaint of Psalm 137, while an old black spiritual asks, "How can I play when I'm in a strange land?" How can anyone laugh here when innocent people are being killed in Vietnam? How can anyone play here when children are dying of hunger in Africa? How can we in Europe dance when men and women are being tortured in the prisons of Latin America military dictatorships and "disappear"? Aren't we living in a single world? Have we a right to rejoice when we don't cry out on behalf of the people who have nothing to laugh about? At that time, the musical *Fiddler on the Roof* was being staged. It shows Tevye the milkman and his Jewish community in the Ukraine. The tsar is imposing heavy taxes, their young men have to serve in foreign armies, the Cossacks hold pogroms whenever they feel like a bit of Jewish persecution, and yet this little community of oppressed men and women dances and sings "the Lord's song in a foreign land." Are these people trying to forget their wretched situation? Are they consoling themselves for their misery with beautiful sounds? Or does it really exist—freedom in the midst of oppression? Joy in the midst of pain? Praise of God in the sighings of creation?

In this chapter, written 40 years later, I am not proposing to ask, How can I sing the Lord's song in a strange land? but, How can I sing the Lord's song in God's presence—or, to put it metaphorically, in the warmth of God's shining countenance? I am not presupposing the antithesis of what existed in 1971, for it has become no less worldwide. Today the persecution of Christians has been added. But I want now to assess the positive dimensions of the "great joy" in the wide spaces of the God who is closer to us than we think, and who makes our life wider than we can guess. *Joy* is strength for living, the empowerment to love, the delight in a creative beginning. It wakes us up, and makes us alive from within. How do we experience this force in the presence of the risen Christ? How do we so tune our lives that they resonate with the inexhaustible joy of God? Are we capable of happiness at all?

God's Joy

According to the Old Testament, it is the turn to God and God's all-comprehensive presence that evokes joy:

> *You show me the path of life.*
> *In your presence there is fullness of joy;*
> *in your right hand are pleasures forevermore. (Ps. 16:11)*

This life-giving presence of God is often described as "God's shining face." God's shining face is the source of the blessing that makes life a fulfilled life, and exalts it into a festive one.

Astonishingly enough, joy is also associated with God's cosmic judgment. When God comes "to judge" the earth, joy will make nature on earth blossom.

Let the heavens be glad, and let the earth rejoice,
and let them say among the nations, "The LORD reigns!"
(1 Chron. 16:31)

Let the heavens be glad, and let the earth rejoice;
let the sea roar, and all that fills it;
let the field exult, and everything in it.
Then shall all the trees of the forest sing for joy
before the LORD; for he is coming,
for he is coming to judge the earth. *(Ps. 96:11-13)*

When God comes to judge the earth, the whole of creation will rejoice.[1]

When God comes to human beings, that brings about a new turn in two ways. God's countenance is no longer "hidden"; now it "shines." This new direction on God's part—God's turn from rejection of the wrongdoing of human beings to the inclination of God's grace—evokes a corresponding change among the human beings who are touched by it:

You have turned for me my mourning into dancing;
you have taken off my sackcloth
and clothed me with joy. (Ps. 30:11)

Let me hear joy and gladness;
let the bones that you have crushed rejoice. (Ps. 51:8)

When the "ransomed of the LORD" return, "everlasting joy shall be upon their heads;[2] they shall obtain joy and gladness, and sorrow and sighing shall flee away" (Isa. 35:10). God will "rejoice over [the redeemed] with gladness; he will renew you in his love; he will exult over you with loud singing" (Zeph. 3:17). Isn't that a wonderful picture for the glory of God—the God who rejoices, shouts for joy, and sings over God's redeemed created beings?

We see from this compendium of verses from the Old Testament psalms and prophets a great and wonderful harmony of rejoicing: God's joy, the joy of the earth, and the joy of the redeemed.

The Birth of Religion Out of the Festival of Life

Modern theories about religion like to place it in sphere of people's unhappiness: religion springs form "the sighings of creation" or, according to Karl Marx, it is "the opiate of the people." According to the popular view, it is distress that brings people to their knees. But, in fact, religion is the festival of life,[3] and prayer is first and foremost jubilation over the joy of existence.

The earliest religions are family religions. Family feast days accompany life from the cradle to the grave. There are also the festive accompaniments of the seasons, the summer and the winter solstices, the phases of the moon, springtime and autumn, seedtime and harvest. These are religions that are bound up with nature. The religions that are bound up with the family and with nature constitute the practical and everyday foundation for all the world religions.

In a festival, life is depicted, not produced. In the presentation of life before the gods, the experiences of life are given expression. There are no experiences without their appropriate expression. The religious festivals express a "demonstrative evaluation" of their significance. This is not necessary, but it is useful to give living expression to the joy in existence through praise, thanksgiving, and rejoicing in the form of music and dance. In the festival of life, the soul is "exalted" and the heart is lifted up—*sursum corda*. It is exalted into God's wide space, which we call heaven. The festival of life elates the soul and sets unguessed-of powers free. It renews life out of its transcendent origin.

Christianity: Religion of Joy

When we think about it, we arrive at the surprising conclusion that Christianity is a unique *religion of joy*.[4] It lives the Christian faith in its festivals. And yet the universal sign of Christianity is, after all, the cross, a symbol of pain, suffering, and a cruel death. How do these things go together? Are joy and pain mutually exclusive antitheses or do they belong together?

Christianity begins with *Christmas*. When Mary becomes pregnant she sings:

My soul magnifies the Lord,
and my spirit rejoices in God my Saviour. (Luke 1:46-47)

When her child is born in Bethlehem, the angels come fom heaven to the poor shepherds in the fields with the announcement:

Behold, I bring to you good news of a great joy, . . .
for to you is born this day . . . a Saviour." (Luke 2:10-11, RSV)

According to the thought of the Eastern church, this birth takes place not in a manmade stable, but in a cave in the earth: the child is the Saviour of the earth as well. Jesus is born out of God's exuberant joy—God "has pleasure" in him. God brings "great joy" to human beings, first of all to the solitary, freezing shepherds in the fields. That is why today we still sing joyful hymns all over the world today, and exchange gifts as a sign of our joy:

Joy to the world! The Lord is come:
Let earth receive her king.

Christmas is the central festival of Western Christianity.

Easter is the central feast day of Eastern Christianity. Christ's resurrection and the appearance in him of eternal life on this earth are the inexhaustible reason for the Easter jubilation.

Christ is risen! He is risen indeed!

Following the canon of John of Damascus, the church sings:

Everything brims over with light,
Heaven and earth, and the world below the earth.

All creation celebrates with joy Christ's rising
For now creation is assured.[5]

The West also knows that the resurrection is not only a human event, but a cosmic one as well:

Earth with joy confesses, clothing her for spring.
All good gifts restored with her returning king.
Bloom in every meadow, leaves on every bough,
speak his sorrows ended, hail his triumph now.

Following the Old Testament pattern, Easter joy is the earth's joy, too. That is why Easter is celebrated in the spring in the northern hemisphere, as the springtime of the new eternal creation.

The experience of the divine Spirit in human life is extolled at *Pentecost* with many joyful hymns. This is the central feast day of the new Pentecostal churches all over the world. Whenever there is talk in the New Testament about the experience of the Holy Spirit, the word *joy* occurs, for it is the Spirit of life that awakens men and women to a new, live, intensive feeling for life. It is an enduring feeling for life that opens the soul and all the senses for the nearness of God in life as it is lived.

My heart and my flesh sing for joy to the living God. (Ps. 84:2)

So it is not just "spiritual" joy that is meant but the joys of the senses, too. We do not have to distinguish between the two—they belong together. But what one must of course do is to distinguish between the joys of life and destructive addictions, which the New Testament also calls "the lusts of the flesh."

But what about *Good Friday*, the central "holiday" of the Lutheran churches? Here, first of all, Jesus' passion is remembered, and his dying on the cross. His suffering with us and for us awakens a deep sympathy with Jesus' torment on the cross, and a compassion with the passion of God in him. That is why we sing:

O sacred head, now wounded,
with shame and grief bowed down,
now scornfully surrounded
with thorns, thy only crown.

It is participation in the pain of Jesus, who participates in our pain. "The Bible points us to the helplessness and suffering of God; only the suffering God can help," wrote Dietrich Bonhoeffer in 1944 from his prison cell, and, in a later poem, "Christians stand beside God in his suffering."

The God who can rejoice can also suffer. The God who experiences happiness and bliss also feels pain and grief. A God who cannot suffer cannot be a God of joy, either. Because we find both joy and suffering in God, on Good Friday, too, "we sing the praise of him who died, of him who died upon the cross."

And that is why the same hymn can call the cross "the balm of life, the cure of woe," and perceive in the cross of death God's tree of life, which bears the fruits of eternal life. "*Ave crux—unica spes*": "hail to the cross, our only hope." Behind the cross of Christ there rises the sun of the resurrection—only here, but here for all.

It is worth noting that the great Christian festivals are not distributed equally throughout the year; they fall in its first half, so that they are concentrated on the spring. The spring begins in the midst of winter with the winter solstice, begins to stir at Easter with the budding of the flowers and trees, and arrives at its full blossoming at Whitsun or Pentecost. It begins with the birth of a child in the manger, and ends with the outpouring of the Spirit "on all flesh." This shows emphatically that with the coming of Christ and of God's Spirit in our world the springtime of eternal life is dawning in this mortal life and in this often chaotic nature, and that this loved human life will be taken up into the eternal divine life, and this chaotic nature will be transformed into the new creation.

Christianity lives in its festivals. The Christian festivals are feasts of joy. And as a consequence,

Faith *is joy in the living God.*
Love *is joy in a life filled by God.*
Hope *is the anticipatory joy over God's future world.*

The Joy of the God Who Seeks and Finds

Joy comes before faith, for what does God the giver expect other than the joy of the recipient? Before there is faith in the trust of the heart and a sure recognition, there is already astonishment and a spontaneous joy that fills the whole life of the recipient. In Greek, *charis*, grace, and *chora*, joy, are closely related linguistically. For Paul, faith and joy are interchangeable when he says: "Not that we lord it over your faith, but we work with you for your joy" (2 Cor. 1:24, RSV).

On the other hand, joy is the original doxology. Before there is thanksgiving, praise, honour, and glorifying, there is joy over the God-given, God-loved life. God does not expect praise and glorification. God doesn't need it. But God is joyful when those God has created rejoice over God's grace and over Godself. Thanksgiving and praise then follow as an expression of this primal joy.

How does God's joy reach human beings? In interpreting Jesus' astonishing attitude toward "sinners and publicans," for which the Pharisees publically rebuke him—that he "ate with publicans and sinners"—Luke offers three parables, those of the lost sheep, the lost coin, and the prodigal son (Luke 15:1-32). In the cases of the found sheep and the found coin, his theological interpretation is: "There will be more joy in heaven over one sinner who repents than over ninety-nine righteous persons who need no repentance" (Luke 15:7; cf. v. 10). The theology here is not quite logical, for in the first place Jesus accepted sinners and tax collectors without any conditions, and it was by no means only with repentant sinners that he ate. And, second, the lost sheep could not contribute much to its finding and the lost coin nothing at all. The joy was first of all the finder's: "When he has found it [the sheep], he lays it on his shoulders and rejoices" (15:5).

These are parables about *God's joy as finder*, which Jesus illustrates on the basis of "the lost" in his society.[6] It is only "the prodigal son" who repents: we are told that he turns his back on the path which has led to his destruction, and intends to say to his father: "Father, I have sinned against heaven and before you" (15:18). But before he can make this confession, the father runs to meet him: "But while he was still far off, his father saw him and was filled with compassion; he ran and put his arms around him" (15:20). It is only after that that the son admits his lostness; but the father is not bothered by this, for "'This son of mine was dead and is alive again; he was lost and is found!' And *they began to celebrate*" (15:24).

The sole activity is that of the seeking and finding and rejoicing God, because "the lost," wherever they are, and for whatever reason, belong to God. We have the impression that it gives God pleasure to look for the lost, and that God is delighted when they are found. What is left for "the lost" and for the neighbour and for the elder brother of the "prodigal son" is *the joy shared* with God. For the one found, this is also spontaneous and a matter of course, but for the neighbours and the "ninety-nine righteous persons," shared joy is rare.

Why is it easier for us to weep with those who weep than to laugh with those who laugh? I think that in sympathizing with people who have lost something or someone very close to them, we come down to their level, offer them our sympathy, and feel like bigger people, or even in solidarity with them, because their suffering is familiar to us. But in rejoicing with them we are supposed to share in the happiness of other people and feel smaller than them. To rejoice with someone else presupposes a degree of selflessnesss in which we do not compare the happiness of the other with our own situation, but participate in the happiness itself. That is the advice the happy father gives the elder brother of the "lost" son, who is envious: "But we had to celebrate and rejoice, because this brother of yours was dead, and has come to life; he was lost and has been found" (15:32). The event of the finding that which had been lost is like a revival of the dead. To rejoice over it is to participate in God's joy whenever it is present. It is a celebration of life where there had been death.

Luke interprets Jesus' attitude over the lost of his time with the parables about the "joy in heaven." The finding of the lost takes place

today as well in the Spirit. Some people talk about "Pentecostal experiences." The best-known example is the famous 17th-century math-
ematician and philosopher Blaise Pascal. When he died in Paris, a
writing was found sewn into his coat: it was this "Memorial":

This year of grace 1654,
Monday 23rd November . . .
From about half past ten in the evening until half past
midnight:
FIRE.
GOD of Abraham, GOD of Isaac, GOD of Jacob,
not of philosophers and scholars.
CERTAINTY, heart-felt, JOY, JOY, God of Jesus Christ,
Thy God is my God . . .
Joy, joy, joy, tears of joy.
I have cut myself off from him.
My God why hast thou forsaken me?
Let me never be cut off from him.
But this is eternal life, that they know thee who alone art true
God,
and him whom thou hast sent, Jesus Christ.
I have cut myself off from him, I have fled from him . . .
Let me never be cut off from him.
He can only be kept by the ways taught in the Gospel . . .
Everlasting joy in return for one day's effort on earth.[7]

Human Joy: Joy and Fun

Here we change over from the theology of joy to the anthropology of
joy—to joy and happiness on the human level. But we keep in mind
as guideline God's joy over the finding of the lost human being, and
the human being's joy in the living God. If we do that, joy cannot be
a superficial, passing emotion, but must be something that can only
be experienced "with all our heart, all our soul, and all our strength."
We cannot properly rejoice half-heartedly and in the absence of our
soul.

Here the distinction between joy and fun is helpful. We are living in the wealthier of the earth's societies, and in the "upwardly mobile" sections of them. This is a "fun society." "I want to have some fun," young people who can afford it say, and throw parties—if possible with music that is so loud one can't hear oneself speak. But then, one is not supposed to talk and listen, after all, but everyone is supposed to be "beside oneself," each for oneself, in the dancing throng. If one has had this kind of fun, one is by no means sated and contented; one is hungry for more and more of it. Life is supposed to be an endless party. The elderly rich have their cocktail parties, where courtesies and platitudes are exchanged, and everyone watches to see what the other one is doing. One no longer knows how to be festive, and one has stopped trying. One engages an entertainer and an event manager, because one no longer knows how to set about these things oneself. But I will stop my mockery at this point, because I don't want to be a "spoilsport," as they say.

The distance between joy and this kind of fun is as wide as the gap between experienced happiness and a game of chance, or between a successful life and a lottery win. Real joy is a feeling about life, but fun is a superficial experience; joy is lasting and enduring, and puts its stamp on one's whole attitude to life. Joy is fulfilled time; fun is short-lived and serves to pass the time, as they say. The feeling about life behind the party-making, fun society is probably boredom and a certain contempt for life. Real joy stimulates the soul, makes relationships flourish, makes the heart light and limbs nimble, mobilizes undreamed-of powers, and increases confidence. Genuine happiness lays hold of the person's whole being. In joy, the ecstatic nature of human existence finds its true expression.[8] We are made for joy. We are born for joy.

Joy and Human Pain: Schiller and Dostoevsky

On the other hand, joy in life and happiness are called into question and their legitimacy is denied if we say that the pain and despair of many people is more acute than joy and happiness. We are told that grief is deeper than joy, and that pain has more weight than happiness.

We weep more readily than we laugh, for human life is more of a tragedy than a game of rejoicing. After two lost wars and an untold number of war crimes, Germans especially were more in love with failure than with success. In the 20th century, what Miguel de Unamuno describes as a "tragic sense of life" was widespread throughout Europe. After the catastrophe of the First World War, existential literature and philosophy counted as being more realistic than 19th-century idealism. Many people threw themselves into what Oswald Spengler calls "the decline of the West."

Nevertheless Friedrich Schiller' s "Ode to Joy," in its setting within Beethoven's Ninth Symphony, was made the European hymn.[9] Did Europe deserve that, after the state crimes of the 20th century and the financial crises of the 21st? Let us look at the hymn more closely:

> *Joy, fair spark of the gods,*
> *daughter of Elysium.*
> *Drunk with fiery rapture*
> *we approach thy shrine.*
>
> *Thy magic reunites those*
> *whom stern custom has parted.*
> *All men will become brothers*
> *under thy gentle wing.*

And one of the following verses runs:

> *Endure courageously, millions,*
> *endure for the better world.*
> *Then above the starry canopy*
> *a great God will reward.*

The world's joyful harmony will come about in a different world, so that the "millions" may endure suffering in this world and will not rebel. Are those the costs of the ideal joys of humanity?

This "theodicy of joy," as George Steiner called it, soon evoked the reactions of protest atheism. The senseless suffering of "the millions" finds no compensation through the reward of a good God—and a God "above the starry canopy" in the next world at that. Suffering is the "rock of atheism" on which "joy optimism" comes to grief.

Dostoevsky challenged Schiller's "joy" idealism and countered its consolation by way of Ivan Karamasov's familiar story: while he was playing, a little boy unintentionally hurt the leg of the landowner's favourite dog. As a punishment the general allowed his hunting dogs to attack the boy and tear him to pieces before his mother's eyes. Ivan comments:

> What kind of harmony is that, where there is a hell like this? And if the suffering of children is to make up the sum of suffering which would be required for the acquisition of the truth, then I would say that the whole truth is not worth such a price. . . . So I hasten to give back the ticket which would give me an entry into this world. Not that I don't accept God; but I respectfully hand him back my ticket. (*The Brothers Karamasov*, book V)[10]

"Then I prefer to keep the unrevenged suffering" and, with it, my indignation. This world in which there are such crimes and such suffering is not a divine world. Nor are they compensated for through a reward in the next world. So, the face of the world is not a face of joy and peace but one of pain and protest.

But are happiness and pain, laughter and tears really opposites? I don't believe that they are. The secret of life is *love*. In love we go out of ourselves and expose ourselves to the experiences of life. That is why it is only in love that we are capable of happiness—but are also vulnerable. We can rejoice, but in love we are also sad. We can laugh and weep. The more deeply love draws us into life, the more alive we become, but our experience of suffering is greater, too. The more alive life is, the more deadly for us is death. That is the dialectic of affirmed and loved life.

We can easily make the countercheck. If we become resigned after a disappointment or a failure, and withdraw our love into ourselves, we lose interest in life and become apathetic. Then we no longer feel the pain, but nor do we live anymore. Everything is a matter of indifference. Our souls lose their vigour and what we acquire is a heart of stone. We become inviolable, but nothing touches us any more. This paralysis of soul is a step toward the death of the person.

This means that Schiller's "Ode to Joy" and Dostoevsky's indignation over the guiltless suffering of a single child are not antitheses. Joy over life's happiness leads us spontaneously to indignation over the ruined life of "the millions"; for the protest against the suffering in this world is nothing other than the ardent longing for a world of happiness. Otherwise, we would accept innocent suffering and a ruined life as our fate. It is hope for a different world that makes us unable to accept it. We do not accuse God because of the suffering in this world, but in God's name we protest against suffering and those who cause it. There is true life in false life. How else should we know what is false in this life?

Nietzsche's "Deep, Deep Eternity"

Finally, we ask: What is the more primal and more profound, joy or pain, life or death? And we reply: existence is more primal than nonexistence, life is more than death: first of all comes love, then grief, and hope runs ahead of despair. So joy is more primal and more profound than pain. Why? For a simple reason: in pain we want what we suffer to pass. In joy we want that which makes us so happy to remain. That is why, according to Friedrich Nietzsche, Zarathustra said:

> *Pleasure—deeper still than suffering of heart!*
> *Hurt cries out: vanish!*
> *But all delight longs for eternity,*
> *For deep, deep eternity.*[11]

Why is Christianity uniquely a religion of joy, although at its centre stands the suffering and dying of Christ on the cross? It is because behind Golgotha there stands the sun of the world of the resurrection, because the crucified One has appeared on earth in the radiance of the eternal divine life, because in him the new eternal creation of the world begins. The apostle Paul expresses this with his logic of the "how much more": "Where sin is mighty, how much mightier is grace" (Rom. 5:20); "For Christ has died, but how much more has he risen" (Rom. 8:34, my trans.).[12] That is why the pains will be transformed into joys, and mortal life will be taken up and absorbed into the life that is eternal.

What came from pain was fleeting
and what my ear heard was naught but a song of praise.
(Werner Bergengruen)

Chapter 6

✳

Freedom Lived in Solidarity

AT THE LAST CHRISTIAN-MARXIST DIALOGUE OF THE PAULUS Gesellschaft and the Czech Akademie der Wissenschaften, which was held in Marienbad in 1967, I gave a lecture on "The Revolutions of Freedom."[1] During the following stormy years of political theology, the subject "God *and* Freedom" was very much in my mind.[2] The word *and* was the decisive one, for the theology of freedom had to be defended against both the atheists and the devout conservatives who felt themselves confronted with the alternative of God *or* freedom and chose either the one or the other. In the Latin American theology of liberation, the *and* linking God and freedom found convincing expression. As long as there is political oppression, economic exploitation, and cultural alienation, liberating "theology" remains on the agenda. In this chapter, written 40 years later, I am thinking about human freedom within God's "wide space." How does human freedom develop *within* God's freedom? Where is God's freedom to be found within the dimensions of human freedom? How does faith participate in God's potentialities? Where does God throw open God's potentialities for human beings, so that that they can cross their own frontiers?

Freedom *or* God? Michael Bakunin and Carl Schmitt

There is a famous, much-quoted saying of the Russian anarchist Michail Bakunin, which claims that "if God exists, then man is a slave;

103

but the human being can and ought be free; consequently God does not exist."[3]

In his writing *God and the State* (1871), Bakunin expounds this thesis at length: everything which is ascribed to God is taken away from the human being. "Since God is everything, the real world and the human being are nothing." "God appears, the human being becomes nothing, and the greater the deity the more miserable the human race becomes."[4] So if we want to liberate human beings, we must negate God. Atheism is the presupposition for true human liberty. Human liberty stems from rebellion. For Bakunin as for Feuerbach, God and the human being are one and the same, so that what one takes from the one profits the other. That is actually illogical, for God and the human being are not one and the same. Ironically enough, Bakunin uses the biblical story of the fall as justification for his doctrine of freedom: "But then came Satan, the eternal rebel, the first free thinker and universal liberator. . . . He frees him [i.e., the human being] and impresses on his brow the seal of freedom and humanity by driving him to be disobedient and to eat the fruit of the tree of knowledge."[5] And "God said that Satan was right" and found that the human being "had become like God." Bakunin concludes from this myth about the fall that human beings have liberated themselves—and will liberate themselves—"through rebellion and thought."

That was undoubtedly meant politically. Bakunin was living in the holy Russia of the autocratic tsars and the Orthodox state church. "As the slaves of God, men and women must also be slaves of the church and of the state, inasmuch as the state is blessed by the church." Consequently, his writing *God and the State* culminates in the anarchistic cry, "*Ni Dieu ni maître*"—neither God nor state! He knew only the political state god and rose against it for freedom's sake—politically speaking, rightly so.

In 20th-century Germany, the conservative constitutional lawyer Carl Schmitt recognized that Bakunin was his enemy and God's, too.[6] He borrowed from Bakunin the epithet "political theology," and "what Bakunin denied in Satan's name Schmitt maintained in the name of God. . . . What for the atheistic anarchist is nothing but a man-made fiction, is for the political theologian God-given reality."[7] Schmitt used the story of the fall and the doctrine of original sin as a theological justification for an authoritarian state. He took Bakunin's Satanism more seriously than did Bakunin himself and made of it a world-political apocalyptic struggle between the Satanic rebel and the state-true God, between autonomous freedom and a godly obedience of faith, between anarchy and authority. Schmitt, too, believed in the alternative God *or* freedom. His "political theology" is a faithful counterpart to anarchistic atheism—and thereby at the same time its justification.

Who is to find a place in the calendar of saints, Christ or Prometheus? That was Karl Marx's question, and he decided in favour of Prometheus, who stole fire from the gods, probably having in mind Goethe's poem. That was the way things remained in many European and Latin American countries: God *or* freedom. That was the question. Yet, in the early-19th-century civil and national revolutions, many fighters for freedom understood the Christian faith as being the "religion of freedom" (Hegel), because in their eyes it justified the courage for a new society without privileges. They wanted what Mazzini described as a free church in a free state. The religion of freedom showed them the hope for "the kingdom of freedom." But the churches allied themselves with the forces of reaction. They suppressed the people's will for freedom by way of conservative ordering myths that lauded "God, king, and country" or "God, family, and country." On the European continent, and in the European colonial territories, organized religion went hand in hand with "the powers that be" and justified their repressions; freedom was on the side of atheism. But in these confrontations both the state and the liberty of its citizens, and also the Christian faith, fell by the wayside. Christians will critically recollect whom they really believe and what their authentic experience of God looks like. And for that they discover with liberation theology the freedom traditions found in the Bible.

The God of the Exodus and the Resurrection

The God of Abraham, Isaac, and Jacob is not a God of the pharaohs, the Caesars, and the slaves, but the God who led God's people out of slavery into liberty, as the First Commandment states. God is "the

Lord", because God is the liberator. Israel's fundamental experience of God is this *experience of freedom*. To believe in God means nothing other than to trust in God's liberating power. Here the modern alternative "God *or* freedom" sounds absurd. It is the opposite that is true: God's name means freedom. As Israel's history shows, this does not just mean inner freedom, freedom of thought, or freedom of mind or spirit; it means real political, economic, and cultural freedom—in short, the realm of freedom to its fullest compass. Israel's exodus story has been communicated through the centuries to many peoples by way of the Christian Bible, and has again and again led to revolutions in the interests of freedom—among the pilgrim fathers, who emigrated from England, among African American slaves in the United States, and among the peoples in Latin America struggling for their liberation from colonial rule and capitalism.[8]

But there is another exodus story as well in the Old Testament: the exodus of Abraham and Sarah from their "fatherland"—from their family and their homeland—into the country God was going to show them (Gen. 12:1-3). This divine promise points forward to a "great people" and the "blessing for all peoples." But the way there is a lonely one through the desert. This is not the freedom born out of liberation; it is the freedom that issues from alienation, alienation from everything which offers support in the world. "So [Abraham] went" (12:4). That is what the New Testament calls true faith: "the assurance of things hoped for, the conviction of things not seen" (Heb. 11:1).

God the Father of Jesus Christ, the God about whom the New Testament talks, is not a God of the political rulers and slave owners, either. But, rather, the God who raised Christ from death on the cross into the glory of God's kingdom. The God of Jesus Christ is the God of the Son of man who was humiliated, tortured, and crucified by the Roman occupying power in Jerusalem in the name of the Roman imperial power. The person who believes in this God and follows Christ leaves behind the gods of power and throws down their idols.[9] God is the One who "raised Jesus from the dead"—that is the Christian revelation of God: God is the liberator from the power of evil and death. God's power creates life, where injustice and violence destroy it. Christian experience of God is an *experience of resurrection*. That is brought out in two key utterances of Christian faith: "For freedom Christ has set us free" (Gal. 5:1); and "Where the Spirit of the Lord is, there is freedom" (2 Cor. 3:17). The *exodus experiences* of Israel and of Abraham stand at the center of the Old Testament. At the center of the New are the *resurrection experiences* of Christ and the *experiences of freedom* shared by believers in Christ's Spirit and in his discipleship.

God's Freedom

As long as human freedom is viewed as conflicting with the existence of God or God's will, the question about God's freedom does not arise. If we conclude metaphysically from finite human freedom that there is an infinite divine freedom, we are taking human self-determination as our point of departure. But faith perceives God's freedom differently—as God's creative way of acting.

The Greeks understood human freedom as the ordering of the individual into the polis, and as the ordering of the human polis into the cohesion of the world. Diogenes Laertes recommended that one should live "in accordance with nature." The cohesion of the world is determined by divine reason and the law of the gods. The person who lives in accordance with what is divine in the cosmos is truly free. If the cosmos is expanded to include world history, the result, in Marxist terms, is as follows: freedom is insight into necessity.

Chinese traditions teach very similarly: freedom is harmony. In the *Tao Te Ching* of Lao-Tse we read:

> Man takes as law the earth;
> the earth takes as law the heavens;
> the heavens take as law the way;
> the way takes as law its own being.[10]

The ordering of the individual into the community, the ordering of the community into the life of the earth, the ordering of the life of the earth into the ways of heaven, and the ordering of the ways of heaven into the inexpressible wisdom of the Tao—that brings about harmony. "Harmony" was the magic word in ancient China in the "forbidden city" of the emperors, the "sons of heaven," and today it is the magic political word of the communist party and of all cultural events in Peking.

In the modern world of the West, freedom is interpreted as the right of self-determination enjoyed by every individual. Freedom is the right of the independent individual to dispose over his or her own life and capabilities. What makes a human being human is his or her freedom toward other human beings. The modern human being is characterized by individual freedom. Freedom means "ownership of one's own person and capacities." This is what C. B. Macpherson calls "the political theory of possessive individualism," referring to Hobbes and Locke in 17th-century England.[11] As the owner of his or her own self, the individual is not part of a greater social totality. In this interpretation of freedom, we see a reflection of the bourgeois revolution against feudalism and monarchy. Slavery and serfdom are forbidden. Everyone is her or his own property. The human dignity of every individual consists of that person's quality as subject. The lordship of one person over another is wrong. The liberal-democratic community is constituted by the bond between free citizens with their own possessions, so that the state is restricted to the protection of private property and to the maintenance of an orderly exchange between individuals. But this individualization of freedom as control and ownership also reflects the privileges of the nobility and the monarch. Every man is his own master, every woman her own queen.

For the Christian faith, freedom does not mean "insight into necessity," nor does it mean the independent and sovereign power of disposal of the individual over oneself and one's capabilities. Just as Israel's faith is anchored in the God of the exodus, so Christian faith is rooted in Christ's resurrection. Through faith men and women become aware of their liberation and enter into God's wide space. Through faith they participate in God's creative powers: "For God all things are possible" (Matt. 19:26), so "all things are possible for the one who believes" (Mark 9:23). The person who trusts in the God who liberates and raises from the dead participates through God's open Spirit in the wealth of God's potentialities. Paul makes this clear from the example of Abraham, whom he depicts as a model for a life lived out of faith:

"For he is the father of us all . . . who gives life to the dead and calls into existence the things that do not exist. In hope he believed against hope" (Rom. 4:16-18, RSV). In the face of nonbeing God's freedom manifests itself as creative power, and in the face of death it shows itself as life-giving force. Paul takes the new beginning of creation and the beginning of the new creation as ways of describing Abraham's faith in God at the very point of his hope when there was nothing to hope for. The One who at the beginning calls the world into existence, the One who at the end awakens the new beginning, can and will do in history what that One has promised, even though everything speaks against it. This comprehends the divine spaces of human freedom in faith: the space of the creative development of divine freedom and the spaces of the new creation and its eternal life. In faith, human beings correspond to the creative, life-giving God, and in God's Spirit participate in God's divine energies. That goes far beyond the limits of what is humanly possible, as the phrase "all things are possible" shows. Human beings discover themselves with their limited, finite freedom in God's fathomless possibilities. So human freedom cannot be limited by God but will be without any limits in God's name.

But doesn't human freedom differ from God's in that the human being is capable of good *and* evil and has a choice, whereas God's freedom, after all, corresponds to the unending goodness of God's being? Is freedom of choice the highest form of freedom that a human being can attain? I don't believe that it is, for "the one who can choose has the burden of choice." So divine freedom cannot be freedom of choice. The maintaining of a human power to choose between good and evil justifies the existence of evil. The freedom to do the good spontaneously confutes evil and, according to Augustine, also means the "freedom of not being able to sin any more."[12] Grace frees for this freedom human beings who have lost their freedom and have become subject to the bondage of evil. To do spontaneously what is right and just accords with God, and is the human freedom that participates in God's eternal freedom. It is freedom in the faith that is forgetful of self and has no doubts.

Human Freedom in God

When I talk here about freedom "in God," I do not mean special mystical experiences; I mean life in faith, a life in accordance with God, a life that participates in God's energies in the open Spirit. In this section we shall look at the various dimensions of freedom in this divine life.

Freedom as the ability to begin

It was Hannah Arendt who taught us to see freedom as an initiative issuing from something new, something unique, and something undeducible from anything else: *incipit vita nova*[13]—a new life begins. Freedom does not mean the ability to do something, nor does it mean the many possibilities open to us. Freedom means that we ourselves take the initiative and begin something new with our abilities and the potentialities we see before us. To put it simply, we must know what to set about doing with our lives, so that we become truly living. According to Arendt, a simple reason why we take the initiative and can make a new beginning is something within ourselves; this is what we are born for. "Because every human being simply by being born is an *initium*, a beginning and a new arrival, human beings can take the initiative and put on foot something new." That sounds curious, for animals are born, too, but they are nevertheless not so free as human beings. She appeals to a saying of Augustine's: "So that there might be a beginning, the human being was created before whom there was no one" ("*Initium ergo ut esse, creatus est homo, ante quem nullus fuit*").

For "in the beginning God created heaven and earth." Only God has the energies for the free beginning without any presuppositions, the beginning before which there was "nothing." And God created the human being in God's image—that is to say, Arendt concludes, as a beginner of something new, before whom there was no one comparable. Consequently, the creation of God's human image begins with a new resolve on God's part: "Let us make humankind in our image, according to our likeness." (Gen. 1:26). So Arendt writes, "With the creation of man the principle of beginning came into the world itself. At the creation of the world this still remained in the hand of God, as it were, and hence outside the world; which of course is only another way of saying that the principle of freedom was simultaneously created when man was created."[14]

The human being's free nature is his or her creative power, and this creative power is the ability to begin something new. In this respect the human being corresponds to the creative God and participates in God's power to live. Conversely, God participates in this human freedom through God's indwelling Spirit and continually awakens it afresh. Hannah Arendt links this unique character of free action, on the one hand, with the creation of the world "in the beginning," and, on the other hand, with the birth of new life. Every human being is "newly born," and that means a beginner of new life. Every human life is unique. However genetically formed and socially conditioned, the beginning of life distinguishes this life from everything that went before it and from everything that comes after it.

Finally, Arendt finds the roots of these ideas in history. With every word and act we intervene in the world process. No word and no act is like any other. Consequently, she compares every word and act with "a second birth." That may sound like an exaggeration, and as appropriate at most in the case of epoch-making decisions or discoveries. But she thereby draws attention to the miracle of everyday happening, and sharpens our awareness for the new thing that continually comes before us, whether we notice it or not.

If the human freedom that corresponds to God is to be found in the ability to begin, then this directs our gaze toward the future. That emerges with an inward cogency. Every beginning is the *anticipation* of the completion—otherwise it would not be a beginning. Every birth is the beginning of a complete life—otherwise it would not be a beginning. Every birth is the anticipation of a full life—otherwise it would not be the beginning of a life. Every exodus out of an outward and inner captivity is already an anticipation of the free life in the realm of freedom—otherwise there could never be an exodus. Every resurrection is an anticipation of the eternally living life. That is why "there is a magic in every beginning," as Hermann Hesse wrote. The believer perceives this magic in God's promise, out of which one will be "born again to a living hope" (1 Peter 1:3).

Without anticipations and promises of this kind the future would hold no magic, and there would be no reason to yearn for it. In birth, in rebirth, in the ability to begin, what we anticipate are not conditions in evanescent time, but fulfillments of our hopes. We do not anticipate what will probably be tomorrow, and ought to be so the day after that, because we want to live and to affirm life. *Future* is not a prolongation of the present according to the surveyor's pole of linear time; it is the fulfillment of our hope for life, which comes to meet us.

Freedom as domination or as community?

Freedom exists in relationships, either in relationships to other people, or another person, or as a relationship to oneself. A common definition of freedom emerges from political history. The person who believes that world history is a continual struggle for power thinks that the victor in this struggle is the one who is free, while the loser is unfree. The free are the people with power, the people without power become the subordinate subjects of the others. In social and political history, the masters are free, the servants are dependents. Paul was familiar with this division of people into freemen and slaves (Gal. 3:28). According to Roman law, only the master of the household is free; his wives, children, and slaves are not free. Freedom as lordship is a sign of a patriarchal culture, as the word *lordship* shows. The free man determines over himself, while the rest, the unfree, are determined by others. Lordship is a one-sided relationship of a subject to objects. This is particularly obvious in a military context: command requires obedience, preferably slavish obedience.

The bourgeois revolution did away with slavery and serfdom and surmounted princely absolutism and feudalism. But its interpretation still took its bearings from the liberty of the princes and the feudal "powers that be." Freedom is the autonomous self-determination of every individual over his or her own life and abilities. Individual freedom is limited only by the freedom of other people. The person who claims that his or her freedom means self-determination has to respect the same freedom where others are concerned. No one determines anyone else, everyone determines oneself. Ideally, this is a society of free but solitary individuals: The Lonely Crowd.[15]

But lordship and slavery constitute only a very one-sided form of social relationship. Since in everyday life and in old age everyone as child, or as a weak and sick person, is dependent on other people, doing away with the lordship over other people in favour of general autonomous self-determination is not helpful in every situation. What is better is the transformation of lordship and slavery into mutual and alternating social representation. People with their own abilities act as representatives of others and *on their behalf*.[16] They do not just stand side by side with them but are there for each other from the cradle to the grave, and act on others' behalf. One can distinguish here between a temporary representation, which is only necessary until the other person can take over his or her own responsibility, and an enduring representation necessary for life, in which people are there for one another because they live together.

In these representative relationships people take over the responsibility for each other; and ever since New Testament times these relationships have been known in the Christian tradition as *love*. German linguistic history shows that freedom is by no means the equivalent of lordship, for the German word for freedom is related to friendliness, which inclines toward the other person.[17]

This kind of freedom is also called *communicative freedom*.[18] I am free and feel free when I am respected and recognized by other people, and when I, for my part, respect and accept others. Then the other person is not a restriction of my freedom, but an extension of it. In mutual participation in the life of other people, individuals become free beyond the boundaries of their individuality. That is the social side of freedom. We call it solidarity. In a community of this kind individuals become persons. An individual is ultimately indivisible, but a person emerges through participation and communication with other people, that is to say, in community.

Something that is ultimately indivisible has no relationships and cannot communicate. So Goethe was right with his dictum that "*individuum est ineffabile*." If a human individual has no relationships it has no characteristics either, and no name. It does not know itself. The completely "privatized" human being is an idiot, in the Greek sense of the word. Without community a human being cannot be a person; but without persons a community cannot be a human community.

What is a person? The free human being is the being that can promise, as Friedrich Nietzsche said, and who also keeps his or her promises, as every child knows. By promising, I pin myself down in my ambiguities. Through the promises I keep I become trustworthy for other people. Through one's promises a person acquires continuity in the flux of the times. One who forgets one's promises forgets oneself; the person who keeps one's promises remains faithful to oneself. This identity between a human person and one's life history is designated through one's name. Through my name I identify myself as the one I was and as the one I will be. I sign my contracts with my name and vouch for what I say with my name.

Free human beings live in such networks of promises made and kept, agreements, and trust. The political paradigm of a free society is the covenant that is laid down in a state's constitution, and the social contract that orders the community or polity. The paradigm of rule is *auctoritas facit legem* ("authority makes the law") while the paradigm of the free society is *pacta sunt servanda* ("agreements must be kept"). A free society is not an accumulation of independent individuals; it is a a community of persons in solidarity—a community of "care and share."

The old familiar method of government was *divide et impera*— "divide and rule." The life of the united community consists of the bringing together of what would otherwise be divided. In shared freedom, the alienation between people is ended and the separation of human civilization from nature is surmounted. The earth is not intended to be subjected to human domination, and animals are not objects for human subjects; they are "fellow creatures." So we shall replace the old rules of domination through new forms of community in society and with nature. Freedom as harmony will be the watchword once competition is replaced by cooperation, and a mutual give and take with nature comes into being, which will serve the common survival of all.

Freedom as creative expectation

The experience of freedom in the Christian faith even leads beyond the unified community. For the Christian faith does not live solely in love; it lives in hope, too.[19] If Christian faith is resurrection faith then it reaches out toward the future and can be termed the creative passion for the future eternally living life. With that it transcends the limitations of the present and crosses beyond the given reality into the potentialities of the future. This passion does not, like dominion or community, take its bearings from what is present but from the future of what is present now."

Christian hope is not a waiting or a matter of "wait and see." It is a *creative expectation* of the things that God has promised with the resurrection of Christ. Those who passionately await something prepare themselves and their community for it. In these preparations the path of the coming One is prepared through attempts to correspond to what is anticipated with all the capacities and potentialities one has. These correspondences to the future God has promised are *anticipations of this future.* The person who hopes for the realm of freedom will desire liberation from political repression and economic exploitation here and now. The person who hopes for the righteousness and justice of the new earth will respect the earth here and now, will develop reverence for earthly life, and will resist its exploitations and destruction. The person who hopes for the eternally living life will be already seized here and now by this "unique, eternal, glowing life," and will make life live wherever he or she can. This freedom is not an "insight into necessity"; it is an insight into potentiality. This freedom is not a harmony of the existing conditions of power; it is their harmonization with what is to come, as the prophecy of Isaiah says:

Arise, shine,
for your light has come,
and the glory of the LORD has risen upon you. (Isa. 60:1)

If we wish to arrive at an abstract summing-up, we might say: lordship relates subjects to *objects*, community relates *subject*s to subjects, creative passion relates subjects to *projects* belonging to the future.

Chapter 7

Freedom Experienced
in Open Friendship

There is a delightful children's book written by Joan Walsh Anglund that appeals to grown-ups, too. It begins:

A friend is someone who likes you.
It can be a boy or a girl,
or a cat or a dog, or even a white mouse.
A tree can be your friend too.
It doesn't talk to you,
but you know it likes you . . ."[1]

These words can speak so quietly and forcibly about friendship because they are speaking about something that exists and surrounds everyone. One doesn't have to create it, one can't acquire it, but it is waiting to be discovered: the boy or girl, the cat or dog, the tree or the brook. It is just there, like the warm sun or the rustling of the wind, or the babbling of the brook. It doesn't demand anything. It likes everyone and everything equally. That is the open friendship which binds the world together. It has also been called "the sympathy of all things." It is a sensitive atmosphere. We live from it, but without noticing it. We can live from it and yet continually destroy it. Then we hear only the noise of our own thoughts and machines, and no longer find anyone who likes us and whom we like.

The words I have quoted are taken from a children's book. They are talking about something "which shines for everyone in childhood and where no one ever was." Ernst Bloch, that restless spirit, called it "the home of identity."[2] It is the world of friendship, a friendly world that is to replace the hostile one. Children sense its existence in their basic trust. The more adult we become, the more mistrustful we are. Then there are not just friends; there are competitors as well, at school and professionally—there is disappointed and misused trust. So we become more fastidious in our choice of friends, more mistrustful about potential enemies, and more indifferent toward animals and trees. As we grow older, it becomes more difficult to form friendships because it is more difficult for us to open ourselves. And yet the radiance of the friendly world of childhood endures as a spark of longing, making the old dissatisfied with an unfriendly environment and lonely in a world that forgets them.

What Is Friendship?

Let us try to arrive at a phenomenological description.

- Friendship is a personal relationship that makes no claims. For "friend" is not an official category, or a title of sovereignty, or a function that is exercised only for a certain period of time, nor is it a social role that one is supposed to play in society. "Someone who likes you" is a category that falls outside the framework of calculable social systems.

- According to Immanuel Kant, friendship combines liking with respect. Friendship is more than what we otherwise call love, *eros*, or *caritas*. Liking combined with respect does not mean wanting to serve other people or to be of use to them. It means accepting and respecting them just as they are. You can be a recognized personality, and enjoy respect and admiration, and can nevertheless be without anyone "who likes you." We have no need to bow down before friends, or to look up to them, or down to them; we look at each other eye to eye. We enjoy being together with a friend, because we feel "at home" in his or her friendship. So friendship has to be cultivated.

• Friendship is not a temporary feeling of liking, for it links liking with faithfulness. We can rely on a friend, and as a friend other people can rely on us. Friendship remains an enduring tie even if one is guilty of something or has undergone some misfortune, for between friends there is no prejudgment that pins the other person down, and no ideal picture that has to be lived up to. All that lies between friends is the promise to walk together side by side and to be there for the other person, and a faithfulness that is related to the person and what he or she is, not to what he or she does and has.

• Friendship is a free human relationship. It arises out of freedom and preserves freedom. We are not already free here by nature; we only become so "when somebody likes us." Friends open up free spaces for one another, for personal development. Friendship is lived freedom. That is why Hegel called it "the concrete concept of freedom." One element in this free human relationship is that we can also leave each other in peace. We do not constantly need to assure ourselves of our friendship, as is generally the case in love. It is enough to know that the friend is there. What friends do for us are not services that have to be paid back. It is not a matter of an exchange of services. It is said that true friendship proves itself in misfortune—as sym-pathy, co-suffering. It also proves itself in happiness as a shared rejoicing without envy. The one is as important as the other.

• Friendship is enduring and is aligned toward permanence. That gives rise to the hope that its gentle power will overcome the short-term power of enmity. Friendship has time and patience. Enmity and violence never have time. So the world will belong to friendship and the people of violence will disappear from the earth (Ps. 82:7). Friendship is the soul of a friendly world. No free *and* just society will come into being without the ethics and the wisdom of friendship. Friendship links personal freedom with social solidarity.

In the Friendship of Jesus

The titles with which the Christian community sums up the meaning and importance of Jesus are traditionally known as his *titles of
sovereignty.*[3] What he did is interpreted as the office with which he
was entrusted by God. Just as in Israel prophets, priests, and kings
implemented God's will for the people, so what Christ did for the
community of his people counted as the activity of the prophet who
revealed God's will, as the activity of the priest who reconciled God
with the world, and as the activity of a king who ruled the people.
Thus Jesus appears to the community in the garment of this title of
sovereignty. Jesus appears to the community as the Christ with divine
authority. The titles describe his uniqueness, but they also create
a distance between him and the people who are his. We may note
critically that these titles of sovereignty derive from an authoritarian
society, and that the supremacy of the prophets, priests, and kings is
accentuated when their titles are transferred to Christ. But this criticism is irrelevant. Who did the Christians listen to as their prophet?
The derided Son of man from Nazareth, "a carpenter's son." Who was
called God's priest? The crucified victim of the powerful on Golgotha.
If, finally, all the radiance of God is conferred on the powerless man
on the cross, then the crowns of the rulers on earth lose their halos.
So, if the society's highest titles are transferred to the crucified Son of
man from Nazareth, then that is an unheard-of potential for a critical
attitude toward sovereignty.

But the titles of sovereignty only express what Christ does for the
people. They do not describe the new community with Jesus and with
each other. Whether prophet, priest, or king, that new community
would be described only in a one-sided way unless another title still
were added—a title which is not a title at all: the name of friend, and
life in friendship.

It is true that Jesus is only called "friend" in two places in the
New Testament, but these are sufficiently important, even though
they are often overlooked. "The Son of Man has come eating and
drinking, and you say, 'Look, a glutton and a drunkard, a friend of
tax collectors and sinners'" (Luke 7:34; Matt. 11:19). This saying
is found in the speech about John the Baptizer, and compares Jesus

with John. John was an ascetic and preached repentance in all life's activities. He ate no bread and drank no wine. His food consisted of "grasshoppers and wild honey." He was therefore viewed as strange. Jesus came and ate and drank with people who in public life counted as sinners, people outside the law, people who were considered as indecent in the eyes of respectable society. So he himself was viewed as indecent and lawless, too. That was the way the outside world generally viewed John and Jesus. But what were the inner reasons for Jesus' behaviour? The inner reason for his conspicuous friendship with "sinners and tax collectors" is his joy in God. He does not just eat and drink with these people. He celebrates with them the messianic feast of God's kingdom. It is not pity that draws Jesus to the people who in the eyes of the law are "sinners"; it is overflowing, inviting joy. The kingdom of God whose proximity Jesus lives and proclaims is celebrated in the feast. He calls it "the eternal marriage feast" and invites his guests to participate with the words, "Go in to the joy of your Lord." The respect Jesus pays to the despised in this way is the justice of grace, the liking he brought to the marginalized is the justice of love. In this way Jesus as "the friend of sinners and tax collectors" combines liking with respect, out of joy over the open kingdom of God.

According to the law, which says what is good in human societies, people are identified with their achievements and their faults. It is the society of the righteous and the sinners, the winners and the losers, the rich and the poor, the good and the bad. Society also judges people in the light of their illnesses or their disabilities. It is in societies like this that the law pins people down to their achievements and their mistakes, and judges them accordingly. But Jesus is called the Son of man because he becomes the friend of sinful, sick, disabled, and poor *people*. By forgiving sins he gives them back their self-respect. By accepting the outcasts, he gives them back a love for life. The contemptuous description "the friend of tax collectors and sinners" expresses a profound truth about Jesus without meaning to do so. As their friend, he manifests the friendship of God to unpleasant people who, because they are unpleasant, are unpleasantly treated. As the Son of man, he sets free their repressed humanity. As the Messiah, he begins the kingdom of God in this upside-down world with "the people one has no use for."

According to the Gospel of John, Jesus declares himself to be the friend of his disciples. By calling them to himself, he calls them to the new life of friendship. "No one has greater love than this, to lay down one's life for one's friends. You are my friends if you do what I command you" (John 15:12-13). The image used here is not that of the priest who offers the sacrifice. In this case the supreme form of love is the sacrifice of one's own life for one's friends. But here love takes the form of friendship. When John makes friendship the motive for Jesus' death, he means a clear-eyed love that is faithful until death, and a deliberate sacrifice for the life of his friends. Because of Jesus' death out of friendship, the disciples will be friends forever. And that friendship will endure if they follow his precepts and become the friends of others. According to John, too, Jesus' friendship with his disciples comes from his joy in God and other people. Shortly before this declaration we read: "I have said these things to you so that my joy may be in you, and that your joy may be complete" (John 15:11). Jesus has come from the overflowing joy of God and he gives his life for the world's joy. That is why the "disciples" are afterward no longer called "pupils" or "servants" but are now called friends. The relationship of the human being to God is no longer the servant's relationship to his or her master, a relationship of dependence and obedience. Nor is it now only the relationship of human children to a heavenly Father. In the fellowship of Jesus the disciples become independent "friends of God." In the community of Jesus they no longer experience God as master, and not even as father, but in God's innermost being as their friend. Consequently, open friendship becomes the hallmark of their community with each other and what determines them in society.

God's Friends

When hearing the phrase "God's friends," the well-informed person may perhaps think of the group of 14th-century mystics known as "God's friends on the Lower Rhine." But the name goes back a long way. Erik Peterson has shown that it derives from the group surrounding

Socrates.[4] The truly wise are the "friends of the gods" and enjoy their friendship, even if the surrounding world looks at them with hostility. In Greece and Egypt the grave inscriptions of the especially prominent often adorned them with this title. Friends of the gods are "favourites of the gods." Speaking of people being "born under a lucky star" is perhaps a remnant of this idea. However, Aristotle strictly rejected the epithet. According to the *Nicomachean Ethics*, *philia* links like only with like, because it can only be a reciprocal bond. So, no free person can be the friend of a slave, and it would also be absurd to describe a human person as being a friend of Zeus, the Father of the gods. There can only be friendship within the closed circle of the like, since only "like draws to like."

Hellenistic Judaism knew exceptions. So the Greek Septuagint calls Abraham "a friend of God," as is Moses, too; and according to the Book of Jubilees every righteous man who keeps the law "is inscribed on the heavenly tablets as the friend of God." This is echoed in the New Testament, when the epistle of James (2:23) says, "'Abraham believed God, and it was reckoned to him as righteousness,' and he was called the friend of God"; and hence he was surely also seen as the leader of the throng of "God's friends."

In early Christianity there was a double version of the concept of being God's friend. First, there was the narrow, exclusive version: Abraham believed the God of the promise, left everything he had behind, and emigrated. That is why the Christian ascetics who left everything and wandered about forsaken and poor, homeless and solitary, are God's true friends. Moses, who on the mountain talked to God face to face, became God's friend. That is why the men and women of prayer, who continually talk to God face to face, are God's true friends. That is why the Christian martyrs were also called true friends of God. Finally, Christ himself gave his life for his friends. That is why the Christian martyrs were also called God's true friends. In this exclusive form only Christians who trod unusual paths counted as being God's friends. Occasionally, the state of being a Christian was divided into three: (1) the servants of God, the unconverted believers; (2) the children of God, the converted believers; and (3) God's friends, who believe and consistently follow him. But in addition there has always been the broad, inclusive version: all Christians have become God's friends through the friendship of Christ. But that manifests the character of this new relationship to God, the relationship of friend, which sounds too intimate and lacking in proper respect.

According to Luke and John, the friendship of God manifests itself preeminently in *prayer*. In obedience to God's commandments, human beings feel that they are the Lord God's servants. In faith in the gospel, they see themselves as children of God the Father. But in prayer they talk to God as they talk to their friends. The parable with which Luke follows the Our Father prayer talks about the everyday request made to a friend for bread. Although the night is of course an inconvenient time for the friend, he nevertheless fulfills the request because he cannot ignore its urgency and stands by his friendship. Wherever a person prays in Jesus' name, God is being claimed as a friend, and the request is urgently made in the name of that friendship. In John, too, the new friendship gives the disciples new assurance when they pray: "The Father will give you whatever you ask him in my name" (John 15:16). Asking and being heard are the two sides of the friendship with God. And the friendship gives the petitioner the confidence that the prayer will be heard. One can put it more simply in Karl Barth's words: "God lets himself be talked to." In the all-comprehensive freedom of God there is room enough for human freedom. God's rule over the world includes the possibility of human influence and cooperation. In the form of Jesus as friend, God encounters human beings as "the hearing God." God calls the human being not just to the servant's humility, or the child's gratitude, but to the friend's confidentiality and boldness.[5] Prayer must therefore be seen as, after faith, the supreme expression of human freedom in God. By bringing before God the sighs and groans out of the depths of the world, the human being is claiming God's affection for the people who are suffering. And God shows God's friendship by listening to human beings. Prayer and the hearing of prayer are of the essence of human friendship with God and of God's friendship with human beings. It seems to me important to put both the prayer and the hearing of prayer on the level of friendship. For then it is a relationship of mutual liking that respects the freedom of the other. It would be slavish to beg for something without the assurance that the plea would be listened to. Prayer in Christ's name is the language of friendship. And God's hearing of the prayer in Christ's name is the hearing of "someone who likes you," whatever may happen to you.

Open Friendship for a Friendlier World

In the concept of Jesus' friendship we find a summing-up of what the earlier titles of sovereignty wanted to say about the fellowship. As prophet of the kingdom of God for the poor, Jesus becomes the friend of sinners and tax collectors; as high priest, he sacrifices himself for the life and salvation of others and perfects his love in the death died by a friend; as the exalted Lord, he liberates men and women from their enslavement and makes them God's friends. The theological doctrine of the threefold office of Christ has always presented his activity in terms of sovereignty and the office he exercised, and by doing so has obscured his simple friendship. So, in the corresponding official church, authority always played a paramount part. It became a "church without community." But if Christ lives and acts as prophet for the poor, as sacrifice for the many, and as leader for freedom, then he also lives and acts as friend, and creates friendship. In the spirit of friendship, the Christian community of brothers and sisters will become more warm-hearted, and in the friendship of Jesus will be led with more compassion to "the least" of his brothers and sisters outside. It would be good if the church, the church's authorities, and the people in their care were at last to remember that all together they are no more and no less than "the community of Jesus' friends." But for this we must take a final, critical look at the phenomenon of friendship today.

Of course the designation "friendship" is as much open to misunderstanding today as the ancient titles of sovereignty. On the one hand, friendship is in danger of becoming exclusive. That was already the case in Aristotle. If only like draws to like, then dog doesn't eat dog, but what about the other animals? It is true that the Greeks praised friendship as the inner bond of the community. Because justice without the agreement of the community of citizens remains sterile, friendship fulfills the intention of justice and is itself the most just of all. But it can associate only those that are similar because the bond depends on mutuality. Because of this principle of likeness and equality of rank, the Greek ideal of friendship inclines toward exclusivity. That is often no different in our society today. We incline toward "a closed society," to class societies. Quite apart from the fact that this is hurtful for "the outsiders," it is also extremely tedious for the insiders, since people who are no different are, for those who are alike, merely a matter of indifference.[6]

This closed circle of friendship between those who are alike is fundamentally broken through by Christ, both in the direction of God and in the direction of the socially despised. If Christ had been content to abide by the principle of "like draws to like" he would ultimately have had to remain in heaven. But his assumption of humanity and his friendship with sinners and tax collectors break through the exclusive circle. Consequently, Christian friendship cannot be lived within the inner circle of believers and the devout, that is to say, the group of like-minded people, but only in open liking and public respect for the others. Through Jesus, friendship has become an open concept of approachability. Community between Christians doesn't mean sitting next to someone with whom I am in accord; it means to remain sitting beside someone with whom I disagree.

In Old High German, "*Freund* und *Feind*" (friend and enemy) were still official designations. Friendships were concluded through alliances and proved themselves publicly through faithfulness to those alliances. But because of the modern divisions between the public and the private spheres, the terms came to be variously distributed. "The enemy"—the enemy of the state, the enemy of one's class, the enemy of the people—remained a political term, whereas friendship moved ino the private sphere and was internalized. The friend became the personal friend, the bosom or best friend, or the "soulmate," and friendship became a matter of feeling. Because through this separation of the public from the private sphere the individual becomes increasingly lonely, one needs a network of personal friends. But they do not really break through one's loneliness. They lead only to two lonelinesses. This is the romantic friendship in the seclusion of the intimate sphere, reflected in the passage attributed to Heraclitus:

> *I wept as I remembered how often you and I*
> *have tired the sun with talking,*
> *and sent him down the sky.*

This privacy and intimacy of modern friendship is foreign to Jesus' friendship with his disciples and with sinners and tax collectors. To live in his friendship today means deprivatizing the romantic concept of friendship. Friendship must again acquire the character of public protection and public respect for other people. Is that possible? In this world of ours, with its professions, functions, and businesses, can friendship be publicly lived and offered?

One can look in the so-called social networks on the Internet—Facebook, Twitter, and so forth—for public, open friendships of this kind, although here, too, the principle of equality often lurks in the background. But—even apart from the fact that in the background here, too, people are sought out on the basis of similar interests and backgrounds—is an anonymous link in a virtual world really friendship? Does friendship not also require the direct interhuman encounter, the look into the face of the other person in his or her difference?

There are examples which show that there are other possibilities. From their earliest times the Quakers have called themselves "the Society of Friends." They have proved in exemplary fashion Jesus' open friendship through their open social work in the English slums and through their political struggle for the abolition of slavery in the United States.[7] In Atlanta, Georgia, I love the Open Door Community, a Christian community that keeps its doors wide open for homeless, jobless people and prisoners. How would it be if the Christian congregations and communities ceased to understand themselves only as "the communion of saints" or as "the community of believers," but saw themselves as a community of friends like this? They would then have to overcome the much-lamented lack of relationship between the attenders at their services so that people could feel at home in their company. They would have to abandon their unconscious, and sometimes even deliberate, exclusiveness toward "the wicked world" and the so-called unbelievers, and be prepared for friendship with the forsaken. They would then constitute themselves in basis congregations that would live the friendship of Jesus in the people and with the people.

Talking doesn't bring about this change from lordship to friendship, and from the closed society to the open community—and above all not when when it is accompanied by the threatening morality of "this is what must happen." For nothing "must" happen. It happens wherever joy in God, in people, and in the world takes hold of men and women. That is why Nietzsche's Zarathustra taught "not the neighbour but the friend." He will be won not only through "co-suffering" but, before that, through "co-rejoicing." And with him the "festival of the earth" will be celebrated. We saw how Jesus became a friend out of joy in God, which is described with the old word *gospel*. His feast was not only "the marriage of the soul with God," as the mystics called it, but the "feast of heaven and earth"—that is to say, the feast of the coming kingdom, which renews the heavens and the earth. The feast makes friends, and lets friendship be discovered everywhere. "A friend is someone who likes you. It can be a boy, it can be girl, or a cat, or a tree, or the brook, or the wind." So we read in Anglund's children's book. Open friendship illuminates the world, which is otherwise often an unpleasant one. Open friendship prepares the ground for a friendlier world. It discovers harmony with other people, with God, with the earth, and surmounts the discords by taking to itself those who are forsaken. It creates endurance and is what abides, and can be relied on in the ups and downs of life.[8]

Chapter 8

The Loved and Loving Life

LOVE IS THE NAME WE GIVE THE MOST INTENSE EXPERIENCE IN LIFE. Human beings as we know them hunger for love and die of lovelessness. Men and women are erotic beings. They are driven by the longing for happiness. The hunger for recognition urges them forward to ever-greater achievements. Curiosity drives them beyond every familiar environment. Unlike animals, human beings are not content in their environments but, as *homo viator*, feel themselves to be in transition and on the way to something else: one is "always covetous to break through the barriers of [one's] present as it now exists, always striving to transcend the reality that surrounds [one]—including [one's] own self in its present reality"—so wrote Max Scheler.[1] If desire is the essence of the human being, that presupposes an experience of emptiness, and a love for the fullness of life. The emptiness longs to be filled, the fullness is sought for. The lust for life joins the emptiness with the fullness.

Christianity has linked this experience of love with the experience of God: "*Ubi amor et caritas gaudent ibi Deus ist*" ("Where love rejoices, there is God"). That deepens both the emptiness of the heart and the fullness of life. The unending God awakens in the human being God's image, an emptiness that nothing finite or transitory can fill—nothing but the unending God alone. In what Johann Baptist Metz calls the "missing of God," the human being reaches out beyond everything finite and strives for infinity.[2] That is the wandering of God's people in their search for God.

> For here we have no abiding city,
> because we seek the future one. (Heb. 13:14; my trans.)

That is Augustine's "restless heart," which finds no rest except in God alone. For that reason measurelessness is the measure of human desire in its search for God.

The God who has become human fulfills this emptiness of the heart, for with it the eternal divine life enters the human and finite life. Christ brings "the fullness of life" (John 10:11). In him is the risen life that overcomes the great deficiency and ultimate suffering, which is death, and with it fills to the brim the absolute emptiness of the human heart:

> What was from the begininng,
> what we have heard,
> what we have seen with our eyes,
> what we have looked at and touched with our hands,
> concerning the word of life—
> this life that is eternal was made manifest to us. (1 John 1:1-2)

Because fulfillment is possible and is grasped and truly lived in the community of Christ, it is useful to compare the experience of God with the experience of love as we experience it in life; otherwise it would be more useful to link the otherworldly experience with the emptiness of the heart, and to seek the liberation from desire instead of its fulfillment. Fulfilled passion is the happiest experience in life; love that has come to grief is the most terrible experience that men and women can experience, for it becomes the violent power of destruction, the fury of annihilation. "It is passion that creates suffering." Either the suffering of passion is too strong for life, or living passion is superior to suffering.

Let us compare two different ways: the way of the Gautama Buddha and the apostle Paul's eulogy of love.

The Doctrine of Suffering (Buddha)
and the Doctrine of Love (Paul)

Of course, the respective texts of these two cannot be compared in view of their different dates and cultural origins. But they are nevertheless comparable in respect of their reception by contemporary Western readers. They are comparable when they are related to similar and universal experiences of life. In our case, this means the surmounting of suffering through a transcendent quenching of desire, or through the acceptance of suffering by way of the transference of individual desires into the fullness of the divine love.

a. In the *Discourses of Buddha* (ch. 4), the subject is "the doctrine of suffering":[3]

> *Whatever suffering there was in the past,*
> *whether it still exists or will only now come into being,*
> *it all has its root, its foundation, in desire.*
> For desire is the root of suffering.[4]

How can suffering be overcome? Through the extinction of desire, of the thirst for life, of the fondness for life. These drives constitute the consciousness, and the consciousness creates the sixfold character of the sensory sphere: "The sixfold sensory sphere determines touch, touch determines feeling, feeling determines the thirst for life, the thirst for life determines the inclination for life, the inclination for life determines the coming-into-being, the coming-into-being determines birth, birth determines age and death, sorrow. Thus lamentation, suffering, despair, and restlessness arise. *Thus this full measure of suffering comes into being.*"[5] Release from suffering takes the opposite direction. Through the extinction of the drives, consciousness ceases to be, the consciousness disappears, the sphere of the six senses is extinguished. If touch is extinguished, feeling ceases to exist, and with it the inclination for life. If the thirst for life is ended, so is the becoming, and then there is no longer any birth. "*So as a result all this suffering comes to an end.*" Once there is "birthlessness," "deathlessness" is discovered as well: "The birthless, ageless, sickness-free, immortal coming-to-rest of all doing, free of suffering and error—*the Nibbana.*"[6] There is release through the extinction of the passion for life, which creates so much suffering. The fullness of life is viewed not as release from the thirst for life but only as the disappearance of the thirst. And because the thirst for life keeps the consciousness alive and activates the human senses, the sensory feelings must be quenched and this consciousness must disappear. The "emptiness" with which the passion for life begins also already holds within itself the path leading to release from the "life" that begins with birth and ends with death, and is full of all kinds of suffering. The "true life" is not this life in its fated, karma-determined "cycles" but the Nirvana, which can no longer be called "life," or "eternal" or "true" life, because it has nothing in common with this life. In Western ears, these words of Buddha sound like the negation of life and the refusal to live—they sound like total resignation. It is better not to be born at all and not to be born again rather than to bear this "quantity of suffering."

But the extinction of the drives, of desire, of the senses and the consciousness is not the sole Buddhist attitude to life. It is only the overcoming of the false life in "not knowing" through the search for the "enlightenment" of true being. There is also Kwanjin, the goddess of mercy; there is also the Bodhisattva who turns back in front of the goal in order to help the "not-knowing" through his compassion. And there is also the plump, laughing Chinese Buddha. And why does Buddha *speak*, if all speaking and listening is after all supposed to cease? The selfless compassion with the suffering is a virtue that can go hand in hand with the extinction of the selfish desire for life—or so we might put it in positive terms.[7]

b. That brings us to Christ's apostle, Paul, and his "song of songs" over love, 1 Corinthians 13:

If I speak in the tongues of mortals and of angels
but do not have love, *I am a noisy gong or a clanging cymbal.*

*And if I have prophetic powers, and understand all mysteries
and all knowledge, and
if I have all faith, so as to remove mountains,*
but do not have love, *I am nothing.*

*If I give away all my possessions, and
if I hand over my body so that I may boast,*
but do not have love, *I gain nothing. . . .*

And now faith, hope, and love abide, these three;
and the greatest of these is love. *(13:1-3, 13)*

Let us first of all be clear about the situation reflected in this love song. The young Christian community in the port of Corinth was a wonderful pentecostal congregation. They experienced the fullness of life in an overflowing wealth of gifts *(charismata).* In their worship they rejoiced "with men and with angels"; there were theologians who opened to them the mysteries of God; there were believers who had the gift of healing; and they were all aware of God's "preferential option" for the poor. What were they lacking? The Christians in this richly endowed congregation were evidently more concerned about themselves than about their community. Self-love, self-praise, and self-interest dominated them, just as they dominated the heathen people round them. That is why Paul adds to his praise of love his self-criticism: "*I* would be nothing—*I* should gain nothing."

It is the divine power of love that lifts people out of themselves and lets them forget their own ego. People are only concerned about themselves when they are frightened. But there is no fear in love. In love I have no need "to be despairingly myself," as Kierkegaard put it in his description of the "sickness into death." In the love I experience and in the love I give, the hunger for recognition—that is, the recognition of my achievements—and the greed for money and possessions disappear. In the flood of love, the whole joy of God is with us. That is why Paul is right when he says that without love the best human gifts and achievements, the most elevated religious feelings, and the wisest knowledge remain empty—"a noisy gong or a clanging cymbal."

Not every love is good. Love is always determined by what is loved. The person who loves money will become greedy for it; the person who loves to smoke will become addicted to smoking; the person who lusts for praise will become greedy for adulation. It is only the love for life that makes people come alive. Mutual love makes both those engaged in it happy, and the love that runs ahead to encounter the other sparks generosity and begins something new. Love for life makes life something that is living—one's own life and the life of other people, the life we share and life on this earth.

Because when Christians say, "God is love," they are associating the experience of God with this intensive experience of life, love is talked about in the singular even though it takes very different forms in differing relationships. In the double commandment of love, it is both the love of God and neighbourly love. It is both the enchanting power of erotic love—"as strong as death, . . . its flashes are flashes of fire," as it is described in the Song of Solomon—as well as the love for a friend and the love of our enemy. It is called *eros* and *agape* and *philia*, and lives in the words *sympathy* and *empathy*, in recognition and appreciation. It is the love that gives and the love that enjoys, it is mutual love and love that takes the firsr step. It is contained in all the relationships in the human and earthly world that promote life and bring people together. But in all these different relationships it is one and the same love. The distinctions between *eros* and *agape* are misleading.

For that reason we must also turn Paul's statement upside down in order to see what is behind it. He says that *without love* all the riches of life are worthless. And what do his words look like if we turn them into the positive and ask: And how is it *with love in all the wealth of life?*

> *If I have love I shall speak with the tongues of men and of angels*
> *. . .*
> *In love I perceive the mysteries of God,*
> *and have pleasure in the knowledge of God for God's sake,*
> *and for my faith nothing is impossible . . .*
> *In love, the poor are my brothers and sisters,*

and in its power the sick will be healed . . .
In love, I do not ask about myself
but am self-forgetfully happy.

Love can be a desire of the will for an enrichment of one's own self through possessions, reputation, and enjoyment, but then one's own ego remains solitary and imprisoned in the circle of self-seeking, and knows only itself: *homo incurvatus in se.* Love can also be a desire of all the senses for union with the other person. Then it leads the "I" beyond itself to the "Thou" of the other person. The union with the other, or with others, makes the love creative. It then departs from the principle of equality, which imprisons the self: "Like draws to like" is fine for the like, because they empower and endorse the one, but the vital power of love becomes living and creative in "the other." Why? Because it is based on God's love for human beings, and from this divine frontier-crossing love finds the strength to cross barriers itself, and to find the way even to the enemy. Love has pleasure in the other, in what is new.

And what about the problem of suffering? Christian love perceives the love of God in the passion and resurrection of Jesus Christ. That means that this is a love which is prepared for suffering. It is a self-giving love, and is hence a love that rises again. The redeeming death of Buddha is visually presented in the statue of the reclining Buddha. He lies there in utter peace, and glides over into the *nirvana.* The death of Jesus Christ on the cross shows vividly the passion of God—which comprises both death and suffering. The Buddha in the Japanese Kamakura has looked over the sea for more than a thousand years. In unmoved relaxation and with inwardly turned eyes, it gazes at the conflicts of the human beings surrounding it and the catastrophes of the tsunamis in front of it. On the cross on Golgatha, Jesus dies with the cry of desolation over the Godforsakenness of this world. It is only in his rising from the dead that the overcoming of the suffering in the world comes into view. On Orthodox icons the exalted Christ is enthroned in eternal life in relaxation and peace like the Buddha—but he bears the marks of the nails from the cross of this world.

The ascetic spirituality of the patristic church developed in a parallel way, but was undoubtedly also inspired by Eastern Buddist spirituality. The ascent of the soul to God overcomes the lower passions, *pathe*. In the love for God, *agape*, God is *loved* above all things and these things are *used* as the earthly things that they are. The love for God is first acquired through the ascetic absence of passion, *apatheia*, which can also be seen as "inner freedom" (Hans Urs von Balthasar). This is a spiritualizing of the bodily drives and needs, which Sigmund Freud called their "sublimation." The person who loves God alone and only God is "free" of all things and is called to every form of self-control, as the desert and "pillar" saints of the patristic church impressively demonstrated. This ascetic spiriuality presupposes that the soul occupies a higher place than the body in the hierarchy of being, and is therefore closer to God. It is eternal and the body is transitory. God's relationship to the soul is inherent in the soul as the image of God, the *imago Dei*, while the lower powers of the soul and the body show only *vestigia Dei*, traces of God.

In this way the patristic church translated the apocalyptic anthropology of the apostle Paul into the Platonic dualism of body and soul. Whereas Paul talks eschatologically about the "old" and the "new" human being in the passing and the coming eras of the world, they thought in ontological stages of the "outer" and the "inner" human being in the body and in the soul. Through asceticism, the soul's absence of passion thereby takes the place of the bodily passions. But according to Paul, in Christ the believer becomes "a new creation" in soul, inwardly and outwardly. Although the believer still exists in this old, evanescent world system, he or she is already living in God's new creation. It is not ascetic apathy that overcomes the evil fears and cravings of the old world, but participation in the passion of the divine love. That is not human love for God; it is God's love for human beings, which is alive and lays hold of us in Jesus Christ (Rom. 8:39). How does this come about?

"Swords into ploughshares," demands the prophet Micah (4:3). Translated into real-life terms, that means transforming criminal energies into the energies of love, changing war into peace and enmity into friendship, and redeeming the acts of deadly violence so that they become forces for living. That happens through the forgiveness of sins, and in liberating repentance.

God's Love and Human Love for God

The mutuality principle: similarity, dissimilarity, and correspondence

Can finite human beings "love" the infinite God? No! Can we "love" the invisible God as we "love" the people we can see? No! Human beings can love those who are like them, but not the "wholly other" God. That is also right and good, for Moses was told: "You cannot see my face, for no one shall see me and live" (Exod. 33:20). We can revere God, we can stand awestruck before the hidden God, we can respect God's mystery—but then we must fall silent. For us to love the absolute God is impossible—or is it? Aristotle says in his *Magna Moralia:*

> There is no friendship with God and with those without souls: "*for friendship exists where love is returned*."
>
> But in the case of friendship with God, there is no place for returned love, or indeed for love at all. For it would be absurd for anyone to claim that he loves Zeus. And of course no requited love is possible from the side of those without souls either, although there can be "love" for what has no soul—for wine, for example. For that reason the investigation has to do neither with friendship with God nor with friendship for those without souls; it has to do only with friendship between persons with souls—persons for whom requited love is possible.[8]

Here he is simply following the "golden rule" of reciprocity. There is love only where requited love is possible. There is community only on the tit-for-tat principle. This is based on *the principle of similarity.* Between the dissimilar, such as gods and human beings, or masters and slaves, or men and women, there can be neither love nor friendship. Indeed, Aristotle is also familiar with the view that "opposites attract each other": "Others believe that friendship develops between opposites. It is said that 'The earth longs for moisture if the ground is dry.'" So they think that it is opposites that wish to befriend each other, for between those that are alike this is not possible, because the like have no need of the like, but reject it because only the like can recognize the like. The similarity principle in "knowing" corresponds to the reciprocity principle in society, and ultimately also to the right of retaliation, which repays good with good and evil with evil.[9] Aristotle forgot hospitality, which goes out to meet the stranger and does not depend on reciprocity. Aristotle also forgot that children are born out of the anticipatory love of the parents, and grow up in that love. Reciprocity exists only between the similar, but we live in dissimilar circumstances. The like exist with one another, but the unlike can be there for one another—parents for children, the strong for the weak, the healthy for the sick, and so forth. The similarity principle, which is the justification for the reciprocity of the "golden rule" and the law of reciprocity, is not suited to act as a universal ethos, because it is exclusive, not inclusive.

If it is applied to the knowledge of God, God is eiher unknowable by human beings and not to be loved, or human beings have divinity within themselves, with which they can perceive and love the divine. A poem by Goethe takes the second stance:

> *Were not the eye sun-like.*
> *how then could it descry the sun?*
> *Were not within us God's own power,*
> *how then could the divine entrance us?*[10]

Between the principles of similarity and dissimilarity stands the principle of analogy. Between the Creator and created being there is an analogy, or similarity, even though the dissimilarity is still much greater.[11] There is a continuum of being between those that are and "being," which is the *analogia entis*—the analogy of essence. Creation *corresponds* to the Creator, but is not like God. It is a simile of its Creator. Although it is not the same as God, creation can act as an image of its Creator and also needs to be such an image in order for it to exist. Creation is full of similarities that point beyond themselves to the incomparable God. So the human being is not compelled to be silent, but can talk about the incomparable God in comparisons and metaphors:

As a father has compassion for his children
So the Lord *has compassion for those who fear him.*
(Ps. 103:13)

Or:

As a mother comforts her child,
So I will comfort you. (Isa. 66:13)

The equality principle and the friendship based on mutuality remain within the closed circle of those who are always the same. The analogy principle presupposes a graduated continuum of being. It is only the principle of contrast that first creates something new.[12] It requires the ability to begin. Who takes the first step?

In epistemological theory this means that physical perceptions emerge from contrasts: we perceive cold from what is warm, said Anaxagoras, sweetness from the sour, and light from the dark. Physical perceptions are in fact bound up with pain, for when the dissimilar impinges on our sensory organs what emerges is attentiveness, curiosity, and, in the extreme case, pain. On the other hand, when what is similar impinges on our sensory organs, we often do not notice it, or it confirms us in what we already knew.

In social theory that means that social encounters between the dissimilar generally produce conflicts, but if human beings nevertheless have to live together, they develop social fantasy and give rise to new forms of living together. In this respect the encounter with "the others" awakens creative powers in people. These come alive in prevenient creative love, in open friendship, and in the surmounting of evil with good.

"God is only known by God," says the similarity principle. "To know God means to suffer God," says the principle of contrast. We perceive the wholly other God with pain—the pain of one's own fundamental alteration, of dying from God and the new birth out of God, as Christian baptism symbolizes. In perceiving our own contradictions of God, correspondences to God come into being out of God's power.

What does that mean with regard to the possibility of loving God?

The love of God: the story of the exodus and the *Shema Israel*

In the *Shema* (Deut. 6:4-5) we read:

> *Hear, O Israel: the LORD is our God, the LORD alone.*
> *You shall love the LORD your God*
> *with all your heart,*
> *and with all your soul,*
> *and with all your might.*

If the Lord "alone" is our God, then the love of God is undivided and all-embracing. For we cannot "love" the "one" God only a little, half-heartedly, with a divided soul, and only by the way. We can only "love" the one God wholly or not at all. But who is "the Lord"?

This expression is not intended to intensify the authority of the one God by referring to "the Lord God." The reverse is the case: the divinity is related to "the Lord." It is not that God is the Lord, but *the Lord* is "our God." As the First Commandment says, *the Lord* is the one who "brought you out of the land of Egypt, out of the house of slavery" (Deut. 5:6). The Lord is Israel's liberator and divine partner in the covenant. This lordship means freedom in the land of promise. The Lord makes the covenant: "I will be your God, and you shall be my people." The Lord will "dwell" in the midst of the Lord's people.[13] The title "Lord" does not mean God per se, or God in the heavenly world, but the "descending" God who has "seen" the misery of God's people and has "heard" their cries, and the God who leads them out and sets off on the way together with God's people: *Deus Viator* (Exod. 3:7-9). In the exodus of God's people God is present in the pillar of cloud by day and the pillar of fire at night. Out of the cloud God talks to Moses "as one speaks with a friend" (Exod. 33:11). This is not God in inaccessible glory; the Lord is God in God's merciful descent and God's *Shekinah*, the *Shekinah* that is prepared for suffering and accompanies the people on their way.[14] In the Torah, the exodus story is told as a a *Shekinah* history, and this history is God's history with Israel. It is the history of a transcendent immanence, the history of God's compassion (Exod. 34:6) and God's love:

> *When Israel was a child, I loved him,*
> *And out of Egypt I called my son. (Hos. 11:1)*[15]

The prophet Hosea makes Israel's history present as God's love story—God's prevenient love, God's disappointed and wrathful love, but God's faithful love:

> *How can I give you up? . . .*
> *My compassion grows warm and tender. (Hos. 11:8)*

Because with the Lord it is a matter of the immanent, experienced love story of the God of Israel, we need not only "fear" God (Deut. 6:2); we can also love God, as we remember our own liberation from slavery, keep the commandments of freedom, and do not run after other gods, the gods of other peoples.

The *Shema Israel* makes it clear that the love for God which the Bible talks about is not related to a God in the next world per se, nor to a *summum bonum* or "something than which nothing greater can be thought" (Anselm of Canterbury). It is related to the immanence of transcendence, God's history in this world, God's history with God's people, and God's indwelling presence, God's *Shekinah*. Although both this love of God for God's people, and the responding love of the people are both called "love," the difference between God-like and human love is obvious: the Lord's love is the liberation of the people from slavery, but the love of the liberated for the Lord is the recollecting calling to mind of the liberation and life in this freedom. The love of the Lord is compassion—the love of the liberated is joy. Compassionate love is love for those who are different, for the compassion is awakened not through beauty but through misery.

The love of God: the history of Christ and the love of God

Wherever "the Lord" is mentioned in Israel's history with God, in Christianity's history we find the name of Jesus Christ—*the Lord*. That is why Luther writes in his Reformation hymn:

Ask ye, Who is this same?
Christ Jesus is his name,
The Lord Sabaoth's Son
He and no other one,
Shall conquer in the battle.[16]

The role of the exodus story in Israel is taken in the New Testament by the history of Christ. Yet the indwelling of the *Shekinah* in the one story differs from the history of the incarnate Son of God. In the Christian doctrine of God, a distinction has always been made between the personal incarnation of the Son and the social inhabitation of God's Spirit. The experience of God's "indwelling" Spirit in the heart (Rom. 5:5), in the body of believers (2 Cor. 4:10), and in their community (2 Cor. 6:16) corresponds to Israel's experience of the *Shekinah*. That is why the words "dwelling" and "indwelling" are used for this experience.[17]

What is manifested in the history of Christ? What transcendent meaning can be perceived in it? From the beginning Christians have discerned in the coming of Jesus Christ into their world God's love for all human beings and for the whole cosmos; and it is in that sense that they have told and proclaimed the history of Christ:

God's love was revealed among us in this way:
God sent his only Son into the world
so that we might live through him. (1 John 4:9)

Or, as the Gospel of John says:

For God so loved the world
that he gave his only Son,
so that everyone who believes in him should not perish
but may have eternal life. (John 3:16)

But what form does God's love take in Jesus Christ?

a. The *sending* of Jesus manifests God's prevenient creative love. Jesus brings the divine love to the unloved, goes to the outcasts, accepts the sinners who are without the law and eats with them, and proclaims to the poor the gospel of the approaching kingdom of God. The sick experience God's love in their healing, and people whose lives have gone astray discover that God loves them and does not despise them, as do other people or they themselves. In the gospel, the poor hear that with them God wants to build God's kingdom in this world. As Jesus opens the kingdom of God to the poor, as he brings the power of God to the sick, and as he uses the justice of God on behalf of those without rights, so he brings the nonviolent love of God into this violent world, which is violent because it is loveless. It is a healing love that gives health to the sick; it is a love that puts things to rights by bringing justice to those who know no justice; it is a prevenient love that makes the ugly beautiful. It is this creative love of God that was encountered by the persons who encountered Jesus—so the Gospels relate.

b. An interim reflection: Jesus lived and acted out what he taught. In him consciousness and being were a unity. For he taught and acted nothing that he was not, and nothing that he did not live. The first people who followed him did not see in him only a teacher of God's love; they saw *the love of God in person*—the eternal love-become-human, out of which the true, eternal love emanated. Just as for Israel the exodus story is the story of God's compassion, so for Christians the history of Christ is the history of God's love.

c. The *passion* of Jesus manifests a sacrificial life of self-giving. The pains of his death manifest the pains of God's love. Jesus suffers like us, Jesus suffers for us, in order to bring us this love: that was how the first Christians perceived God in the cross on Golgotha—the perception Paul expressed in his theology of the cross. How does this come about? Jesus' own experience in Gethsemane and on Golgotha was the experience of being forsaken by God. He died with the cry: "My God, why have you forsaken me?" and in doing so took to himself the cry of so many forsaken men and women. Paul interprets this "forsaking" as "surrendering" or "giving away" (*paradidonai*): "He who did not spare his own Son but *gave him up* for us all, will he not give us all things with him?" (Rom. 8:32) According to Galatians 2:20, Christ was not only "surrendered," given up, by God, he also quite actively gave himself up—"out of love," as Paul adds: ". . . who loved me and *gave himself* for me." With this he expresses a unity of will between God, the Father of Jesus Christ, and Jesus, the Son of God—the unity of will also expressed in the Gethsemane account: "Not what I will, but what you will" (Mark 14:36).

d. To sum up: we talk about God's self-giving in the passion of Jesus Christ and in his death. Giving and giving away are the characteristics of a selfless love that is not oriented toward one's self-advantage. The giving of oneself is the greatest love of all: "Greater love has no man than this, that a man lay down his life for his friends" (John 15:13). The crucified love of God is beside God's beloved human beings in the Godforsakenness of this world, in "the dark night of the soul," and in the persecutions and humiliations imposed by godless powers. Consequently, Paul sees in the crucified love of God the indestructible reason for the assurance of being eternally loved:

Who shall separate us from the love of Christ?
Shall tribulation, or distress, or persecution, or famine, or
nakedness, or peril, or sword? . . .
No, in all these things we are more than conquerors through
him who loved us.
For I am sure that neither death nor life,
nor angels nor principalities,
nor things present nor things to come,

neither height nor depth nor anything else in all creation,
will be able to separate us from the love of God
which is in Christ Jesus, our Lord. (Rom. 8:31-39)

e. An interim reflection: If the love of Christ suffers death, is that love then itself dead? If the love of God dies, does God then also die? No. The self-giving love suffers the death of Christ on the cross and yet surmounts it as the eternal love of God. That sounds paradoxical, but it is no paradox if we can distinguish in trinitarian terms between Jesus, the Son of God, who in truth dies on the cross, and the God of Jesus Christ whom he calls Abba, Father. The self-giving Father and the self-giving Son are one in the movement of self-giving, but they are not a single person. When the Son suffers, the Father suffers, too— the Father who loves him and has pleasure in him, as was said at Jesus' baptism. But the Father suffers in a different way. When the Son dies, he suffers the dying, but not the death, for he does not survive that in an earthly sense. But the Father who loves him suffers his death, for he has to "survive" the death of the beloved Son. That is the pain of God into which we can enter when death takes our dearest from us and we have to "survive" it. That is "the sorrow of God" in the " bereavement" of the Son.[18]

Why is this trinitarian insight into what took place between Jesus and his God on the cross on Golgotha important? Because it makes it possible for us to comprehend the *"raising"* love of God the Father and the *"rising"* love of the Son. If the divine love is in any case above a human death, it requires no resurrection of Jesus. If the divine love dies with Jesus on the cross, then God's history with Jesus is at an end and God also is "dead." In the trinitarian history of God, divine self-giving to the point of death *and* resurrection from death become comprehensible as the reality of divine love.

Is there a continuum in the absolute discontinuity of death and life, self-giving and raising? In the New Testament the power of the divine love is ascribed to God's Spirit.[19] If we look more closely, we discover the Holy Spirit in Christ's giving of himself to death on the cross and in his raising through God the Father. The epistle to the Hebrews talks about Christ "who through the eternal Spirit offered himself . . . to God" (9:14), and it is this eternal Spirit of God through whom the dead Christ is raised to life by the Father (Rom. 1:4).

f. The raising of the dead Jesus manifests the life-creating power of the divine love.[20] It is the raising from the dead to a life that never again dies and hence counts as eternal life. The raising of Jesus from death does not just endorse the general resurrection of the dead or "a life after death"; it also brings eternal life into this mortal life of human beings. With the resurrection of Jesus, the God-imbued, eternally young life appears in the midst of this history of death. With the resurrection of Jesus, the life that is eternal is proclaimed to all the world. It is open to everyone who lays hold of it in faith and rejoices in it. Raising is a historical event that has taken place in Jesus of Nazareth, but it is at the same time an eschatological happening, *anticipating* the raising of the dead in this one Person, and the new creation through that one Person. Consequently, the resurrection of Jesus is comprehended only if the Spirit of the resurrection lays hold of men and women and they experience a rebirth to the fullness of life. For them, resurrection is like a new birth and a new beginning of life. Through the transforming power of divine love mortal life will come alive from within. The experience of God will become the experience of being loved and affirmed from all eternity. That is the fullness of life. This experience is a support beyond death, one's own death and the death of others, beyond fear and beyond grief. The raising of Jesus and the fullness of life that has appeared in him and is accessible in him is the greatest experience of God's love. It is understandable that the first Christians should have seen this love not only as an act and not only as an attribute of God but as God's eternal being. God does not only love as one who is capable of not loving; but rather "God *is* love" (1 John 4:16). God's nature *is* faithfulness. God is not just "the one who loves in freedom" (Karl Barth) but also "the one who in love is free" (Otto Weber).[21] Even if human beings do not believe God, and God's love remains unrequited, God is still faithful—God cannot deny Godself (2 Tim. 2:13).

That brings us to the conclusion: Eternal life is eternally loved earthly life. Those who are eternally loved, "even though they die, will live" (John 11:25).

Christian love for God

According to Matthew (22:37-40), Jesus puts together the love for God and love for our neighbour in the double commandment of love—citing the *Shema Israel* (Deut. 6:5) for the love for God, and citing Leviticus 19:18 for neighbourly love. Matthew says of the first that it is "the greatest and first commandment," and that the commandment to love one's neighbour "is like it." But can the love for God and love for one's neighbour be equal? We have said that love takes its character from the thing that is loved. In this respect the love of God and the love for one's neighbour are not alike. The one is responsive love, the other is prevenient love.

Christian love for God relates to God as God and is accessible to us in Christ, not to God in Godself, who is inaccessible. What is the response to God's love that has appeared in Christ? It is joy at being loved to all eternity. The joy at being loved, the joy in loving, and Christian experience of God in the experience of loving are well described when we say, "We love because he first loved us" (1 John 4:19).

In the New Testament this interpenetrating and enduring happiness is called "faith." Just as Israel celebrates the Lord of the exodus and its own freedom at the feast of the Passover, so Christians celebrate the love of God they experience in the Lord's Supper, the Eucharist, and hold Christ in their memories (2 Tim. 2:8), The eucharistic recollection of Christ brings the being loved to awareness in physical terms and, hence, also means an enjoyment of God's love.

The foundation and measure of human love is the love of God:

In this is love,
not that we loved God
but that he loved us. (1 John 4:10)

We can deduce from this that human love for God does not mean loving the loving God in return, so that what comes into being is a closed circle of mutuality between the God who loves human beings and the God-loving soul. It means yielding to the stream of God's love for God's failed human beings—not loving God per se but loving *with* God, as God loves, preveniently and creatively, loving not that which is the same as Godself but loving the other, without the expectation of thanks or reward. That is love of our neighbour and love of our enemy, for there we have the overcoming of evil through good.

Perichoretic God mysticism

At this point we find tensions and contradictions between a Christian *mysticism*, which seeks the union of the soul with God, and Christian love of one's neighbour, which seeks the neighbour in the love for God.[22] If mysticism has its roots in the doxological joy over being loved by God, it is Christian mysticism. If it goes beyond that in the divinization of the soul, it must be called trans-Christian. On the other hand, Christian love for one's neighbour cannot be only a divine commandment without requiring too much of the human being. It has to spring from joy over being loved by God and live from the overflow of this joy; otherwise it becomes a morality without force or a banal "be nice to each other."

In the love that God gives there is a unity of mysticism and neighbourly love. Johannine mysticism is not a mysticism of identity and does not mean a dissolution of the human soul, as if it were it a "drop in the ocean of divinity"; it is a perichoretic mysticism:

God is love,
and those who abide in love
abide in God
and God abides in them. (1 John 4:16)

God and the human being continue to be differentiated. But they are one in their reciprocal being-in-one-another. In love, God opens Godself to be a wide space in which the beloved human being can live and expand, while the little mortal human being becomes the room where God can live and move in the world. Jesus' high priestly prayer gives definition to the idea of the reciprocal indwelling:

> . . . *that they may all be one.*
> *As you, Father, are in me and I in you,*
> *may they also be in us . . . (John 17:21)*

In Latin, the Greek word *perichoresis* is translated both by *circuminsessio* and *circumincessio*.[23] This is a way of describing the reciprocal space for living and moving: the beloved human being lives and moves in God, and God lives and moves in the loving human being. They become the living space for love. This perichoretic unity of God and human being in love corresponds to the perichoretic unity of the triune God, as John 17:21 makes clear. It does not merely correspond to it; it actually lives in it: "That they also may be in us." The perichoretic unity not only binds together different persons of like nature, but persons of different natures as well. The perichoretic unity of love surmounts the frontiers between God and human beings, and between human beings and God.

Love is a great movement that is in God and which determines the inner-trinitarian life of God—a movement which God draws out of Godself, so to speak, in order to create, reconcile, and glorify a nondivine world; a movement which in the incarnation of the Son binds together the divinity and the humanity; and which unites divine and human life in the indwelling and the power of the Spirit.

Love for Life

Human beings are in harmony with God's love for those God has created when they love life, the life of their neighbour, the life they share, and the life of the earth. They sanctify personal, social, and political life when they give themselves up to the flow of God's love and interpenetrate life with this love.

Recognition of the person

We recognize achievements by rewarding them. We recognize people by loving them. Human life has to be affirmed, for it can also be denied. A child can only grow up and thrive in an atmosphere of affirmation. If a child is born in an atmosphere of rejection and is unwanted, it becomes stunted psychologically and fails to develop physically. When it is welcomed, affirmed, and loved, it learns to affirm and love itself, and that is vitally necessary for the healthy development of its potential. What is true for a child applies to everyone all their lives.[24]

> *Thou O Christ art all I want.*
> *All I want in thee I find.*

The affirmation of life that is inherent in God's love is greater than the denial of life from which we suffer.

Participation in our common life

Personal life is participation in shared life. We come inwardly alive when we experience the participation of others, and we remain alive when we participate in the life of others. Joy is only good when it experiences the joy of others, and shared suffering is halved. Human existence can be defined as being interested. "Inter-est" is a living being-in-relationship. If one loses interest in the common life, one becomes indifferent, apathetic, and resigned. Nothing is of concern to him or her, neither happiness nor pain. Indifference is a sign that the soul is no longer alive. Many sick and old people suffer from this before they die. If young people come up against a lack of interest in their lives and encounter social disinterest, they feel that they are "surplus people," shut out of the life of society: youth unemployment denies opportunities for living. The love for life makes human beings both capable of participation and in need of it.

The striving for happiness and compassion with the unfortunate

Human life is motivated by the striving for happiness. That is natural, for human beings have been created for joy out of the love of God. The striving for happiness lends men and women their dynamic. In the U.S. Declaration of Independence this is called "the pursuit of happiness" and it is numbered among the fundamental human rights, along with life and liberty. Everyone has the right to strive after his or her happiness. That is not only one's private right but one's public right, too. Everyone has the right to equality of opportunity—the opportunity to realize one's potential. But a human being will not be happy in oneself alone, but only with other people. Consequently, the striving for happiness is not only one's right as a free person but also as an equal one.

If we take the "pursuit of happiness" seriously, then we come upon not only the people who have achieved happiness, but also the unhappy people who have failed to do so. We begin to suffer with them and to cry out on their behalf. Compassion is not just sympathy; it is also and above all co-suffering. It is only the reverse side of "the pursuit of happiness," even though the fortunate generally overlook this side. Those who cannot themselves be happy cannot feel proper sympathy, and those who cannot experience sympathy—that is, co-suffering—cannot be happy either. It is the love for life that makes us happy and at the same time lets us suffer with others.

Community in the competitive society

The love for life creates community, but our late-capitalist societies are becoming class societies with ever-fewer people who are immensely rich, and more and more poor. With this development, the cohesion and the common good of a society gets lost. In a society in which "everyone must look out for himself," solidarity is no longer a social virtue on which people can mutually rely. But the alternative to poverty is not wealth—the alternative to both poverty and wealth is community. One can live in poverty when it is endured jointly with other people. It is the unjust distribution of means for living and chances in life that makes poverty a torment. The refusal of the rich to play their part in society—for example, through tax evasion—justly rouses people's wrath. If everyone is in the same situation, people help one another mutually. Once there is no more equality, because some are the winners and others the losers, the mutual help stops.

It is the task of the Christian community not only to proclaim the gospel of God's love, but also to live it in community. The model for the Christian community is described in the account of the first Pentecost congregation in Acts 4:32-25: "Now the whole group of those who believed were of one heart and soul, and no one claimed private ownership of any possession, but everything they owned was held in common. . . ."[25] Since today we live in competitive societies, with growing inequalities between people, it is becoming all the more important to develop contrast communities and to create places of mutual trust. In the Christian congregation all are equal before God. A person's value is not determined by one's wealth or poverty, one's ability or disability. All are respected in their human dignity, and are greeted and accepted as brother or sister. Trust, not control, is the rule in the Christian congregation. Christian congregations will also become diaconal communities when they form centers of mutual help. The modern competitive society isolates. The community of Christ binds people together. It is the reality of social love, not only in its compassion but also in its mutual joy over the loved life.

Maximus Confessor and the Erotic Universe

Finally, we come to God's earthly love. We talk about the "cosmos of love" because what we are talking about is the beauty of God's creation. The person who understands the world as God's creation does not merely trace it back to its transcendent Creator, and does not just see in the reality of the world "the work of God's hands." Rather, that person perceives the beauty of the world as the appearance of God's truth. He or she understands creation as the "place" of God's presence. Its beauty makes present the eternal life of the inner-trinitarian love that God *is*. This aesthetic way of looking at nature presupposes a purification of one's interest from self-seeking and a love of domination, in order to arrive at the "enlightened eye" of faith. Consequently, Orthodox theology, which we are trying to follow here,[26] put asceticism before the contemplation of nature:

The true and most desired beauty
is seen only by the purified spirit.[27]

The goal of this ascetic contemplation of the world is the revelation—or discovery—of the trinitarian energies of God through the beauty of created things:

The Trinity interpenetrates creation utterly and wholly with
beauty.[28]

The trinitarian self-movement in God emanates from God and is continued in the creative overflow of the love that calls into being the things that do not exist, and fills the living with life. Because this movement emanates from God, it lends a divine splendour to all created beings. Love is the foundation of the creative energies that act in all things. Hence the universe can also be viewed as a "cosmic community of love."[29] What is then described is not the quantitatively measurable outward side of things, as in the natural sciences, but the quality of things in respect to their transcendent inner side. This beauty of things is perceived in scientific theories, from Kepler's *harmonia mundi* down to the "beauties of fractal geometry."[30] Beauty is a proof of truth in scientific findings as well.

We owe the vision of an erotic universe to Maximus Confessor. He sees the whole creation issuing from the inner-trinitarian eros, and developing dynamically, bound together within the cosmic heavenly and earthly, human and natural eros. The universe, from the greatest to the smallest created being, becomes the place where the unique, divine eros is manifested, the eros that moves God and the world. Because this vision is so unique, I am quoting here the essential passage from his discourse on a text of Dionysius the Areopagite. Talking about eros, he writes: "We call eros divine and angelic, spiritual, natural—we perceive it as a unifying and interblending power, which moves what is higher into becoming a presage for what is lower. But it binds whatever enjoys the same rank to reciprocal participation; and with regard to those which have the lowest rank, the power of eros leads them back to what is more powerful and fundamental."[31] From this Maximus develops a vision of the universe derived from the divine eros and which through it is moved in different stages:

> The primary origin of the heavenly eros is God, and God in his mode of limitlessness without origin. For if this eros is really love, and if it is written that God is love, then it is clear that the all-uniting eros—that is, love—is God. From God eros now descends to the angels, so that we may also call it angelic, and this divine eros is discovered as a love which leads to unity. For among the angels everything harmonizes and nothing conflicts. From this there follows the spiritual eros among men of the church who are knowledgeable about God, the men among whom Paul says that there should be no dissension (1 Cor. 1:10). The Lord says, too, that they should be one, even as we are one. But he says that about those who are Christians for the sake of truth, but beyond that also in respect of all men and women who are ruled by the law of love. He called the souls who are gifted with reason spiritual, since they are moved by his divine Spirit. But he called the eros of those without reason, sensual love, and that is certainly devoid of spirit. For out of the power of this love, the birds rise in swarms into the air, the swans, geese, cranes, ravens, or similar beasts. But animals which live on the earth are also so—the deer, cattle, and all the others, as well as the beasts which live in the water, such as tuna fish, mullets and so forth. Hence will they all be gathered together with those like themselves who do not live in swarms. He calls natural eros that which is characterized by soulless and senseless being. For creatures of this kind love the Creator because they have been brought into being by him. In the movement of their lives, that is to say their natural movement, these beings are also orientated towards God.[32]

Over against the exclusive *eros–eidos* correlation, Maximus understands eros as being twofold: on the one hand, it links those who are similar in kind; on the other hand, those who are different. Consequently, it can "descend" and "bring up," so that the different stages of being are linked vertically and horizontally through love. There is the eros which is God, there is the heavenly eros of the angels, the spiritual eros of people endowed with reason, the spiritual eros of non-human beings, and the natural eros of matter. This eros binds together created beings of the same kind and of different kinds. Because he calls this power of existence and life in all its stages eros, they are bound together with the one eros. The erotic universe comes from God, and is directed toward God.

This is a bold, unified world picture of love. But it also raises critical questions. The eros unites those who are different, but does it also differentiate within what is united? Maximus can finely explain the vertical and horizontal power of eros, but that does not as yet explain the protean and still unsurveyable diversity of the creations of love. Nor does Maximus differentiate between the creative love of God and the responsive love of created beings. If the love that comes from God is the same as the love that goes to God, this gives rise to the suspicion that God does not love the created beings, but that in the responding love of the created beings God loves Godself. But then the eros which is God, in its issuing from God and in its return to God, would remain within what is ultimately a closed circle. That then raises the question about the eschatology: Does the universe revert to its origin in the end, which is the way many people from Plotinus to Thomas Aquinas have viewed it? Or will the perfected "new" creation become the eternal creation in which God will finally come to the world?

Chapter 9

A Spirituality of the Senses

"You awaken all my senses"[1]

The Spirituality of the Soul— The Spirituality of the Senses

Close the gateway of thy senses
and seek God deep within.

So advised the 17th-century mystic Gerhard Tersteegen.[2] This is the path that is based on the spirituality of the soul. The person who chooses this path forsakes the sensory experiences of the outside world and forgets all bodily needs. The way to God leads inward, not outwards, not into the world but out of it. One must arrive at the depths of the soul, for at its deepest foundation every soul reaches out to the divine. That is its mystery. One must withdraw from the world, and into oneself in order to find God's sanctuary in the soul's innermost part. "Withdraw into yourself: in the innermost man dwells truth," wrote Augustine, from whom this Christian mysticism of the soul derives.[3] According to mystical tradition, this way of withdrawal into God's sanctuary in the innermost part of one's own soul takes place in six stages, in order finally to arrive at the seventh stage, at the core of the soul. There the mystical marriage takes place: the eternal union of the soul with God. Teresa of Avila left us her wonderful book of inner experiences, *The Interior Castle of the Soul* (1577), and in 1948 the Christian mystic Thomas Merton wrote his famous autobiography under the title *The Seven–Storey Mountain*.

a. As the word *spirituality* suggests, what we are talking about here is the seizure of the human being by God's Spirit. Spirituality develops where God's Spirit is experienced. If "God's love has been poured into our hearts through the Holy Spirit that has been given to us" (Rom. 5:5), what comes into being is a *spirituality of the heart*. If the Holy Spirit is "poured out on to all flesh," what comes into being is a *spirituality of life*. If the Spirit is present everywhere and sustains everything in heaven and on earth—if it holds them together and directs them toward their future—what comes into being is a *cosmic spirituality*. The *spirituality of the soul* and the inner human being is a one-sided perception of the holy, which is acquired through detachment from the outward world and the human senses. But if the soul is defined through detachment and an ascetic denial of the body and the senses, then narrow limits are set to God's Spirit. The result is a spirituality hostile to the body. That was the spirituality of the Egyptian desert ascetics and the spirituality of the monastic cell. But it is also the spirituality of prisoners for whom, in their cells, the "inner life" is all that is left.

According to the biblical traditions, the Holy Spirit is not the Spirit of the passing time of this world; it is the dawn of God's coming new world. But that does not mean that the divine Spirit acts in a way that is hostile to the body, or alien to the world, or to the senses. God's Spirit sanctifies the earth, makes life come alive, and awakens all the senses; for it is the Spirit of Christ's resurrection. The Spirit of the resurrection comes like waves of "living water" into the hearts, into the community, breaking through all the barriers of race, gender, class, and nation, in the emerging energies and forms of creation in heaven and on earth. The important thing today is to open the narrow limits of the "God and the soul" pattern for patterns of

God and the body, and of God and the senses. The "salvation of the soul" that belongs to the Augustinian tradition must be thrown open for God and the body, for social salvation and the salvation of groaning nature. We need a spirituality for the world, a piety or spirituality of the everyday Spirit that preserves and renews the world. I believe that such a this-worldly spirituality is the legacy Dietrich Bonhoeffer left behind him in his *Letters and Papers from Prison*: in his letter of 31 July 1944, he writes: "In recent years I have increasingly come to know and understand (this) profound worldliness. The Christian is not a *homo religiosus* but a human being per se, as Jesus himself was— probably unlike John the Baptist. It was not the flat and banal this-worldliness of the busy 'man of the world,' of the indolent or the lascivious, but the profound this-worldliness which is disciplined and is always present in the awareness of death and of the resurrection."[4]

b. God created the human being in God's own image, as man and as woman God created them (Gen. 1:27). So the whole human being in his or her psychosomatic form is an image of God on earth, and so are human beings in their social relationships with one another. There is no suggestion that the soul has preeminence and there is nothing in Old Testament anthropology to suggest that the relationship to God goes together with a depreciation of the body.[5]

For Paul, too, no defensive ring is drawn round "God and the soul."[6] On the contrary, the body is the temple of the Holy Spirit: "The body is meant . . . for the Lord and the Lord for the body. . . . For you were bought with a price; therefore glorify God in your body" (1 Cor. 6:13-20). And talking about Jesus' apostles, he writes: "[We always carry] in the body the death of Jesus, so that the life of Jesus may be manifested in our bodies" (2 Cor. 4:10, RSV). Why this marked stress on the body's relation to God? For Plato, the *meditatio mortis* makes the immortality of the soul certain. For Paul, the bodily resurrection of Jesus makes "the resurrection of the body" certain. "Moreover, my flesh also will live in hope" (Acts 2:26). If the body is viewed as the temple of the Holy Spirit, God does not just dwell in some remote apex of the soul but also in the whole sensory and socially open bodiliness. The bodily life is sanctified and affirmed. It is not the unlived life of the soul that is the bond with the living God but lived life of love. The human soul shows itself in the ensouled body, not in an innerliness devoid of body: *anima—forma corporis.*

Before the living God the living human being always appears as a psychosomatic whole. It can also be said, conversely, that it is only "before God" that people appear in their entirety, that is to say, in their whole life histories, since in the face of eternity all the times that we experience successively are simultaneous.

In their consciousness, human beings experience themselves and their bodiliness in dialectical form, as *being* a body and as *having* a body, as Helmut Plessner aptly described the human being's excentric position.[7] That is based on the human being's experience of the self, both in the spontaneity of one's feelings and in the reflectivity of one's spirit. If I go out of myself, then I am one with myself in the direct life; if I reflect on myself, I distinguish myself from myself and am my own counterpart. The two forms of consciousness must be related to each other and must not be separated; otherwise, the human being becomes sick. If I only act and react spontaneously, I am like an animal. If I continually reflect myself, I become schizophrenic. The essential thing in the lived life is to keep the balance or continually to seek it. That is what is being expressed when busy people say: I must have time to reflect, must quiet down, and come to myself. But in an over-organized, over-considered society, the other side is just as important: the new spontaneity, the adventure of life. "It has to be lived," says the strong woman in the 1995 film *Antonia's Line.*

The Spirit of the living God is "the Spirit of life," and it is experienced in the loved life, and lived in the love for life.

c. According to Christian understanding, the creation of the cosmos is a trinitarian happening. God the Father creates the world through God's eternal Logos in the energies of the Holy Spirit. The world is a nondivine reality but it is interpenetrated by God's Spirit. If all things are created by God, through God, and in God, then they also exist from God, through God, and in God.[8]

According to this interpretation, in Christ, God has "reconciled" the cosmos (2 Cor. 5:19). The exalted Christ is the head of everything that is in heaven and on earth (Eph. 1:10; Col. 1:20). The cosmic Christ is the coming Christ who will judge with righteousness not only the living and the dead but the earth, too. So Christians live in a world that is not evil and not paradisal either, but in a world that is "reconciled." That creates trust in the world in spite of the many catastrophes in nature. From this there develops a cosmic spirituality such as Francis of Assisi expressed in his famous "Canticle of the Sun."[9] If we human beings are "a part of the universe," we shall respect everything for its own sake, apart from its utility for human beings and shall encounter all "fellow ceatures" with reverence for life. We shall seek the bond with God's Spirit through the sensory perceptions of the world. We shall not withdraw into ourselves in order to seek God, but shall go out of ourselves in order to experience God's presence with all our senses in the world outside. The person who seeks God must want to live; the person who finds God awakens to life in its fullness. The person who is seized by God's Spirit opens his or her senses to the wonder of life. We become aware of the presence of God's Spirit.

The Human Senses

The human being has five senses, but which is the original one from which all the others develop? Ever since antiquity, the sense of touch, *sensus tactus*, has been called the primal one. With what organ do we touch and feel? With the skin of our whole body, from head to foot. The skin is the site of our nerve cells. They vary in their density and sensitivity. We say that some people are thick skinned, others are especially thin skinned. Our skin both links us to the outer world and separates us from it. We feel and develop feelings, we taste and develop taste. With our skin we perceive environments as a whole: heat and cold, the pleasant and the unpleasant.

Particularly sensitive organs have developed from the skin that envelops our bodies—the taste buds in the mouth, the sense of smell in the nose, the organs of hearing in the ears, and the eyes. The brain, with its convolutions and separate spheres with which we process the sensory impressions, has developed from the skin. We receive and we send with our brain.[10]

We can distinguish the five senses from each other, some being the direct ones and others the remote ones. With the direct senses—feeling, taste, and smell—we can make direct contact with objects. For the remote senses we need the intervening media of sound and light. Let us begin with the direct senses.

1. *Feeling and tasting.* Children put everything in their mouths first of all. Their sense of taste is developed in the best possible way. They already knows what tastes good and what doesn't. The ability to taste is one of the most elemental functions of our life. It is not confined to the intake of nourishment but, as everyone who enjoys food knows, expands into pleasure in life generally and the taste for existence.

From the aspect of brain physiology, the taste stimuli are taken up by the taste buds and are transported to the thalamus, the "great gate" of the sensory input, and to the taste centers of the somato-sensory cortex. They then arrive at the parts of the limbic system where emotions and memories slumber. There they awaken the taste attributes of the food in question.

2. *Feeling and smelling.* The sense of smell and the memory are apparently closely connected. The remembrance of emotionally charged experiences is linked with the part of the brain called the olfactory cortex. In smelling we distinguish between the pleasant smell and the stink, and that again extends to our attitude to the whole person.

In English we say that we can't "stand" someone but in German one says in such cases that one can't "smell" them. With other people we can say that "the chemistry harmonizes." Through smell we pick up scents. Smell molecules are absorbed through smell receptors in the nose, are processed into electro-chemical information, and are guided to the center of the limbic system. The sense of smell is the shortest connecting path in our sensory system, as the relation of the nose to the brain shows. Human beings are said to recognize and distinguish up to 10,000 different smells—dogs very many more. Smells awaken pleasure and dislike in the whole person. They rouse memories and expectations. Through fragrances and perfume we enrich the world of smells and expand our sense of smell. When our sense of smell atrophies, our emotions atrophy as well.

3. *Feeling and hearing.* Our hearing is a remote sense with which we perceive sound waves. The medium is the air, the speed of sound waves being 333 metres per second. The outside world is full of noises. What we hear depends on the finest selection of what we can and will absorb at the same time. Our hearing is only capable of taking in a limited frequency of vibrations. Elephants and whales communicate via different frequencies. People with impaired hearing need hearing aids and selection apparatus in order to be able to receive something. Hair cells pick up sound waves and transform them into electrical impulses. The eardrum registers variations in the air pressure. The spiral inner ear differentiates into their individual frequencies the sounds as they arrive, and by doing so distinguishs sounds that differ from one another by only as much as a tenth of a semi-tone.

As the hearing of good music shows, what is heard is disseminated through the whole body and finds its resonance in the whole organism. Music can move us to tears and is experienced by many people as comforting. It can also move us deeply and make our bodies tremble. When we listen to music, we sense particularly the harmonies and antitheses between the world outside and our own inner world. But we also hear the stillness, when we can listen and come to rest ourselves.

4. *Feeling—seeing—perceiving—marveling—contemplating.* The human being's remote sensory organ is the eye. Its medium is light, which has the speed of of 3,000,000 kilometers per second. Out of the wealth of electrical waves, our eye picks up only the frequencies between ultraviolet and infrared. That is a narrow selection, but it is all we can endure.

The actual sight that proceeds is astonishing: by way of the open eyes, light arrives on the nerve structure of the retina; there photo-receptors react to the wavelengths and intensity of the light and are transformed into neurological impulses. Separated into millions of individual signals, via the thalamus they reach the visual cortex and the prefrontal cortex in the brain. There the images we have of what we see come into being. Through filtering and selection we acquire certain visual perceptions in the otherwise incalculable wealth of visual impressions.

There are stages of intensity in impressions. In order to perceive something, we must learn how to see. The person who wants to see must be alert and attentive. He or she must focus on something, and look carefully. Both eyes must be concentrated and focused on the object. In order to recognize what we see, we must pause in our con-templation of it and let its impression work on us. One can hurry through a museum or gallery, and see a hundred pictures, and still have failed to perceive any of them. Shock or astonishment increases our concentrated contemplation of them. When we are shocked, we withdraw in order to protect ourselves. In astonishment, our senses are opened. What is truly astonishing knows no bounds. It happens suddenly, in a moment. At first we simply can't believe it and must gradually come to terms with the new impressions. These are things that happen for the first time. What we perceive in astonishment we therefore call intuitive knowing.

The recognizing and the being astonished are completed only in the seeing. It is only in the seeing that we are so fascinated by what we see that we forget ourselves and are totally absorbed in the looking. We should like to remain where we are, and say to the moment, "Tarry a while—thou art so fair," as Goethe puts it in *Faust*. In the contem-plation of the beautiful and in the loving seeing "face to face," a fluid unity emerges between the contemplator and the thing contemplated. Here there comes into being the ecstatic conditions of over-wakeful wakefulness.

The Diminution and Attrition of the Senses

It is true that if we are in good health we are in possession of our five senses, but they are not always equally strong and vigorously developed. We have to learn how to see and hear. Smelling, tasting, and feeling can wither. We need a school for our senses. That is part of our experiences of life and death when we love life.

If we begin truly to live, if we come to life from within, then our senses wake up. If we lose interest in life, then our senses become dormant and wither. Just as all the individual senses influence the way we feel as a whole, so our overall state of health, our motivation system, also affects our senses.

Let us consider this on the basis of four experiences:

1. Grief

2. Captivity

3. Routine life, without any interest

4. The social demands and hindrances to our senses in modern society

1. *Grief and the extinguishing of the senses.* I still remember very well an elderly friend. He loved his wife devotedly. When she died suddenly, he was as if paralyzed and felt as if he had undergone an amputation. He had lost the content of his life and did not want to go on living. Death had taken possession of the rest of his life. Later, he told how his senses were snuffed out. He no longer saw colours; he was not aware of any melodies, although he had loved music passionately; his feelings died; and what he ate became a matter of indifference. He was no longer interested in life and his will to live became weaker and weaker. He "opted out" and turned to stone, although he was still

alive.[11] It was only later, when he sensed the love of other people who looked after him, and was able to believe again in God's love, that he woke up and experienced what he himself called a resurrection in the senses. For our senses are snuffed out in the cold breath of death, and awaken when love breathes life into them.

2. *The apathy of a prisoner.* This is based on my own experience.[12] In the Second World War, as a 17-year-old I was conscripted into the German army for only six months, but then spent more than three years as a prisoner of war behind barbed wire. My initial experience was of a totally hostile environment. One was surrounded by barbed wire, outwardly and inwardly. It was a world as cut off from the world as if it had been behind monastery walls. We lost all hope because our lives seemed devoid of prospect. Each of us tried for himself to protect and hide his wounded soul behind an armour of untouchability. One became completely indifferent. One did not hope for anything and did not fear anything. One no longer loved anything nor felt anything. Everything was a matter of indifference. One was surrounded by an icy wall of apathy and smothered all sensory experiences. The camp food anyway tasted of nothing, one gulped the stuff down only so as not to die of hunger. The huts with their 2,000 prisoners stank so infernally that it was best to forget how to smell. Everyone reduced his interest in life so far that in the captivity he felt the determination to live as little as possible. It is possible to survive like this, but one is no longer alive. One felt the senselessness of this existence by way of the quenching of one's senses.

I can well remember a day in May 1945, after the end of the war. We had to push a railway truck out of the prisoner-of-war camp. Suddenly I found myself standing in front of a tree covered with wonderful cherry blossom, and my eyes filled with tears. I saw its beauty and almost fainted. I had regained a first contact with the living world. I could see again, and slowly returned to life.

3. *The routine life and the quenching of the senses.* We come back from these extreme situations to our everyday world. Sometimes everything is fine—the home, the family, the job; everything becomes

a matter of course. We have grown accustomed to things as they are, and react to them with the routine we have learned. Everything goes quite well, but nothing new ever happens. One day is just like another. We don't know how to begin anything new. Life holds no more charm. This experience also paralyzes our pleasure in life and puts our senses to sleep. Everyday life becomes flat and grey and a matter of indifference. We do the same things over and over again, although every morning sees the dawn of a new day, and every moment means something new. We look into ourselves and ask, with the poet Wolf Biermann:

> *That surely can't have been all,*
> *that little bit of Sunday and children's voices—*
> *surely it must lead somewhere.*
>
> *That surely can't have been all,*
> *Surely something or other has to come:*
> *No, what has to come is* life into life.[13]

When we get to this point, it is time to fall into the arms of life and to rediscover the senses. When our life again takes on colour and sound and scent and taste, we feel as if newborn. Then our joy in life reawakens, and with that all our senses reawaken. We discover afresh the fullness of life that we have hastened by so negligently, and we are seized by joy over every new day. Those who rediscover their senses discover every day something new in this world, and their lives take on meaning. They come alive and really begin to live.

4. *Challenges and hindrances to our senses in modern society.* Our sensory life is not determined only by the inner disposition of our body, and not just by our own attitude to life, but also by the world in which we live. It makes demands on certain senses and neglects others. The modern media—radio, television, telephone, fax, e-mail, computer, Internet, and so forth—make demands on our *remote senses*: we have to be able to see and hear in order to participate. Our modern means of transport, such as the car or the aeroplane, are navigated by means of our eyes and ears. We react with great confidence to light and

noise signals. We can remain attentive for hours. That is not true of people in other cultures.

But what has happened to our direct senses? If we live in great cities we can no longer smell much, because the emissions in the streets and the dust in them have paralyzed our sense of smell. We need a powerful perfume or a strong stench in order to smell anything at all. City life has become a hurried life. Because we have no time for enjoyment, we nourish ourselves from fast food and ruin our sense of taste.

Even with children we find that they can no longer discover things by means of touch. If one covers the eyes of schoolchildren, and lets them touch wood, earth, iron, plastic, and other things, one discovers that the sense of touch is quite underdeveloped. Compared with the native dwellers in Papua New Guinea, we modern men and women are masters where the remote senses are concerned, and beggars with regard to the direct senses. We can hear and see everything, but we can hardly smell, taste, and feel things at all.[14]

The Awakening of the Senses

The life-giving Spirit is not only the Spirit of the world beyond; it is also the energy of this one. It is not only the Spirit of the soul; it is also the Spirit of the whole of life. So from the powers of this divine Spirit we expect the rousing and awakening of our senses. I propose to show this on the basis of its vital powers (1) in love; (2) in hope; (3) in rest; and (4) in faith, and from that I will lead on to the spirituality of the sensory life.

1. *Love awakens all the senses for life.* Each and every one of us has experienced it: the love we experience and the love we give awaken our senses; we perceive the others and feel that we are perceived; we speak to one another and listen to one another; we feel other people and feelings awaken in us: the full life pulsates in our veins. Love opens and leads out those who were previously closed in on themselves. Love awakens in us interest in life, interest in the life of other people and in our own. Appreciative love activates our motivation system and sets free new energies within us. We trust ourselves to do things before

which we earlier shrank back. The living power of love makes us capable of happiness for the first time, so that we can laugh, rejoice, and dance. But it also leads us into possible pains of disappointment and loss, and makes us able to suffer and to feel pain. Because of the interest in life that love awakens, we sense the marvelous vitality of life and at the same time the terrible deadliness of death. It is only the person who has no more interest in life who feels neither happiness nor pain. The love for life is passion and com-passion, and is therefore the exact opposite of the apathy that obstructs life.

2. *Hope opens the senses for the future.* Hope does not mean holding out the prospect of better times in the future. It is a tense expectation of the new day. Hope for a fulfilled life makes us curious, and opens all our senses for what is coming to meet us. By virtue of this hope we are prepared for astonishment and meet each new day with wonderment. We wake up, because we know that we are expected. In the strength of hope we do not capitulate in the face of the powers of death, humiliation, and disappointment but go on with heads held high, because we can look beyond the present day. In the strength of hope we don't give ourselves up, but stand our ground even in adverse circumstances. The person who gives up hope in life and despairs stands at the gate of the hell, about which Dante wrote, "Abandon hope, all ye that enter here." The person who maintains hope in life is already saved. This hope keeps us alive. It continually makes us live again. It awakens all our senses every morning.

3. *Rest purifies the senses.* Part of the new spirituality of the sensory life is that we can come to rest and can take the time to experience and enjoy life with all our senses. Coming to rest is the asceticism for the purification of the senses. It is not for nothing that the Bible teaches us to keep the sabbath and on the seventh day to come to rest and to leave our environment in peace. God also rested on the seventh day of creation, and it was in doing so that God completed God's work of creation.

The mystics taught us to encounter God in the inner ascent of the soul, in the seventh room. In so doing they only transported Israel's teaching about the sabbath experience of time to the inner experience of the soul.

It is much easier and more natural to take the seventh day for that purpose, and there to experience God's rest, and in that rest to experience the presence of God. But this sabbath and Sunday coming-to-rest has to be learned. It doesn't happen just by itself. The body has to find rest and relax its tensions. The spirit must free itself from worries and expectations and must learn how to be still. Then all the senses will become open to perceive the beauty of the things by which we are surrounded. Our everyday focus on purpose and intentions will be interrupted and then our life relaxes. We shall take time to look at what we see, time for the taste of food and drink. "The discovery of slowness" and calm give back health and happiness to the tense and harassed life, as wisdom tells us.

4. *The mystery of things entices the senses.* It is true that we are told that faith is directed toward God in heaven. But heaven seems to be very far away, and then God is very far away from each of us. But Christian faith is not directed toward a faraway God, but lives in the presence of the God who surrounds us from every side. "You hem me in, behind and before, and lay your hand upon me. Such knowledge is too wonderful for me; it so high I cannot attain it," we read in Psalm 139:5. It is true that we cannot see God, yet that is not because God is so far off but because God is so close. We cannot recognize what is too close because some degree of detachment is necessary for every recognition. God is closer to us than we can be to ourselves, said Augustine. In him we live and move and have our being, declared Paul to the Greek philosophers in Athens (Acts 17:28).

But that is not only true for us ourselves; it also applies to everything God has created. There is nothing without God's presence in it, nowhere we could not encounter God. Consequently, we shall encounter everything with reverence and absorb it into our faith. Then we see everything in God's presence and God's presence in everything. The moment we believe that, a new cosmic spirituality begins. We begin to see everything with astonishment, and are seized by profound reverence in the face of life. We have no need to leave this world behind in order to look for God in a world to come. We only need to enter into this world with its beauties and its terrors, for God is already there. God waits for us in everything God has created, and speaks to us through all of them. The one who has eyes to see, sees that. The one who has ears to hear, hears it. The whole creation is a great and wonderful sacrament of God's indwelling presence.

Praying and Watching

This cry runs through the biblical writings like a scarlet thread: *Watch and pray—Pray and watch!* What else is Christianity other than this watching and praying, praying to watch and watching to pray: praying never stands by itself, it is always linked with watching. Praying is good, watching is better.[15]

It is true that we sometimes encounter the prejudiced judgment that those who pray don't have their feet in this world, or already have one foot in the next. Only work helps, not prayer. The fact that praying could have anything to do with watching, attentiveness, and the expectation of life is more or less unrecognized.

1. *"Could you not watch with me one hour?"* We find the most impressive story about watching in the accounts of Jesus' hardest hour. It is the night in Gethsemane. In Luther's Bible it is entitled "The Struggle in Gethsemane," for it has to do with Jesus' inner struggle with Godforsakenness. His prayer to God, whom with complete trust he calls "Abba, dear Father," is not heard. The cup of eternal death does not pass him by. What descends on him, on those who are his, on this world, is the night that Martin Buber describes as the eclipse of God. It is like "the dark night of the soul," in which one completely loses one's orientation, and all our feelings dry up. We are told that during this hour Jesus began to be "greatly distressed and troubled," as Mark writes, or, as Matthew reports, "sorrowful and troubled." "My soul is very sorrowful, even to death," he says to the disciples. So he begs the disciples: "Stay here and watch." Jesus prays, and struggles with the dark, threatening will of God, and his disciples are to take over the watching that belongs to prayer.

But it doesn't work out like that. Jesus enters, praying and watching, into this eclipse of God and struggles through it: "Not my will be done but yours." But the disciples fall into a deep unconscious sleep. "Simon Peter, are you asleep? Can't you watch with me for a single hour?" This scene, which is for Jesus so saddening and for the disciples so shameful, is repeated three times: watching, Jesus struggles with God's dark side—and the unconsciousness of sleep falls on the disciples until the night is past and the day of Golgotha begins, the day into which Jesus goes resolutely: "Get up, let us be going."

Why do the disciples sleep? When the master himself they have followed without fear and trembling himself begins to fear and tremble, then some cruel and impenetrable fate is threatening.

The reaction is stupor and the sleep of hopelessness. We know this ourselves, too: a threatening danger can excite us, but inescapable dangers numb us, and we escape best into deep sleep, a sleep that protects us from what is unendurable. That is not a natural restorative sleep but a freezing of all our senses, which makes us sick. We see with open eyes—nothing. We hear with open ears—nothing. We are wholly without feeling and turn to stone while we are still alive. The paralyzing sleep that overcomes Jesus' disciples in Gethsemane was the expression of a paralysis of soul, the like of which we know today as well.[16] How, then, do we react to unknown dangers? Over millions of years, our awareness has learned to react to a variety of dangers in a way that will preserve life. How? It is fear that keeps us alert and all our senses alive so that we can react to threats in good time and respond to them appropriately. In all human civilizations survival techniques have been built up with which we control the dangers we are aware of, from the building of dikes against flooding to lightning conductors. But today there are dangers that we cannot see. In 1986, in the catastrophe in the Chernobyl power station, deadly radioactive emissions were released that could be neither smelled nor tasted nor seen. The climate changes are much more threatening than we could have once conceived.

According to the Third Report of the International Panel of Climate Change 2001, global warming is undoubtedly due to human activity. In the next 40 years the atmosphere is going to warm up by 3 to 5 degrees Celsius. But although our eyes are open, we see nothing. Although our ears are open, we hear nothing. And that means that we no longer perceive the real world; we see only our dreams, and believe that our wishful thinking about reality is reality itself. But that again means that in reality we are not watchful. What do we look for when we pray?

When we pray we are not looking for the fulfillment of our own wishes. We are looking for the reality of God, and are breaking out of the hall of mirrors of our own wishes and the fears in which we are imprisoned. We wake up out of the numbness and deafness of our feelings. We burst apart the armour of apathy that holds us fast. If in prayer we seek the reality of God's world, as with the first lines of the Lord's Prayer, then prayer is the very opposite of the "opiate of the people." It is, rather, that in prayer we begin a withdrawal cure, withdrawal from the opiates of the secular world.

In praying we come awake for the world as it is manifested before God in all its heights and depths. We become aware of the sighings of created beings and hear the cries of the victims that are being silenced. We hear, too, the song of praise of the blossoming spring, and sense that divine love in everything that lives. So the prayer to God awakens all our senses and brings a great wakefulness into our spirits.

2. *The person who prays lives attentively.* To pray watchfully: that is only possible if we don't pray mystically with closed eyes, but pray messianically with our eyes wide open for God's future in the world. Christian faith is not a blind trust in God but the watchful expectation of God in which all our senses are involved. The original attitude for prayer, as we can see from pictures in the Roman catacombs, was to stand with outstretched arms, open face, and wide-open eyes, the stance showing a readiness to go or leap forward. What this attitude reveals is not a silent withdrawal but a tense expectation. We live in God's advent, we are on the watch in expectation of the coming One and go with tense watchfulness to meet the coming God.

Watch and be sober: that is the next instruction we hear (1 Thess. 5:6, 8). People are sober if they are not drunk, if they do not suffer from hallucinations, and if they have no illusions. If sobriety is added to the watchfulness that springs from prayer, we shall have no illusions and shall not allow ourselves to be fobbed off with illusions, either by way of political propaganda or through the consumer pressure of advertisements. We shall accept reality as it is, and come to terms with the form it takes in everyday life, as well as with its surprises, and then we shall discover that it is much more protean and much more fantastic than all our expectations of it. We shall then discover, too, that the pain it also brings is still much better than the self-immunizations with which we want to protect ourselves, but through which we in actual fact only wall ourselves in.

In German, however, the same word, *nüchtern,* "sober," is used for people who have not eaten and who begin the day with empty stomachs. They are hungry. If we begin the day sober in this sense, we are hungry for the reality that God truly is. One single experienced reality is richer than a thousand dreamed-of possibilities. That is why the sober contact with reality is so important. But only the watchful, the sober, and the hungry can achieve it.

Watching and seeing: curiously enough, praying and watching have little to do with faith but everything to do with seeing. Israel's Wisdom already knew that: "The hearing ear and the seeing eye—the LORD has made them both" (Prov. 20:12). And Jesus complained about his contemporaries that "Seeing they do not perceive and hearing they do not listen, nor do they understand" (Matt. 13:13). But by this he also meant his own presence among them. In the image of the great judgment (Matthew 25), the Son of man and judge of the world says: "I was hungry, and you gave me no food, I was thirsty and you gave me nothing to drink, I was a stranger and you did not welcome me. . . ." Then they will also answer: "Lord, when did we *see* you hungry or thirsty or a stranger or sick or in prison?" Then he will answer them: "Truly I tell you, just as you did not do it to one of the least of these, you did not do it to me" (vv. 42-46). So the important thing is the *seeing*.[17]

To go open-eyed through life, to recognize Christ in unnoticeable people, in presence of mind to do the right thing at the right time—that is what praying and watching is about. We believe in order to see, and to affirm what we see.

3. "*Those who watch have a world in common.*" Darkness and night are always symbols for the Godforsakennness of the world and the lostness of humanity. In the darkness we see nothing and do not know where we are. There is an apt passage in the prophet Isaaiah: in exile and far from home, strangers among strangers, the prisoners from Israel come to the prophet and ask, "Sentinel, what of the night?" How long will the night last? And he answers: "Morning comes, and also the night. If you will inquire, . . . come back again" (Isa. 21:11-12).

But Paul, Christ's witness, proclaims: "The night is far gone, the day is near. Let us then lay aside the works of darkness and put on the armour of light" (Rom. 13:12). So it is time to rise up from sleep, to forget the dreams and the fears, and to experience life in the dawn of God's day.

In dreams, each of us is alone, but when we wake up we are in a shared world. Heraclitus remarked long ago that "those who are awake have a world in common, whereas in sleep everyone turns to a world of his own."[18]

Chapter 10

※

Hoping and Thinking

Thinking Means Transcending

In 2014 my book *Theology of Hope* was 50 years old.[1] Consequently, I should like to look back to my beginnings in 1964, and discuss these first in connection with Ernst Bloch and then also philosophically. In 1964 I was fascinated by Bloch personally and by his messianic-Marxist philosophy articulated in *The Principle of Hope*.[2] I asked myself: Why has Christian theology allowed this theme of hope to escape it? Are not God's promises and human hopes the scarlet thread running right through the prophets of the Old Testament and the apostles of the New? Aren't Jews and Christians the people of hope in this world? Doesn't everything in Christian theology draw toward the future of God—that is to say, eschatology?[3] There are medieval theologies of love, there are Reformation doctrines of faith, but in none of the theological traditions is there a tradition shot through by hope. And yet for 400 years the modern world has been impregnated by projects and processes of hope for "better times in the future"; and this is true of the spirit of America especially. Has the hope of the prophets and apostles emigrated from the churches and synagogues, and did it only become fruitful in the secular world of modern times?

I neither wanted to copy Bloch nor to go along with him. I wanted to set in motion an act in theology parallel to his *Principle of Hope*, but on a biblical basis. With his philosophical categories, Bloch offered a conceptual framework for thinking through a theology of hope in human terms. But now I should also like to bring out the difference between a theology of hope and his atheistic philosophy of hope.

What is left of Bloch's philosophy of hope after 50 years? The Marxist project to which he had pledged his faith ever since the Russian revolution of 1917 fell apart in 1990. The Soviet Union has broken down. In Eastern Europe, socialism has abolished itself. Was that the end of the utopian age per se, as Joachim Fest maintained?[4] Or was it the victory of the capitalist utopia, as Francis Fukuyama triumphantly proclaimed in 1991?[5]

Ernst Bloch had returned to socialist East Germany from his American exile in 1948, yet he was never at home in "socialism as it really exists." On the contrary, he was attacked and rejected because of his "religious" philosophy. In 1961 he crossed the frontier to the West, and from that time on lived in Tübingen in West Germany. In his late works *Natural Law and Human Dignity* (1961) and *Atheism in Christianity* (1968), he left behind him the flat and uninspiring world of socialist ideology, and was known for his linking of the socialist project with the democratic one in such a way that it was possible to assent to it even without Karl Marx. To the very end he held fast to what he called "the religion of the Exodus and the Kingdom, united in the will for the Kingdom."[6] His religion culminated in the expectation of an apocalyptic self-encounter: "We all *with unveiled face* reflect the glory of the Lord." If we abstract his somewhat idiosyncratic Marxism, what remains as the guiding idea of his philosophy of history is a secularly inherited religious messianism, fed from Jewish and Christian springs.

1. If, as a theologian, one takes this messianism seriously, a "principle of hope" appears to be not too utopian but, rather, insufficiently utopian. Compared with the divine fullness of life in the prophetic and apostolic hopes, Bloch maintains an atheistically reduced hope. That is due to his turn to the religious criticism of Feuerbach and Marx, not to his own early *Spirit of Utopia* (1918, 1923). His early work ends with the words about "our God-invoking philosophy and truth as prayer." We recognize it from the use and non-use of biblical

images of hope. The social utopias are aligned toward human happiness—human rights are aligned toward human dignity. The two belong together:

> The social utopia imagines in advance conditions in which there are no more *weary and heavy-laden.*
> Natural law constructs conditions in which there are no more *humiliated and insulted.*

But we may ask: And what about the dead, the murdered? In the end are the perpetrators going to triumph over their victims? asks Max Horkheimer, and he pinned his faith to God and God's righteousness and justice.[7] Why doesn't Bloch talk about the hope of resurrection, which promises conditions in which "death will be no more"? For a "God-invoking philosophy," this would surely have been possible. Then social utopia and natural law, human happiness and human dignity would have found a comprehensive horizon that does not reduce them but, rather, expands them.

2. Bloch reduces Christian eschatology to an end-of-history millenarianism—that is, to the expectation of the Thousand Years' Empire and the Golden Age. He referred to the revolutionary utopian movements in Christianity, and called them the "taboritic–communist–Joachitic type of radical anabaptism in which millenarianism always plays a part."[8] That is an interpretation of communism as "teaching about the Thousand Years' Empire,"[9] which Karl Marx did not maintain. Bloch secularized religious millenarianism, reducing it to an inner-historical perfecting of goodness and peace such as Lessing and Kant had proclaimed during the German Enlightenment. He called it "the home of identity." It is a world of progress without the resurrection of the dead.

But in Christianity there has never been an end-time millenarianism without the transcendent framework of the eschatological raising of the dead. That is already made plain in the transition in the book of Revelation from chapter 20 to chapter 21. Without this eschatology the millenarian hope for "better times in the future" loses its thrust.

Why should the transient future that we don't have be better than the transient present we have now? Future history loses its attraction if there is no transcendent future for history as a whole. Without hope for the ultimate, hope for the penultimate soon loses its force, or it becomes violent in order to extort the ultimate from what is penultimate. Bloch's anticipatory and utopian awareness functions only as long as traces still remain of "the religion of the Exodus and the Kingdom." His secular "inherited religion" lives consciously from presuppositions that it has not itself created.

I would maintain the contrary: there is no hope for the future of history as a whole without hope for "better times in history." There is no Christian hope for eternity without the forward-looking hope for the kingdom of God.[10] Without hope for the penultimate, hope for the ultimate makes the whole of history a matter of indifference. There is no Christian eschatology without millenarianism. But for that, Bloch's "religion of the Exodus and the Kingdom" must be expanded by the religion of *resurrection and the kingdom*, as in the "theology of hope." There is no relevant eschatology without the messianic qualification of present experience and action.

3. Bloch's gravestone in the mountain cemetery in Tübingen bears the inscription: "Thinking means transcending." That epitaph sums up Bloch's *Principle of Hope* in a single sentence. The thinking of hope leaps over frontiers. But which frontiers are to be surmounted, and in which direction? Bloch always decided in favour of a "transcending without transcendence."[11] I found this transcending without transcendence illogical, and set over against it "transcending with transcendence."

But, in fact, it is not a matter of the verb and the substantive, and the things for which the two stand, the process and its origin. The question is: Which frontiers are to be crossed? If frontiers in the process of history from the past to the future and from reality to possibility are crossed, then the transcending remains within the continuity of things that are the same. It is not then a transcending into what is not the same, and is qualitatively different, into the "wholly other," the divine. Transcending without transcendence is not "truth as prayer."

Bloch carries over the "two-worlds" theory of transcendence and immanence into his idea about the two times: past and future.[12] The past is immanent, the future is transcendent. Reality is immanent, possibilities are transcendent. The metaphysics of the dipolar world, heaven and earth, the invisible and the visible cosmos, mould the ideas about creation in the Bible and Christian theology, but not their eschatology. That, in contrast, is determined by the apocalyptic doctrine of the two times or aeons, past and future. The past is immanent, the future transcendent. *Here* is the old, transient aeon, *there* the new, abiding aeon; here the pattern of this world is dominant, with violence, injustice, and death—and there comes God's new world with righteousness, peace, and eternal life. These aeons embrace the whole creation, earth and heaven. That is why in the visions of the future "a new heaven and a new earth" emerge—to put it in different words, a new transcendence and a new immanence. With this the prophets of the Old Testament and the apostles of the New have introduced the category *novum*[13] into the perception of history:

> *Do not remember the former things*
> *or consider the things of old.*
> *I am about to do a new thing;*
> *now it springs forth, do you not perceive it? (Isa. 43:18, 19)*

History has no "religious" timetable and no atheistic one. History is neither the aging of the world in the course of seven aeons, nor its progress toward its perfecting in three. History is the confrontation of the old pattern of the world with God's new creation (2 Cor. 5:17; Rev. 21:5). Bloch took over this doctrine of the apocalyptic aeons and applied it to his "philosophy of hope." He thereby confused the transcendence of heaven with the transcendence of God. And because of that, the new creation of all things escaped him.

With "God" we have to think of the transcendence of "transcendence and immanence." In this transitory world-time God is "the God of hope" (Rom. 15:13), but in the coming world-time God is "the indwelling God"—that is, God in God's cosmic *Shekinah*. Then we shall no longer exist *before* God, but *shall live in God*. Then we shall no longer talk about "God" using the attributes of the far-off country and the desert wanderings, but shall live in God's trinitarian homeland. That is surely what Bloch meant with his contradictory formulation about "the Kingdom of God without God."

Hoping and Perceiving:
Hegel and "Minerva's Owl" and Aurora's Lark

It is a task of philosophy to understand what exists. If what is, is history, then it is the task of philosophy "to grasp time in thoughts," as the elderly Hegel said in his *Rechtsphilosophie* (1821), when he had left behind the revolutionary dialectic of his early writings. But if philosophy wants to grasp its time in thoughts, then, according to Hegel, it is only dealing with what has become the past, not with the still-nonexistent future:

> In order to say anything about what the world should be—for that, philosophy is always too late on the scene. As the idea of the world it appears in time only after reality has already completed the formation process and has come to a finish. . . .
>
> When philosophy paints its grey in grey, then a form of life has become old, and with grey in grey it cannot rejuvenate itself, but can only perceive what is: Minerva's owl begins its flight only when twilight falls.[14]

That sounds resigned, yet it is only half the truth. The magic of reality does not lie in reality but in its potentialities. But we only perceive these if we look into reality's future. Every living present is localized between the times of the past and the future, so a "time grasped in thought" cannot be only remembered past; it has to be anticipated future as well.

According to Augustine's theory of time, the human mind makes the past that has already happened present through remembrance, and in hope it anticipates the possible future. Through the power of remembrance and hope, the human mind, imaging God, calls into present awareness what no longer exists and what does not yet exist, thereby becoming creatively active, in correspondence to the God who calls into existence the things that do not exist (Rom. 4:17).

But a second reflection offers a more complex picture: we remember not only what has happened, but also what might have happened. We remember past possibilities as well. Things might have turned out differently—we ourselves might have acted differently. We remember in shame and contrition the missed possibilities for good. We recollect in hope the not-yet-realized potentialities for good. So what is past is by no means only reality as it came to pass. It is always, at the same time, past future. Our remembrances are consequently not only subsequent perceptions. When we recollect their potentialities we perceive their hopes. "Past future" awakens remembered hopes.[15] Existing reality is always surrounded by an ocean of possibilities, of which only the lesser part has been realized.[16] Because reality is realized potentiality, ontologically speaking, potentiality is higher than reality. Consequently, "the primary phenomenon of the primal and true temporality is the future," as Martin Heidegger established in *Being and Time*.[17]

The perceiving reason, which "comprehends its time in thoughts," does not stand above the historical process but influences it through the perception of reality and through the anticipation of possibilities. It must understand itself as a moment in a process. What it knows is not a matter of established facts or of speculation over possibilities but a realistic and, at the same time, utopian *knowledge of change*.

Nor does the perceiving reason stand at the end of days, as the elderly Hegel thought. If he were right, we could only recognize a "form of life" when it had become not merely "old" but had already died and was dead, for then it would no longer change. If we wished to apply Hegel's "owl of Minerva" to the world process, it would be able to perceive nothing as long as everything is still in flux. Only at the end of history—that is to say, at the great final judgment—does the reality of the world appear, in its progresses and abysses. But until then even Minerva's owl perceives in a mirror, darkly, and in part, as Paul says in 1 Corinthians 13. All the knowledge of the perceiving reason is anticipatory knowledge. It is not only in the perception of possibilities but also in the understanding of the realities that reason anticipates the end of world history, and in an attempt at a judgment, anticipates the great last judgment of the world.

In order not to leave Hegel's owl alone in the twilight of the world, let us take an additional image: Aurora's lark soars into the air in the dawn of the world, and greets the new day with its song. So the perception born of hope perceives the possibilities of the new day, of the new life, and of the new creation. Its category is not the grey wisdom of old age but the green category *novum* with which it "rejuvenates" the life that has grown old.

That throws a new light on time. We talk about *transitory time* or, to be more precise, about the time of transience, when we look at the transition from the present to the past, or when we measure all times against the transcendence of timeless eternity. But if we experience the transition from the present to a new future, we have to talk about *beginning time*. Every successful transition from the present to a desired expected future is a beginning. After all, time began "in the beginning" of creation (Gen. 1:1), and it ends, theologically speaking, in the transition from the temporal to the eternal creation (Rev. 21:1). Between the beginning of all things and their new creation time takes place in the *kairos* in which what is old passes away, and something new comes into being. Paul expresses his messianic sense of time by saying: "The night is far gone, the day is near" (Rom. 13:12). For him, time is the dawning glory of eternity. Kierkegaard called the moment between the times of past and future "an atom of eternity."[18] Correspondingly, we call the *kairos* a beginning of the new, eternal creation. That is not the eternity of God but the aeon of the new creation, which from time immemorial has been described with the word *aevum*. In the *kairos* of every initial time the new creation of all things is intended because it is implicit. In every *temporal novum* the *novum ultimum* is heralded. Until the resurrection of the dead we find ourselves "in the beginning," and remain" beginners" until God has finished God's work in us (Phil. 1:6).

Hegel's "Minerva's owl" waits for the past of time; Aurora's lark proclaims the time that is beginning. Past time is the time of death and of eternal forgetting; beginning time is the time of life and of eternal remembering.

The primal image of hope is not only the wide space of future possibilities; it is first of all birth: *incipit vita nova*. With birth, new life comes into the world—that is a reason for hope. With the "being born again to a living hope" (1 Peter 1:3), an old, guilt-laden, and weary life will become young again. That is a reason for a greater hope still. And at the end all that remains is eternal life. That is the greatest of all reasons for hope. A living hope does not develop out of the promise "better and better, greater and greater, further and further," but out of the experience of resurrection in the *kairos*: at the end—the new beginning.

For perception it is never too early, yet it is not evoked by the tempting mystery of the object but always, in addition, by the concerns that guide the perception of the inquirer. These precede the perception, determine the perspectives, and evaluate what is perceived. Of course, there are many personal and social concerns. To be aware of them purifies the senses and makes the mind self-critical. The supreme goal of all perception is truth. Here we may put forward three practical concerns that guide perception:

1. *Knowledge as the basis for rule.* The modern world began with the rise of the exact sciences. The sciences became exact through the "reduction of science to mathematics" (*reductio scientiae ad mathematicum*). The concern that guided perception was freedom from natural forces that were not understood, and the mastery over them. For Descartes it was the concern to make the human being "the lord and possessor of nature"; for the devout Francis Bacon it was the restoration of the likeness to God by way of lordship over the earth (*dominum terrae*). How can power over nature be acquired through knowledge? Through the application of the old Roman method, *divide et impera*—"divide and rule." If natural formations are split up into their individual parts, and one perceives how they are put together and function, they can be "dominated," and a separate formation can be constructed from their individual parts. But has one thereby perceived the truth of nature, or merely overpowered it because it was weaker?

2. *Participatory knowledge.* In the ancient world, philosophers wanted to know nature in order to participate in it. Wonder was the beginning, seeing the goal. What was sought was not initially the utility of things but their beauty, for beauty is an indication of truth. This kind of knowing changes the perceiver, not what is perceived. Perception always confers community between the perceiver and the thing perceived. Dominating knowledge is a one-sided, violent form of community. Participatory knowledge is a relational knowledge with empathy and receptivity. "*Tantum cognoscitur quantum diligitur,*" said Augustine—we know the other or others only insofar as we can love them and, in respect, can let them be themselves. The object of our knowing is a subject per se. So, it is not just a matter of an objective knowing; it also has to do with the perceiving of relationships.

3. *The knowledge that brings about change.* If life takes place in processes, its conditions are not fixed but are involved in development or in disappearing. So, it is impossible to determine how things are but only the way in which they move and change. But that means that through our knowing we participate in their processes and influence their movements. We establish what is passing away and anticipate what can be and should be. We perceive not only what they have become but also their becoming; not only their reality but also their potentiality. In this way knowing itself becomes a moment in a process.

Dominating knowledge establishes facts. Participatory knowledge leads to community with what already exists. The knowledge of possible change perceives the future of things and communities, and evaluates their potentialities. In this way knowing itself becomes a moment in a process. One perceives conditions in transition from the present to the future, from reality to possibilities, and asks how things could go better. One asks about changes for the better, because one wants the good. Knowledge of change is *the reason of hope.* The evaluating ethos of hope does not become relevant for the first time in action, but already in the perception. It becomes the concern that guides perception.

Dominating knowledge is directed toward *objects* and turns things into objects. Participatory knowledge is related to *subjects,* and creates community. The knowledge of change sees objects and subjects as *projects* for a common future.

Hoping and Thinking:
The Productive Power of the Imagination

In everyday speech we talk about remembering, anticipating, and imagining. In so doing, we think about being in different times. In all three respects it is a matter of the astonishing imaginative power of the human mind.

1. *Reflecting*, we consider memories. When we remember, we fit them into ourselves and identify ourselves with them. If it is our past, we also evaluate them in pride and gratitude or, it may be, in shame and regret.[19] For we are remembering not only the past as it has happened but also the past future, and are thinking about the possibilities that, for good or ill, were grasped or missed. Were things bound to develop as they did? No, they could have developed differently, and we could also have acted differently. When we consider our memories, we also come across the past possibilities, and imagine what would have happened if we had realized them. We also reflect in memory about the epoch-making happenings that opened up a new age, or plunged the world into the abyss. The French and the American revolutions opened up a new age and new possibilities. In the primal catastrophe of the First World War (1914–1918), "the lights went out all over Europe," as the British Foreign Secretary Edward Grey already perceived in 1914, adding: "and we shall not see them lit again in our generation. " Epochal events like this are not just "past" future; they are also future that has already happened.

2. *Anticipating*, we grasp in advance in our minds the future with its undreamed-of possibilities and transpose ourselves into it. In *fear* we anticipate the loss of the present and its possible terrors; in *hope* we anticipate possible improvements to the present. We always anticipate the next steps and our attitudes to changed conditions. Without such suppositions we could not live. That is the everyday imaginative power of our anticipating awareness. In the case of epoch-making events such

as the French and American revolutions, more is always latent in the beginning than develops later. Consequently, we like to go back in memory to the original point in order to take the next step forward. It is remarkable that periods which have brought into being something new in Europe have "re" as their prefix: Renaissance, Reformation, Revolution, and so forth.

3. *Imagining,* we produce images of the future we wish for and want. Our productive power of the imagination brings before us dreams, visions, blueprints, and projects—at best in that order. What is this mental power of ours? "Imaginative power is the ability to bring an object before the mind in the imagination, without its being present" was Kant's somewhat dry definition in his *Critique of Pure Reason.*[20] It can also be termed creative fantasy, creative imagination, or creative expectancy. Because all our imaginations are sensory, their imaginative power belongs to what is sensory. But because it cannot merely be defined like the senses but, for its own part, can determine the senses, it must be transcendental. So Kant called it the "transcendental power of the imagination." Like the senses, the power of the imagination should be restricted to "possible experiences." Nevertheless, we can also imagine impossible experiences—experiences that are impossible because they are fantastic. If one is a realist, one must reach out with the power of one's imagination to the limits of what is possible if we wish to exhaust its potentialities. The courage of hope is needed if one is to grow beyond oneself and do what one can.[21] Political repression and personal resignation also repress the people's imaginative power. But "where there is no vision the people perish" (Prov. 29:18, KJV). What do realistic visions look like? In the prophetic and apocalyptic visions we find two principles:

a. the negation of the negative,
b. the completion of the positive.

In this form, visions remain simultaneously realistic and futurist. The negation of the negative: "He will wipe every tear from their eyes. Death will be no more; mourning and crying and pain will be no more" (Rev. 21:4)—that describes the open space for the positive: "I saw a new heaven and a new earth" (Rev. 21:1), and "[God] will dwell with them [the peoples]" (Rev. 21:3). Nothing positive emerges from the mere negation of the negative: no eternal life springs from "the death of death"; the "classless society" is not yet a humane one. On the other hand, the visions lose themselves in irrelevant dreams unless they have their feet in present-day life. A hope without contradiction is only a dream, a contradiction without hope is no more than, in Christian terms, rage.

4. *To think eschatologically* means, generally speaking, thinking something through to the end, that is, "the end of all things," as Kant called it. In Christian terms that means considering life, human history, and the history of nature in the light of Christ's resurrection. The eschatological power of the imagination sees moral life in the future of eternal life, human history in the future of the judgment and the kingdom of God, and the history of nature in the appearance of the new creation of all things. How does this come about?

a. The eschatological hope draws the future of the God "who is to come" (Rev. 1:4) into the present, thereby qualifying the present to be the present of this future, in accordance with the Christ, "the one who has come into this world," as Martha's confession of faith says (John 11:27). The proclamation of the gospel to the poor, Jesus' healing of the sick, and the Beatitudes in the Sermon on the Mount are signs of the presence of God's future in this world. "The kingdom of God is in your midst."

b. On the other hand, the eschatological hope opens every present for God's future:

Lift up your heads, O gates!
and be lifted up, O ancient doors!
that the King of glory may come in. (Ps. 24:7)

That is supposed to find its resonance in a society open for the future. Closed societies break off communication with other societies; closed societies enrich themselves at the cost of coming generations. Open societies are participatory and anticipatory societies. They see their future in the future of God, the future of life, and the future of the eternal creation.

c. Life in this eschatological hope is certainly depicted by Paul in ambiguous terms. On the one hand, we should have all things "as if we did not have them"; on the other hand, we are supposed to live joyfully, because "the Lord is at hand." The two are hardly compatible:

> *The appointed time has grown short;*
> *from now on, let even those who have wives*
> *be as though they had none,*
> *and those who mourn as though they were not mourning,*
> *and those who rejoice as though they were not rejoicing. . . .*
> *For the present form of this world is passing away.*
> *(1 Cor. 7:29-31)*

Theologians call this "the eschatological proviso."[22] But one cannot live it. One surely cannot make a declaration of love with an eschatological proviso: "I love you as if I didn't love you." One cannot weep or rejoice as if one didn't weep or rejoice. One cannot live as if one didn't live—and that merely because the time is short and this world passes away.

It sounds quite different if the imminent expectation is filled positively, as Paul does when he writes in Philippians 4:4:

> *Rejoice in the Lord always;*
> *again I will say, Rejoice.*
> *Let your gentleness be known to everyone.*
> *The Lord is near.*

What is dominant here is not the "eschatological proviso" but the *eschatological anticipation.* Life in joy is already an anticipation of eternal life; the goodly life here is already the beginning of the glorious life there; fulfilled life here points beyond itself to the fullness of life there. In joy over the hoped-for future, we live here and now, completely and wholly, weep with those who weep and rejoice with those who rejoice, as Romans 12:15 says. Life in hope is not half a life under a proviso; it is a whole life awakening in the daybreak colours of eternal life.

Chapter 11

✴

Life: A Never-Ending Festival

The Risen Christ Makes of Human Life
a Never-Ending Festival

"One must be very thick-skinned not to feel the presence of Christians and Christian values as a pressure under which every sense of celebration goes by the board. . . . The festival is paganism *per excellence*," wrote Friedrich Nietzsche at the end of the 19th century.[1] As the son of a Protestant pastor, he must have been speaking from experience. In the Protestantism of the industrial age, festivals such as the Catholic Carnival or Shrove Tuesday were viewed as a waste of time and money. Church services were, rather, hours set aside for reflection. One was supposed to "fear and love" God, but not "enjoy" God, as Augustine had said. In Protestant ears, the desire for God and the enjoyment of God sounded frivolous. After all, we are not in this world for fun. We ought to take life seriously and beware of mere pleasure seekers. Is there something wrong about Protestant services and the Protestant way of life? Or is the festival and the festival atmosphere actually "paganism per excellence"?

In his address on the Saturday after Easter to the "newly enlightened," Athanasius, bishop of Alexandria, that great father of the church, said:

Christ, risen from the dead,
makes the whole of human life
a festival without end.[2]

Christian worship was in fact and from the beginning a festival: the festival of Christ's resurrection from the dead.[3] It was celebrated on the day following the Jewish sabbath, that is to say, on the first day of the Jewish week, at daybreak, and always as a eucharist, with bread and wine. Easter begins with a feast, for Easter is a feast and makes the life of those who celebrate it a festal life. Both are important: one can encounter the glory of God, which appears in the raising of the crucified Christ, only with profound astonishment and can only celebrate the victory of life as a festivity. Jesus himself compared the presence of God, which he proclaimed and lived, with the rejoicing over a marriage. His earthly life was a festal life, even if it ended in suffering and death. How much more must the early Christians have understood his raising from the dead and the presence of the now-exalted Christ as the beginning of an unending joy and a happiness without end. They also experienced the risen Christ as "the first among those who had fallen asleep" and as the leader of life; as the leader in the mystic dance and himself as the bride who dances with the others, as the church father Hippolytus put it.[4] Long before the somber dances of death were painted in medieval times of plague, the figure of the resurrection dance can be seen in old churches. The modern Shaker song "The Lord of the Dance" brings out very well the dancing Christ:

I am the life that'll never, never die;
I'll live in you if you'll live in me,
I am the Lord of the Dance, said he.[5]

"Dying was annihilated through the victory of the dance," as a German translation aptly puts it, the moved cosmos issued from the dance of the Divine One. We have the Indian Shiva Nataraja, who creates and then destroys the world in dance. In Plato we find "the blissful round of the stars" and in Philo "the heavenly dance which revolves round the divine Being." In Israel's Wisdom, the Wisdom of creation "plays beside God," and finds its delight in earthly children. So it was not too far-fetched when the patristic church saw in the risen Christ the leader of the cosmic dance of all things and the leader, too, of the human polonaise into eternal life. There is not only a play of creation; grace plays, too: it plays for the dance of life:

> *Grace dances,*
> *I will flute, let everyone dance . . .*
> *The one who doesn't dance*
> *has failed to comprehend*
> *what it is that is happening.*[6]

It is understandable that Paul should call the exalted Christ "the Lord of glory" (1 Cor. 2:8). In the light of the resurrection, the Orthodox Church has set the glorification of life and the cosmos at the center.[7] It is not through the forgiveness of sins and the commandments of the new obedience that the risen Christ heals weak and fragile human life but, rather, through his beauty. Christ's resurrection acts like the sunrise of God's glory over this tormented life.

> *Arise, shine, for your light has come,*
> *and the glory of the LORD has risen upon you. (Isa. 60:1)*

Easter is a festival of freedom[8] where the risen Christ sits at table with those who are his. Easter epiphanies and eucharistic celebrations probably originally belonged together. It is the eating and drinking in the kingdom of God that the risen Christ anticipates with all those for whom he is Lord and Master. In the Easter feast he takes them with him into his indestructible divine life by giving himself to them in bread and wine. The free spaces of God that are opened up with Christ's resurrection and with the presence of the Christ who was exalted lead to a hardly exhaustible freedom. This freedom we can not only proclaim and believe; we must also taste and enjoy it. If Christian worship is the Sunday feast of the resurrection it must also be celebrated eucharistically. Whether the present forms of the Protestant Lord's Supper and the Catholic Mass are the appropriate ones is doubted in the young churches in Africa and Asia, because their experiences of resurrection are greater than these old European forms, and from their new forms, again, the young Christian generations in the new Europe can learn.

The feast of the resurrection is not a religious excursion into the religious heaven. It is rooted in the earth and in its history. It joins remembrance with hope, and past with future, and presents this bond as a transformation. The making-present in the eucharist of Jesus' suffering and his dying "in the night when he was delivered up" is hope in the mode of remembrance. The eucharistic making-present of the coming kingdom of God is remembrance in the mode of hope, "until he comes." The eucharist is the sacrament of remembrance of his giving of himself for us. At the same time, it is a sacrament of hope for the glory of his future life with us. The harmonization of this remembrance and this hope is a sacrament of grace, which fundamentally transforms those involved in that it interpenetrates their mortal life with divine power, making it immortal in the resurrection Spirit.

With Easter, and therefore really in every Christian service of worship, there begins the laughter of the redeemed, the dance of the liberated, and the creative play of the imagination for life. From earliest times Easter hymns have extolled the victory of life by laughing at death, by mocking hell, and by driving out the demons of terror. In the Middle Ages Easter sermons encouraged Easter laughter (*risus paschalis*). That is not just a joke; it contains a not-yet-exhausted potential for resistance.[9] The laughter takes away the expected fear of the powerful and disarms the enemies. It shows a death-despising freedom where the "principalities and powers" had expected fear and submission. The fear of death is the weapon of all tyrants. Consequently, the festival of the resurrection is also the festival for all those who take the first Easter hymn seriously:

> *"Death has been swallowed up in victory.*
> *Where, O death, is your victory?*
> *Where, O death, is your sting? (1 Cor. 15:54-55)*

When the oppressed laugh at their oppressors, their mockery is also an echo of God's laughter over the tyrants:

He who sits in the heavens laughs;
the LORD has them in derision. (Ps. 2:4)

But the festival of freedom has another effect as well, if Sunday is celebrated not as a passing interruption of the everyday week but with realistic seriousness. When freedom is near, the chains begin to chafe. When the Spirit of the risen Christ lays hold of men and women at the center of what oppresses them, they become aware of their loneliness. When they become aware of their diminished life, then the celebrated life awakens the hunger for real life, and the celebrated freedom awakens the cry for true liberation. Then a remembrance of this festival emanates into everyday life from this festival: this act is a remembrance. It acts as a counter-image to the lonely and reduced life, awakens the will for an uprising against the oppressions, and gives courage to the hope for change. The festival of Christ's resurrection builds up a tension with everyday life; the sufferings over the limitations of life become conscious pains. In this festival the joy over the liberated and transfigured life is deeply bound up with pain over the lack of freedom experienced. Pains of this kind are signs of life. Joy over eternal life leads deeply into solidarity with "groaning creation."

The Festive Life

Joy is the meaning of human life. Human beings were created in order to have joy in God. They are born in order to have joy in life. This means that the frequent questions—What am I here for? Am I of any use? Can I make myself of any use?—lose their point. There is no purpose and no utilitarian goal for which human life is required. There are no ethical goals or ideal aims with which human life has to justify itself.[10] Life itself is good. Existence is beautiful and to be here is glorious. We live in order to live. The working world of the modern industrial society already trains kindergarten children with threatening existential questions of this kind, according to which the meaning of life is to be found in purpose and usefulness. But those who find the meaning of their lives in purpose and utility inevitably end up in life crises once they become disabled or old. The "meaning" of life cannot be found outside life but in life itself. Life must not be misused as if it were a means to an end. For those who are seized by the joy in God and in life are no longer faced by the anxious existential question, "With what purpose?" They become inwardly immune against the demands of the "achievement" that wants to misuse them for alien purposes. They become critical of a society that assesses people according to their utility, and rewards them or penalizes them in their function as worker or consumer.

Of course, one must also add: if the whole of life becomes a festival, then the festival is nothing special, and becomes tedious as time goes by. It is precisely the alternation of everyday and holiday that makes life varied and interesting. Nor does the festal life mean passing life from one party after another, or spending one's whole life in a church service. But a radiance of the divine life can emanate from the feast of the resurrection and fall on the human life, which is filled with worries and work, and, as Luther insisted, there is also a service of worship in the everyday world. That is the spiritual worship (Rom. 12:1, 2) in which the whole of life becomes a resonance responding to the divine song of the resurrection, and in that finds its happiness.

If a life is led in the light of Christ's resurrection, we can recognize that there the power of death has been broken, and the powers of death have lost their rights over us. In the wonder of the resurrection a life becomes new. It is no longer a life leading to death; it is a life leading to the fullness that God has promised. The radiance of the resurrection makes it a life that is buoyant. It is full of interest and participation, and happy because it can forget itself, as it were, for anxiety about one's own self and recognition of one's own ego no longer dominate a life of this kind. The earthly life is totally absorbed into the divine life, which has appeared in the risen Christ. That is more than merely a "flow experience," but it is similar to one.[11] It is a life in the assurance of being caught up and of rising again if one falls or breaks down under a load. It is a life in "reasonable service," in the real world, not in a dream one.

Paul describes this reasonable service when he says:

Do not be conformed to this world,
but be transformed by the renewing of your minds,
so that you may discern what is the will of God—
what is good and acceptable and perfect. (Rom. 12:2)

The laws of this world are no longer valid, so one does not have to adapt to them or let oneself be made to conform to them, for one can "be transformed" through a renewal of life orientation. The spirit of the resurrection offers possibilities enough. The spaces of God lie open, and there we find the new life if we look for it. That was what the patristic church anticipated when it called for asceticism. Do not conform to this world, free your lives from their constraints; become new people who ask solely about God's will, the will revealed in the resurrection of the crucified Christ!

Paul names, first of all, "the good," and that sounds very general and a matter of course. But, as in Jesus' Sermon on the Mount, it has its point in love for one's enemies:

Do not repay anyone evil for evil. (Rom. 12:17)
Do not be overcome by evil, but overcome evil with good.
(Rom. 12:21)

This overrules not only the law of retaliation but the ethic of reciprocity,[12] too, and an ethics of the surmounting of evil is maintained. "Do not be overcome by evil." For with every evil that I suffer, evil penetrates my life, first in the form of the desire for retaliation. The person who has made me suffer is to experience the same suffering; we are on even terms: tit for tat. But through retaliation the evil is not overcome; it is doubled. We cannot drive out hate through hate, but only through love. "Do not overcome by evil—not, either, by the evil with which evil is repaid."[13] Do not put yourself on the same level as the evildoer. Those who repay evil with evil have a feeling of satisfaction, but at bottom they know that they are no better than the perpetrator. The person who murders a murderer is a murderer, too.

"Overcome evil with good." When we forgive our debtors, we do good not only to them but to ourselves as well. We overcome the evil that has entered into us. We do not increase it but put an end to it in ourselves. Overcoming evil with good, loving our enemies, and doing good to those who hate us is not a sign of weakness but presupposes great inner sovereignty, as we saw with Martin Luther King Jr. and Nelson Mandela. The forgiveness of sins is not just about the relationship between victims and perpetrators. It also has to do with the ending of evil. Evil is not just a fault in those who are essentially good. The evil that they did was overpowering in these perpetrators and drove them on because they had surrendered to it. That means ultimately that evil must not depart from the human being but the human being must depart from evil. That is why we read in the Lord's Prayer: "deliver us from evil." The overcoming of evil with good is an essential point in the "reasonable service" in confronting the evil entanglements of this world. This overcoming presupposes that one does not succumb to the pressures of "this world" but conforms to the God of Jesus Christ (Matt. 5:48). The forgiveness of guilt is a resurrection experience for victims and perpetrators, for it creates new life for them both.

Truth as Prayer

We shall take up this thesis of the young Ernst Bloch in order to point to the universal breadth of prayer. If truth is the unconcealed mystery of the world, then prayer is the human way of access to it. Let us look at prayer in the context of creation in order to abstract from it the strangeness that the modern world attributes to it.[14] What, actually, is prayer?

We thank and praise,
We laugh and rejoice,
We shout for joy and dance.

We cry out and lament,
We groan and we weep,
We are dumb and fall silent.

We beg and implore,
We wish and we want,
We desire and implore.

To call all these expressions of living before God "praying" is misleading, because praying is the equivalent of asking. We are placing ourselves, consciously or unconsciously, before God, but not merely as people asking for something, but, in the festival of life, first as people who come in thanksgiving, singing, and laughter. The person who considers God only as the heavenly helper in times of need has not yet understood the true love of God. Modern men and women think that in order to pray one must be particularly religiously endowed—the person who goes to church goes to pray, and behind monastery walls there is prayer without ceasing. But modern men and women help themselves through work. Prayer seems for them too passive, and for some men prayer is only something for women. This modern impression is quite wrong. Prayer is not something peculiarly religious; it is something that is profoundly human. It has been said that prayer is the breathing of the soul. Praying is not even something solely human. The whole of creation prays without ceasing in the breath of the divine Spirit.

A sigh goes through the world

People who begin to long for the redemption of this unredeemed world will become sensitized and, with wakeful senses, become aware that this longing impels every living thing that wants to live and yet has to die. Paul describes a surprising discovery in his epistle to the Romans: "All who are led by the Spirit of God are children of God" (Rom. 8:14). He then sets this human experience of God in the framework of the universal cosmic expectation: "For the creation waits with eager longing for the revealing of the children of God. . . . [for] the creation itself will be set free from its bondage to decay and will obtain the glorious freedom of the children of God" (8:19, 21). The pains of death and the longing for life let all earthly beings chime in with human sighs and groans. Wherever such sighs and groans are heard, there is also hope for redemption. Sighs and groans are signs of the life that stands over against transience. And where human beings in their torment fall dumb, the Spirit intervenes on their behalf with sighs too deep to be uttered (8:26).[15] So, where we human beings, in the Spirit that makes us live, begin to weep over our dead and lament their death, we shall be awake and hear how the earth, too, with all its living things weeps before God. No longer to sigh and groan before God is in fact peculiar, because human beings are then setting themselves apart from sighing creation. Even the young Karl Marx understood that when he discussed religion: "Religion is the sighing of distressed creation, the feeling of a heartless world, as it is the soul of a soulless condition."[16] This recollection of Romans 18:19 came to him via Jakob Böhme and Ludwig Feuerbach.

The world is full of jubilation

There would be no fear of death if there were no joy in life, and there would be no sighings in the world if there were no love for life. The pain of death is only the negative reverse side of the positive love for life. The sighings under the burden of transience and the song of praise for life are not contradictory, but enhance one another mutually. The world is full of jubilation, for God is in this world.[17] God is not far off in the world beyond, but through the Spirit of life is already present in this world of the living. Israel expressed this by saying that God's Spirit, God's Wisdom, and God's powers fill everything created in such a way that all things live from God and have their existence in God. "The spirit of the Lord has filled the world" (Wisd. 1:7) and "[God's] immortal spirit is in all things" (Wisd. 12:1) So, one day the glory of God will also "fill the whole earth" (cf. Isa. 6:3).

What are the signs of this? All created beings extol and praise God by rejoicing before God in their existence, by enjoying their life in God, and by expressing that joy. "All your works give thanks to you, O Lᴏʀᴅ" (Ps. 145:10), and "The heavens are telling the glory of God" (Ps. 19:1). The biologists F. J. J. Buytendijk and Adolf Portmann have called this "the demonstrative value of being."[18] They have discovered a playful behaviour among animals. "To put it simply: birds sing more than they ought to do according to Darwin," states Buytendijk.[19] Together with Portmann, he analyzed the exuberant profusion of types, the luxurious wealth of colour, and the nonutilitarian fullness of their artistic forms of expression as the play of their freedom. Every living thing does not merely desire to live, to survive, and to reproduce itself, but also to present itself and to parade its riches, and that is a token of freedom. Among human beings, isn't the playful joy over our possibilities precisely this demonstrative value of being about which the biologists talk in connection with animals? Then inherent in the rejoicing over creation is the glorification of its Creator, and the joy in God is reflected in the song of nature.

For modern human beings, nature has, for the most part, fallen dumb. This world has produced "the silent spring," to echo Rachel Carson in one of the first books (1962) on the ecological crisis. But nature is not dumb. It is our fault if we don't hear it. In the multiplicity of its forms it reflects God's beauty. But we lack the eyes to see it; we are blind, as John Calvin explained the missing connection. Praying, sighing, and singing mean waking up out of the modern world and being in harmony with the cosmic solidarity of all created beings.

We shall therefore turn to prayer in the human being's relationship to God and consider, first of all, external body language.

The body language of people at prayer

Our body language shows what is going on inside us, and at the same time determines our inner life as well, for we are, inwardly and outwardly, physically and spiritually unified beings. In what bodily attitude do people pray to God? Out of the multiplicity of attitudes, we shall pick out three, because they were established on a biblical foundation.

1. The Muslim attitude in prayer is reminiscent of the subjugation of the subject under absolute power of Asiatic despots. One throws oneself on the ground before them, offering one's unprotected neck, and makes oneself as small as possible. This age-old gesture of subjugation is the expression of a religion of absolute dependence. In

complete submission, the human being bent down to the earth is also assuming the position of the fetus in the womb, thereby bringing one's own will into a kind of embryonic condition. This prayerful attitude is by no means merely a political gesture. According to the Old Testament, out of fear and alarm in the face of the overwhelming divine power, the whole people "fall on their faces before the LORD." So it was with Abraham (Gen. 17:3, 17), Joshua (Josh. 7:6), Daniel (Dan. 8:17), Moses and Aaron (Num. 16:22), and the whole people of Israel (1 Kgs. 18:39). According to the New Testament, the disciples "fell to the ground" when Jesus was "transfigured" on the mountain by God (Matt. 17:6). Divine appearances are experienced as a *mysterium tremendum*; those affected are entirely delivered over to them. It is only the grace of the One who is still stronger that gives them life.

2. The Christian posture in prayer in the West may, for political reasons, derive from a political gesture of submissiveness in the Germanic culture, although the hierarchical church developed its own tokens of submissiveness. Subjects were never permitted to look at their masters eye to eye. Folding the hands was a sign that one was disarmed. To bend the knee was the sign of reverence and a gesture of humility. One demonstrates one's own weakness when one kneels down before the one who is stronger. According to biblical traditions, kneeling down shows that while the body sinks to earth, the spirit is elevated to the Almighty God. "Come, let us worship and bow down and kneel before the LORD our maker" (Ps. 95:5). With this gesture, too, Jesus is promised universal sovereignty to the glory of God the Father: "At the name of Jesus every knee shall bow, in heaven and on earth and under the earth."

But to what are we giving bodily expression when we fold our hands, bow our heads, and close our eyes? We withdraw into ourselves, assume an attitude of penitence, and are twisted as if we were in pain. If one sees the kneeling human being at prayer, with closed eyes and folded hands, and inwardly turned, one is also reminded of the figure of the *homo incurvatus in seipsum*, which Luther used to depict the sinner as. This is anything but the figure of someone who has been redeemed. This is someone turned within oneself, who shuts off one's senses in order to seek God within. It is the mysticism of closed eyes.

3. We find a completely different attitude of adoration among early Christians as they are depicted in the catacombs in Rome and Naples. They stand upright, with raised heads and open eyes. Their arms are stretched out wide, their hands are open and turned upward (1 Tim. 2:8). It is an attitude showing great expectation and a loving preparedness to embrace the other. Those who open themselves to God in this way are patently free men and women. They grow beyond themselves, as it were, and become bigger. The raised arms let their chests expand, so that they can breathe more deeply. The upright stance is the starting point for movements in space, for the striding forward or for dancing. This attitude was traditionally used in prayers for the coming of the Holy Spirit. It is the attitude of Orthodox priests at the *epiklesis* of the Spirit. The modern Pentecostal movement has taken it up in its worship. It also becomes the attitude of people who are filled with the messianic hope and who contravene the uncertainties of their time: "Stand up and raise your heads, because your redemption is drawing near" (Luke 21:28).

In the New Testament, praying is never mentioned in isolation, but always in combination with watching: "watch and pray." So, in metaphorical terms it is never directed only upward, but is always at the same time forward looking. Thus, it is an open-eyed certainty. Here God is not feared as the one who is supremely powerful, but as the "broad place" into which in prayer a person enters and can develop him- or herself (Ps. 31:8). The early Christian attitude of worshiping adoration shows that Christianity is, in sensory terms, a religion of freedom. The upright stance before God is astonishing and incomparable. The person who prays is then praying in the Spirit whose name is freedom. It is freedom *in* God.

Does God accede to the requests of human beings?

Let us talk now about the inner side of prayer: petitionary prayers, cries of lamentation, and cries of suffering. Is there any point in asking God for something, in bewailing our suffering, or in crying out for God?

If we accept the metaphysical attributes of unalterability and immovability described in Part One as being divine attributes, then all attempts to influence God in God's guidance of individual or universal destinies are pointless. If God is unchangeable, then prayers, however fervent, cannot change God. If God is immovable, then laments cannot move God to mercy, either.[20] If God is "the all-determining reality," then all that is left for human beings is dumb resignation to their fates. What is a human being that he or she could dispute with God?

As we saw in Part One, the God of Israel is the living God who "sees the affliction of his people who are in Egypt." He "hears their cries" and "has come down" to deliver them (Exod. 3:7, 8). In God's descent (*Shekinah*), God makes God someone who can be talked to and is receptive; God is both sympathetic and capable of suffering. Moses can talk to God "as with a friend" (Exod. 33:11). In the covenant with the people of God's choice, God is both high and low, active and passive, God speaks and listens, is active and suffers. A reciprocal relationship comes into being between the God of the covenant and God's people. It is indeed embedded in the election, which issues one-sidedly from God. But God lays the sanctification of the divine name in the hands of the people.

The God of Jesus Christ is the same God. Between Jesus, the Son, "in whom I [that is, God] am well pleased" (as is said at Jesus' baptism, Mark 1:11), and the God whom he calls "Abba, dear Father," an intimate relationship of praying and being heard comes into being, until the silence of God in Gethsemane and the lament on Golgotha. Those who live in the community of Christ pray like Jesus, "Abba, dear Father," and enter into his reciprocal relationship with God. They pray, lament, and cry out for God in Jesus' name, and are assured that the Father of Jesus Christ hears them and listens to their laments. One might now think that with the coming of Christ into our world and with the community of Christ that is open to all, all the prayerful concerns of human beings have been heard, and all that is left is gratitude for the divine gift which is Jesus Christ. But that is by no means the case. It is, rather, that in the community of Christ the divine spaces for asking, lamenting, and crying out are opened for the first time. Christ gives us the courage to ask, lament, and cry out for the first time. "And if the human being in his torment should fall dumb, give me a God to utter how I suffer," wrote Goethe. It is just this that happens in the community of Christ. Before the God of Jesus, we can express everything that weighs on us, in the certainty that God hears us and will respond to us. The community of Christ is not a closed society. It is eschatologically open for the redemption of the world. The last prayer in the New Testament is directed toward the future of Jesus: "Amen. Come Lord Jesus!" (Rev. 22:20). "Then he will wipe every tear from their eyes. Death will be no more, mourning and crying and pain shall be no more" (Rev. 21:4). But until then the praying and the crying out, the suffering and weeping in the name of Jesus, have a point because it is in this name that God will answer them through the resurrection of the dead and the new creation of all things. In the history of our lives and in world history there are many portents and beginnings of this future that we call answers to prayer. Only the person who falls silent and who has no more tears is lost.

How do we talk to God when we ask for something, complain, or cry out? That depends on how we address God: as *Lord*, as *Father*, or as *friend*.

If we address God as *Lord*, then we generally feel ourselves as God's subjects or servants or followers. When we think of the biblical stories in which God shows Godself as the Lord, then, following the First Commandment, we are addressing the God of Israel as the liberator, and we are those whom God has liberated. The relationship of dependence remains, but it is a free relationship, not a dictated one. When we call Jesus our Lord, we have before our eyes the risen Christ and know that we have been liberated from sin, death, and hell. We are his redeemed property.

When in the community of Christ we address God as *Abba, dear Father*, we are recognizing ourselves as God's children. Jesus is called the firstborn among many brothers and sisters because he takes us with him into the Son's relationship with God. Only servants beg from their masters; children discuss their affairs confidentially with their parents. We share our joys and sorrows with God the Father, because we know that God participates lovingly in our lives. Servants only approach their master in case of need—otherwise they keep their distance. Children enjoy being with their parents.

Friends have a different relationship. They share their joys and sorrows. Only the person who can rejoice with us can also suffer with us. Friends turn to one another for advice in difficult situations. They are bound together in mutual liking and respect. We open our hearts to God as we talk to friends who understand us because they know us. We share our worries and wishes with them but we do not put them under pressure with what we intend but respect their freedom. It is true that, in the Old Testament, only those who have "seen" God are called "friends of God" because they can speak so confidentially with God in the Holy Spirit "as with a friend."

The servant begs, the child confides, the friend consults. Those do not have to be three stages in the self-consciousness that is discovered in praying, but they are certainly layers of self-experience that open up for the person who prays.

What do we have to bring with us when we pray? Really nothing except open hands and empty hearts. But when one prays, one does it with a firm trust and a strong will. We take our bearings from the stories about Jesus' healings. "Your faith has made you well," he says to the woman "with an issue of blood" who touches his garment because she promises herself healing from it (Mark 5:34). "Let it be done for you as you wish," he says to the Canaanite woman who asks for healing for her daughter (Matt. 15:28). Those who pray bring with them the belief that what they ask for can come about: "All things are possible with God." But what they want, they must want under all circumstances. We should trust and desire with all our hearts and with all our souls and with all our strength, and not immediately, out of fear of disappointment, reckon with God's nonfulfillment of the petition. It is better to be disappointed than to abandon the hope. To live with unheard prayers means watching with Jesus in Gethsemane. Watching in tense expectation is a fervent form of praying.

Adoration and doxology

In praying, in thanking and complaining, in sighing and singing, we always arrive at a point that can be called a mystical silence: we fall dumb in what we want to say about life and become aware of God's holiness. The prayer becomes adoration, and the enjoyment of God's gifts becomes worship of the Giver. God is then loved for God's sake, not only as creator, reconciler, and redeemer. The way to this point is simple and familiar: we begin with our asking and giving thanks for the gifts and powers of life. Then we acknowledge the gracious hand of God from whom these gifts and powers come, and we grasp this open hand of God. There we feel ourselves to be in safe-keeping, even when we fall, when the gifts are absent and our powers fail us. We are led from this open hand of God to the heart of God, where there is glowing love, as Luther said. With these images we circumscribe a path from God's immanence to God's transcendence: from the gift to the giver, from the giver to God. We love God not only because of the powers of life that we receive but, ultimately, for God's own sake. In adoration we fall dumb because we forget ourselves and find bliss in God, just as we fall dumb when we look at something overwhelmingly beautiful. Marvelling, our breath is taken away. When we pray, we always arrive at the point where we are overcome by astonishment over God.

But in the adoration of God we stand face to face not only with the holy mystery but also with God's inexhaustible fullness. So we must not only fall silent before that over which we cannot speak, but must also speak about that over which we cannot be silent. That takes place in worship, in the doxology.

In joy over the inexhaustible abundance of God, from which we take not only grace upon grace but also life upon life, the whole of life is transfigured and becomes a festal life. It is this radiance of the divine life now shed on human life that finds expression in the doxology.

Notes

Preface

1. Dietrich Bonhoeffer, letter to Eberhard Bethge, Tegel, 21 July 1944, in John W. deGruchy, ed., *Letters and Papers from Prison*, trans. Isabel Best, et al., *Dietrich Bonhoeffer Works*, vol. 8 (Minneapolis: Fortress Press, 2010), 485–86.

Introduction

1. The standard work is still Georges de Lagarde, *Naissance de l'esprit laique au decline du Moyen Age* (Paris: Éditions Béatrice, 1934).

2. Robert Bellah, et al., *Habits of the Heart. Individualism and Commitment in American Life* (Berkeley: University of California Press, 1985).

3. Perry Miller, *The New England Mind: From Colony to Province* (Cambridge: Harvard University Press, 1953).

4. Hermann Lübbe, *Säkularisierung. Geschichte eines ideenpolitischen Begriffs* (Freiburg: Alber, 1965). Charles Taylor offers a one-sided Catholic interpretation in *A Secular Age*, Cambridge: Harvard University Press, 2007). See also Günter Thomas, "Die Versuchung religiöser Nostalgie. Eine protestantische Lektüre von Charles Taylors 'Eine säkulares Zeitalter'," *Evangelische Theologie* 73, no. 6 (2013): 421–36.

5. On the general background, see Karl Aner, *Die Theologie der Lessingzeit* (Hildesheim: Olms, 1964). On *Nathan the Wise*, see *Nathan der Weise*, ed. Wolfgang Kröger, *Literaturwissenschaft: Gotthold Ephraim Lessing* (Stuttgart: Metzler, 1995), 51–62.

6. From *Nathan the Wise*, act III, scene 7.

7. Ibid.

8. *De Tribus Impostoribus. Von den drei Betrügern* (1598), ed. and introduced by Gerhard Bartsch, trans. Rolf Walther (Berlin: Akademie, 1960). For comment, see Friedrich Niewöhner, *Veritas sive Varietas. Lessings*

Toleranzparabel und das Buch von den drei Betrüger (Heidelberg: Lampert Schneider, 1988). For another interpretation, see Karl-Josef Kuschel, *Im Ringen um den wahren Ring, Lessings „Nathan der Weise"—eine Herausforderung an die Religionen* (Düsseldorf: Patmos, 2011); but in my view his interpretation is too positive, and not merely historically so. Lessing's interpretation of the ring parable also has behind it the atheistic presumption that "the true ring was probably lost." With this presupposition, no interreligious dialogues are possible.

9. Ibid., 8.

10. Ibid., 9.

11. From *Nathan the Wise*, act II, scene 5.

12. Romano Guardini, *Das Ende der Neuzeit. Ein Versuch zur Orientierung* (Basel: Werkbund, 1950).

13. Immanuel Kant, *Critique of Pure Reason* (1781).

14. Ludwig Feuerbach, *Das Wesen der Religion* (Leipzig: Otto Wigand, 1848/Berlin: Deutsche Bibliothek, 1913), 308.

15. Ludwig Feuerbach, *Das Wesen des Christentums* (Leipzig: Otto Wigand, 1841/Berlin: Akademie, 1956), xxv, 536, and frequently. On Feüerbach, see Simon Rawidowicz, *Ludwig Feuerbachs Philosophie. Ursprung und Schicksal* (Berlin: Reuther & Reichard, 1931).

16. Jürgen Moltmann, "Gottesbeweise und Gegenbeweise," *Das Gespräch* 46 (1965): 27. The quotation is taken from Ludwig Feuerbach, *Gedanken über Tod und Unsterblichkeit* (1830). The expression "enjoyment of God" goes back to Augustine, who set the world and God over against one another with the alternative "*uti–frui.*" The godless person "uses" God in order to "enjoy" the world; the believer "uses" the world in order to "enjoy" God. But Augustine went a step further—the enjoyment of God also includes human beings: "*Fruitio Dei et seinvicem in Deo.*" If we take this up and extend it to include God's creation, we can say that the enjoyment of God includes the enjoyment of life. We enjoy all our fellow creatures "in God," and do not "use" them. They are but the means to an end, yet are in their own way an end in themselves. They praise and "enjoy" God in their own way, and join wih us and we with them so that we can "enjoy God forever" (*Westminster Catechism*). That is why we seek fellowship with them.

17. Ludwig Feuerbach, *Grundsätze der Philosophie der Zukunft* (1843), in *Kleine philosophische Schriften*, Philosophische Bibliothek 227 (Leipzig: Felix Meiner, 1950), §64, 170.

18. Ibid., §60, 169.

19. Ibid., §62, 169.

20. Ludwig Feuerbach, *Vorläufige Thesen zur Reform der Philosophie* (1842), in *Kleine philosophische Schriften*, Philosophische Bibliothek (Leipzig: Felix Meiner, 1950), §63.

21. Ibid., §62.

22. Ibid., §67. Cf. also Feuerbach, *Philosophie der Zukunft*, §33.

23. Feuerbach, *Vorläufige Thesen*, §70. In his *Wesen des Christentums*, Feuerbach contends with the theological thesis that God is incapable of suffering: "St. Bernard has recourse to a delightfully sophistical word-play: *„Impassibilis est Deus, sed non incompassibilis, cui proprium est merereris semper et parcere"* (*Sup. Cant, Serm.* 25 [39]). As if sympathy were not also suffering! Though indeed the suffering of love, the suffering of the heart. But what does suffer if not the participating heart? Without love there is no suffering, for the substance, the source of suffering, is the sympathizing heart" (ibid., 119 n.2). Pope Benedict XVI also quotes the sentence in his encyclical *Salvi Spes*, §39, though without reference to Feuerbach.

24. Feuerbach, *Das Wesen der Religion*, 313. These are the final sentences in his Heidelberg lectures.

25. Ibid., 308.

26. See here Max Scheler, *Die Stellung des Menschen im Kosmos* (1927) (Munich: Nymphenburger, 1949), 47, 56.

27. Jürgen Moltmann, "The Knowing of the Other and the Community of the Different," in *God for a Secular Society*, trans, Margaret Kohl (Minneapolis: Fortress Press, 1999), 135ff. (Ger.: *Gott im Project der Modernen Welt*, 1997). The similarity principle goes back to Empedocles. "Like is known by like" leads to "like draws to like," and to "like is requited with like," and to "God is only known by God" and *"nemo contra Deum nisi Deus ipse."* The opposite, that the unlike know themselves through their opposite, goes back to Anaxagoras: "We perceive the cold through the hot, the sweet through the sour, the light through the dark . . . for sensory perception is linked with pain. When the unlike is brought into contact with our sensory organs, the result is pain" (Theophrastus, *De sensibus,* 27). An old Greek wisdom saying states

that "to know God means to suffer God" and Israel's Wisdom tradition says that "the one who looks upon God must die." If Feuerbach had recognized this tradition, he would have been able to make his theory about pain the basis of a truly dialectical theology.

28. Günther Anders, *Die Antiquiertheit des Menschen*, 3d ed. (Munich: Beck, 1984). Mikhail Bakunin already reduced human intelligence to the animal body and "the whole material organization of the brain." Cf. *Gott und Staat* (1871) (Berlin: Aufbau, 1995), 98.

29. Ernst Haeckel, *Die Welträtsel. Gemeinverständliche Studien über Monistische Philosophie, mit einem Nachwort: Das Glaubensbekenntnis der Reinen Vernunft* (Stuttgart: 1899); also idem, *Die Lebenswunder. Gemeinverständliche Studien über Biologische Philosophie* (Leipzig: 1904).

30. Ernst U. von Weizsäcker, *Erdpolitik. Ökologische Realpolitik an der Schwelle zum Jahrhundert der Umwelt*, 3d ed. (Darmstadt: Wissenschaftliche Buchgesellschaft, 1992).

31. Dietrich Bonhoeffer's ideas about "the world that has come of age," which developed historically from the Middle Ages to modern times, does not correspond to Kant's concept. People have never suffered so much from self-imposed infancy as have the Germans in modern times. In the Middle Ages and in the ancient world there were people of independent thought, or are Plato and Aristotle supposed to have lived and thought in a world without independent thought? Cf. Bonhoeffer, letter to Eberhard Bethge, Tegel, 6 June 1944, in John W. deGruchy, ed., *Letters and Papers from Prison*, trans. Isabel Best, et al., *Dietrich Bonhoeffer Works*, vol. 8 (Minneapolis: Fortress Press, 2010), 422.

32. Hannah Arendt, in *The Origins of Totalitarianism* (1950), rightly compares the Nazi and the Stalinist dictatorship in the 20th century. Total rule means "self-imposed infancy" on the part of the people. This was only broken in the resistance movement and in the awareness that "we are the people," as in Leipzig in 1989.

33. Rudolf Weth, ed., *Totaler Markt und Menschenwürde*, with contributions by Herta Däubler-Gmelin, Heino Falcke, Friedheim Hengsbach, Jürgen Moltmann, Dietrich Ritschl, Friedrich Schorlemmer, Wolfgang Schrage, Jakub Trojan, Rudolf Weth, and Ina Willi-Plein (Neukirchen-Vluyn: Neukirchener Theologie, 1996); Frank Schirrmacher, *EGO: Das Spiel des Lebens* (Frankfurt: N.P., 2012).

34. Hannah Arendt, *Eichmann in Jerusalem: A Report on the Banality of Evil* (London: Penguin, 1963).

1. The Living God

1. Pierre Hadot, "Leben," in Joachim Ritter, et al., eds., *Historisches Wörterbuch der Philosophie* (Basel/Stuttgart: Schwabe, 1980), 5:52–55, which I am following here.

2. Aristotle, *Metaphysics*, Book XII, 1072 b.

3. Quoted in Hadot, "Leben," n.7.

4. Friedrich Nietzsche, *Gedichte und Sprüche* (Leipzig: Kröner, 1916), 180.

5. Ibid., 141: "Das trunkene Lied."

6. Boethius, *Philosophiae consolationis* ("The Consolations of Philosophy"), Book V,1.

7. Ernst Bloch, *Geist der Utopie* (1923) (Frankfurt: Suhrkamp, 1964), 254 (Eng.: *The Spirit of Utopia* [Stanford: Stanford University Press, 2000]).

8. Søren Kierkegaard, *Der Begriff der Angst* (*The Concept of Dread*, 1884).

9. Leopold von Ranke, *Über die Epochen der Neueren Geschichte. Historische-kritische Ausgabe*, ed. Theodor Schieder and Helmut Berding (Munich: Oldenbourg Wissenschaftsverlag, 1971), 60.

10. Reinhart Koselleck, *Vergangene Zukunft. Zur Semantik geschichtlicher Zeiten* (Frankfurt: Suhrkamp, 1979).

11. See G. W. F. Hegel, "Phenomenology of Spirit (1807)," in *G. W. F. Hegel: Theologian of the Spirit*, ed. Peter C. Hodgson, The Making of Modern Theology (Minneapolis: Fortress Press, 1997), 101.

12. Ibid.

2. God's Attributes

1. Paul Imhof and Hubert Biallowons, *Karl Rahner im Gespräch* I (Munich: Kösel, 1982), 245f.; see also the comment on God's co-suffering and inability to suffer in Jürgen Moltmann, *History and the Triune God: Contributions to Trinitarian Theology*, trans. John Bowden (London: SCM Press, 1991).

2. In his *Church Dogmatics*, Karl Barth pioneered the liberation of Christian theology from Aristotelian metaphysics. Cf. Wolf Krötke, *Gottes Klarheiten. Eine neuinterpretation der Lehre von Gottes 'Eigenschaften'* (Tübingen:

Mohr Siebeck, 2001). I am pursuing Barth's approach further, taking up the biblical theology of Bernd Janowski, Michael Welker, and others. Nevertheless, work on a general metaphysics remains a task for Christian theology, which must combine its particularity with universality,

3. Joachim Jeremias, *Die Reue Gottes. Aspekte alttestamentlicher Gottesvorstellung*, 2d ed. (Neukirchen: Neukirchener, 1997). Jan-Dirk Döhling, *Der bewegliche Gott. Eine Untersuchung des Motifs der Reue Gottes in der Hebräischen Bibel* (Freiburg: Herder, 2009); with comment by Frank Crüsemann, "Biblische Herausforderung für das Gottesbild," *Evangelische Theologie* 72, no. 1 (2012): 75–80. Ingo Baldermann, *Der Gott der Lebenden. Die Einzigartigkeit der biblischen Gotteserfahrung* (Neukirchen: Neukirchener, 2013); and Otto Weber's *Grundlagen der Dogmatik* (Neukirchen: Neukirchener, 1955, 1962) already circle round the understanding of God's faithfulness; see also Otto Weber, *Die Treue Gottes und die Kontinuität der menschlichen Existenz. Gesammelte Aufsätze* (Neukirchen: Neukirchener, 1967), 99–112.

4. Jürgen Moltmann, *The Crucified God: The Cross of Christ as the Foundation and Criticism of Christian Theology*, trans. R. A. Wilson and John Bowden (Minneapolis: Fortress Press, 1993 [Ger.: 1973/Eng.: 1974]), was directed against this axiom; see also idem, "II: The Passion of God," in *The Trinity and the Kingdom: The Doctrine of God*, trans. Margaret Kohl (Minneapolis: Fortress Press, 1993 [Ger.: 1980/Eng.: 1981]), (21–60).

5. John Paul II, *Dominum et vivificantem*, 18 May 1986, 41, http://w2.vatican.va/content/john-paul-ii/en/encyclicals/documents/hf_jp-ii_enc_18051986_dominum-et-vivificantem.html.

6. Benedict XVI, *Salve Spes*, 30 November 2007, 39, http://w2.vatican.va/content/benedict-xvi/en/encyclicals/documents/hf_ben-xvi_enc_20071130_spe-salvi.html.

7. Abraham Heschel, *The Prophets*, 2 vols. (New York: Harper & Row, 1962).

8. Dietrich Bonhoeffer, letter to Eberhard Bethge, Tegel, 16 July 1944, in John W. deGruchy, ed., *Letters and Papers from Prison*, trans. Isabel Best, et al., *Dietrich Bonhoeffer Works*, vol. 8 (Minneapolis: Fortress Press, 2010), 479.

9. Fides Buchheim, *Der Gnadenstuhl. Darstellung der Dreifaltigkeitt* (Würzburg: Echter, 1984); Francois Boespflug talks about the "compassion

of the Father": see his *Trinität. Dreifaltigkeitsbilder im späten Mittelalter* (Paderborn: Schöningh, 1999).

10. Christoph Schwöbel, *Gott in Beziehung.* Studien zur Dogmatik (Tübingen: Mohr Siebeck, 2002).

11. Rudolf Bultmann, *Glauben und Verstehen* I (Tübingen: J. C. B. Mohr, 1958), 26, 29, 33.

12. Søren Kierkegaard, "Eine literarische Anzeige," in *Gesammelte Werke,* 17.

13. Hans Jonas, *Zwischen Nichts und Ewigkeit. Zur Lehre vom Menschen* (Göttingen: Vandenhoeck & Ruprecht, 1963), 55–62.

14. Gershom Scholem, *Die jüdische Mystik in ihrer Hauptströmungen* (Frankfurt: Suhrkamp, 1957), 265–93.

15. Gershom Scholem, "Schöpfung aus Nichts und Selbstverschränkung," *Eranos Jahrbuch 1956,* bd. 25 (Zürich: Daimon, 1957), 87–119.

16. Emil Brunner, *Dogmatik* II (Zürich: Zwingli, 1950), 31.

17. Jürgen Moltmann, *God in Creation: A New Theology of Creation and the Spirit of God,* the Gifford Lectures for 1984–85, trans. Margaret Kohl (Minneapolis: Fortress Press, 1993 [1985]), 72ff.

18. Bonhoeffer, letter to Eberhard Bethge, Tegel, 16 July 1944, in deGruchy, ed., *Letters and Papers,* 8:479.

19. Johann Baptist Metz, *Memoria Passionis. Ein provozierendes Gedächtnis in pluralistischer Gesellschaft* (Freiburg: Herder, 2006), 28–34.

20. Bonhoeffer, "Christians and Heathens," Tegel, summer 1944, in deGruchy, ed., *Letters and Papers,* 460–61.

21. Tadeusz Styczen and Stanislaw Dziwisz, *The Prayer of Gethsemane Goes On* (Lublin: John Paul II Institute, Catholic University of Lublin, 2003), on the spirituality of this pope.

22. Blaise Pascal, "On Religion," in *Pensées* 7,553.

23. For *omnipotentia* and *omniscientia* from kenotic perspectives, cf. John Polkinghorne, "Kenotic Creation and Divine Action," in Polkinghorne, ed., *The Work of Love: Creation as Kenosis* (Grand Rapids: Eerdmans, 2001), 102–106; and commentary on the same by J. M. Watkins, "John Polkinghorne's Kenotic Theology of Creation and Its Implications for a Theory of Human Creativity," in Fraser Watts and Christopher C. Knight, *God and the Scientist: Exploring the Work of John Polkinghorne* (Farnham, UK: Ashgate, 2012), 217–42.

24. Here I am taking up the concept of promise I used in *Theology of Hope: On the Ground and Implications of Christian Eschatology*, trans. James W. Leitch (Minneapolis: Fortress Press, 1993 [Ger.: 1964/Eng.: 1967]).

25. Max Frisch, *Tagebuch 1946–1949* (Frankfurt: Suhrkamp, 1985).

26. Gregory of Nyssa, "De Vita Moysis," PG 44, 377.

3. The Living God in the History of Christ

1. Jürgen Moltmann, "No Monotheism Is Like Another," in *Sun of Righeousness, Arise! God's Future for Humanity*, trans. Margaret Kohl (Minneapolis: Fortress Press, 2010 [2009]), 85–100. On the question whether the number one is applicable to the Deity, cf. Hans Urs von Balthasar's account of the patristic discussion in *Kosmische Liturgie. Das Weltbild Maximus des Bekenners* (Einsiedeln: Johannes, 1961), 101–109. For the new discussion about monotheism, see Laurel C. Schneider, *Beyond Monotheism: A Theology of Multiplicity* (New York: Routledge, 2008).

2. "Im dreieinigen Gott leben," sermon on 2 Cor. 13:13, in Jürgen Moltmann, *'So komm dass wir das Offene schauen.' Perspektiven der Hoffnung* (Stuttgart: Calwer, 2011), 40–46.

3. Joachim Jeremias, *Abba. Studien zur neutestamentlichen Theologie und Zeitgeschichte*, (Göttingen: Vandenhoeck & Ruprecht, 1966).

4. See Jürgen Moltmann, *History and the Triune God: Contributions to Trinitarian Theology* (London: SCM Press, 1991).

5. Lyle Dabney, *Die Kenosis des Geistes. Kontinuiät zwischen Schöpfung und Erlösung im Werk des Heiligen Geistes*, diss. (Tübingen, 1989).

6. Jürgen Moltmann, "The Triune God," in *Sun of Righteousness, Arise!* 149–69. The following section is also my grateful response to the two festschrifts for my 80th birthday, *Der lebendige Gott als Trinität*, ed. Michael Welker and Miroslav Wolf (Gütersloh: Gütersloher, 2006); and *God's Life in Trinity*, ed. Michael Welker and Miroslav Wolf (Minneapolis: Fortress Press, 2006), with contributions by American and British colleagues.

7. Jürgen Moltmann, *The Trinity and the Kingdom: The Doctrine of God*, trans. Margaret Kohl (Minneapolis: Fortress Press, 1993 [Ger.: 1980/Eng.: 1981]); Wolfhart Pannenberg, *Systematic Theology*, vol. 1, trans. Geoffrey Bromiley (Edinburgh: T&T Clark, 1988).

8. Wolfhart Pannenberg, "Der offenbarungstheologische Ansatz in der Trinitätslehre," in Welker and Wolf, eds., *Der lebendige Gott als Trinität*, 14.

He presents the doctrine of the Trinity from the starting point of the history of Christ, not, like Karl Barth, from the concept of God's self-presentation. See Hegel's *Lectures on the Philosophy of Religion* 1:126-27 (1824).

9. Karl Barth, *Church Dogmatics* I/1: *The Doctrine of the Word of God*, trans. G. W. Bromiley, et al. (Edinburgh: T&T Clark, 1969); Eberhard Jüngel, "Gott selbst im Ereignis seiner Offenbarung," in Welker and Wolf, eds., *Der Lebendige Gott als Trinität*, 32. He develops Karl Barth's approach further.

10. Myung Yong Kim, "Ein Vergleich der Trinitätslehre von Karl Barth and Jürgen Moltmann," in Welker and Wolf, eds., *Der lebendige Gott als Trinität*, 155–73, at 162.

11. A long but still incomplete list can be found in *Sun of Righteousness, Arise!*, 240f.

12. This was the thesis of my book *The Trinity and the Kingdom*.

13. Jürgen Moltmann, "The God of Resurrection," in *Sun of Righteousness, Arise!*, 37–85.

14. Paul Ricoeur, "La Liberté selon l'espérance," in *Le Conflit des interpretations. Essais d'herméneutique* (Paris: Seuil, 1969), 393.

15. Barth, *Church Dogmatics* I/1.

16. Jürgen Moltmann, "Trinitarian Glorification," in *The Trinity and the Kingdom*, 126–28.

4. This Eternal Life

1. Blaise Pascal, *Memorial*, 254: "Eternal joy in return for a single day of toil on earth."

2. John Paul II, *Dominum et Vivificantem*, 18 May 1986, §50, http://w2.vatican.va/content/john-paul-ii/en/encyclicals/documents/hf_jp-ii_enc_18051986_dominum-et-vivificantem.html.

3. Karl Rahner, "Die Christologie innerhalb einer evolutiven Weltanschauung," in *Schriften zur Theologie* V (Zürich: Benziger, 1962), 183–221.

4. In "Ich stehe an Deine Krippe . . . ," Karl Barth expounds and deepens this verse in his teaching on predestination. See *Kirchliche Dogmatik* II/2 (Zürich: EVZ, 1942).

5. Jürgen Moltmann, *In the End—The Beginning: The Life of Hope*, trans. Margaret Kohl (Minneapolis: Fortress Press, 2004).

6. Here I am picking up ideas already published in "Gott und Gaja. Zur Theologie der Erde," *Evangelische Theologie* 53, no. 5 (1993), with contributions by Leonardo Boff, Elisabeth Moltmann-Wendel, and myself. Cf. also Rosemary Radford Ruether, *Gaia and God: An Ecofeminist Theology of Earth Healing* (New York: HarperCollins, 1992); Leonardo Boff, *Von der Würde der Erde* (Düsseldorf: Patmos, 1994); Larry L. Rasmusssen, *Earth Community—Earth Ethics* (Maryknoll, NY: Orbis, 1996); Geiko Müller-Fahrenholz, *Heimat Erde. Christliche Spiritualität unter endzeitlichen Lebensbedingungen* (Gütersloh: Gütersloher, 2013).

7. I have described and discussed the Gaia theory in *Ethik der Hoffnung* (Gütersloh: Gütersloher, 2010).

8. Jürgen Moltmann, "Theologie mit D. Bonhoeffer," in John deGruchy, ed., *D. Bonhoeffers Theologie heute. Ein Weg zwischen Fundamentalismus und Säkularismus* (Gütersloh: Gütersloher, 2009), 17–34, showing the link between Bonhoeffer and Christoph Blumhardt in their reverence for the earth.

9. Rosemary Radford Ruether, *New Woman, New Earth: Sexist Ideologies and Human Liberation* (New York: Seabury, 1975).

10. Richard Bauckham, *Bible and Ecology: Rediscovering the Community of Creation* (London; Darton, Longman, and Todd, 2010), 37, on cosmic humility.

11. Fyodor Dostoevsky, *The Brothers Karamazov* I, book 6. Dostoevsky took over this Orthodox nature-spirituality from Isaac the Syrian.

5. Life in the Wide Space of God's Joy

1. Bernd Janowski, *Die Welt als Schöpfung. Beiträge zur Theologie des Alten Testaments* 4 (Neukirchen: Neukirchener, 2008); Jürgen Moltmann, "Earth Ethics," ch. 10 in *Ethics of Hope*, trans. Margaret Kohl (Minneapolis: Fortress Press, 2012 [2010]).

2. Ernst Bloch put this verse below the picture of his first wife, Else von Stritzki, with whom he had written his book *Geist der Utopie*. She died in 1921. See his *Gedenkbuch* in *Tendenz—Latenz—Utopie* (Frankfurt: Suhrkamp, 1978), 17, 37.

3. Theo Sundermeier, *Religion—was ist das? Religionswissenschaft im theologischen Kontext. Eim studienbuch* (Frankfurt: Lembeck, 2007).

4. William Morrice, *Joy in the New Testament* (Grand Rapids: Eerdmans, 1984); Heinrich Bedford-Strohm, ed., *Glück-Seligkeit. Theologische Rede vom Glück in einer bedrohten Welt* (Neukirchen: Neukirchener, 2011).

5. Ernst Benz, *Heiteres Licht der Herrlichkeit, Die Glaubenswelt der Ostkirche* (Hamburg: Furche, 1962); Nikos A. Nissiotis, "Die österliche Freude als doxologischer Ausdruck des Glaubens," in Hermann Deuser, ed., *Gottes Zukunft—Zukunft der Welt. Festschrift* für Jürgen *Moltmann zum 60. Geburtstag* (Munich: Chr. Kaiser, 1986); Alexander Schmemann, *Aus der Freude leben. Ein Glaubensbuch der orthodoxen Christen* (Olten/Freiburg: Walter, 1974).

6. Julius Schniewind, *Die Freude der Busse* (Göttingen: Vandenhoeck & Ruprecht, 1956 [1940]); Helmut Gollwitzer, *Die Freude Gottes. Einführung in das Lukas-Evangelium* (Berlin: Burckhardthaus, 1940); Otto Weber, *"Weicht, ihr Trauergeister!" Eine Betrachtung über die Freude* (Berlin: Furche, 1938).

7. Blaise Pascal, *Pensées.* Fire visions have belonged to experiences of the Spirit since the first Pentecost (Acts 2:3). Harvey Cox, *Fire from Heaven: The Rise of Pentecostal Spirituality and the Reshaping of Religion in the Twenty-First Century* (Reading, MA: Addison-Wesley, 1995).

8. Helmuth Plessner, "Die Gebärden der Freude," in *Lachen und Weinen. Eine Untersuchung nach den Grenzen menschlichen Verhaltens*, 3d ed. (Bern: Francke, 1961), 93–100.

9. Schiller's "Ode to Joy" is as much influenced by freemason humanism as is Mozart's *Magic Flute.* Freemasonry provided the organizational forms for the bourgeois Enlightenment and revolution.

10. George Steiner has pointed to the link between Dostoevsky and Schiller's "Ode to Joy"; see his *Tolstoy or Dostoevsky: An Essay in the Old Criticism* (New York: Knopf, 1971).

11. Friedrich Nietzsche, "Das trunkene Lied," in *Gedichte und Sprüche* (Leipzig: Kröner, 1916), 141.

12. Paul Ricoeur, "La liberté selon l'éspérance," in *Le conflit des interpretations. Essais d'hermeneutique* I (Paris: Seuil, 1969).

6. Freedom Lived in Solidarity

1. Jürgen Moltmann, "Die Revolutionen der Freiheit," in *Perspektiven der Theologie. Gesammelte Aufsätze* (Munich: Chr. Kaiser/M. Grünewald, 1968), 189–211.

2. For more detail, see Jürgen Moltmann, *God for a Secular Society: The Public Relevance of Theology*, trans. Margaret Kohl (Minneapolis: Fortress Press, 1999 [1997]).

3. Michail Bakunin, *Gott und Staat*, with an introduction by Paul Avrich (Berlin: Kramer, 1995), 51.

4. Ibid., 50, 82.

5. Ibid., 34.

6. Heinrich Meier, *Die Lehre Carl Schmitts. Vier Kapitel zu Unterscheidung politischer Theologie und politischer Philosophie* (Stuttgart/Weimar: Metzler, 1994), 21–24.

7. Ibid., 23.

8. Gustavo Gutiérrez, *A Theology of Liberation: History, Politics, and Salvation* (Maryknoll, NY: Orbis, 1973).

9. Jon Sobrino, *Sterben muss, wer an Götzen rührt. Das Zeugnis der ermordeten Jesuiten in San Salvador* (Fribourg: Exodus, 1990).

10. Lao-Tse, *Tao-Te-Ching*, ch. 25.

11. C. B. Macpherson, *The Political Theory of Possessive Individualism: From Hobbes to Locke* (New York: Oxford University Press, 1962).

12. Augustine, *Enchiridion*, 106.

13. Hannah Arendt, *Vita Activa oder vom tätigen Leben* (Stuttgart: Kohlhammer, 1960, 1977), 168.

14. Ibid., 166.

15. David Riesman, *The Lonely Crowd: Individualism Reconsidered* (New York: Free Press, 1954).

16. Dietrich Bonhoeffer, *Ethics*, trans. Reinhold Krauss, *Dietrich Bonhoeffer Works*, vol. 6, ed. Clifford Green, et al. (Minneapolis: Fortress Press, 2008).

17. For the meaning of the German word, see the article "frei," in Friedrich Kluge, *Etymologisches Wörterbuch der deutschen Sprache*, 9th ed. (Berlin: de Gruyter, 1963)

18. Wolfgang Huber, *Folgen christlicher Freiheit* (Neukirchen: Neukirchener, 1983), esp. 133ff.; idem, *Von der Freiheit. Perspektiven für eine solidarische Welt* (Munich: Beck, 2012).

19. Jürgen Moltmann, *Ethics of Hope*, trans. Margaret Kohl (Minneapolis: Fortress Press, 2012 [2010]).

7. Freedom Experienced in Open Friendship

1. Joan Walsh Anglund, *Ein Freund ist jemand, der dich gern hat* (Olten/ Freiburg: Walter, 1963).

2. Ernst Bloch, *The Principle of Hope* (Oxford: Oxford University Press, 1986).

3. Jürgen Moltmann, *The Way of Jesus Christ: Christology in Messianic Dimensions*, trans. Margaret Kohl (Minneapolis: Fortress Press, 1993 [Ger.: 1989/Eng.: 1990]).

4. Erik Peterson, "Der Gottesfreund. Beiträge zur Geschichte eines religiösen Terminus," *Zeitschrift für Kirchengeschichte* 42, no. 5 (1923): 161–202.

5. Karl Barth, *Kirchliche Dogmatik* III/2. *Die Lehre von der Schöpfung* (Zürich: EVZ, 1948), 323.

6. Anaxagoras. Cf. Jürgen Moltmann, *Experiences in Theology: Ways and Forms of Christian Theology*, trans. Margaret Kohl (Minneapolis: Fortress Press, 2000).

7. For friendship work at the present day, cf. Peter Slade, *Open Friendship in a Closed Society: Mission Mississippi and a Theology of Friendship* (Oxford: Oxford University Press, 2009); Peter R. Gathje, *Sharing the Bread of Life: Hospitality and Resistance at the Open Door Community* (Atlanta: Open Door Community, 2006).

8. For the theological basis of "open friendship," see also Jürgen Moltmann, "Offene Freundschaft," in *Neue Lebensstil. Schritte zur Gemeinde* (Munich: Chr. Kaiser, 1977); idem, *The Spirit of Life: A Universal Affirmation*, trans. Margaret Kohl (Minneapolis: Fortress Press, 1992 [1991]); Elisabeth Moltmann-Wendel, *Wach auf, meine Freundin. Die Wiederkehr der Gottesfreundschaft* (Stuttgart: Kreuz, 2000); Liz Carmichael, *Friendship: Reinterpreting Christian Love* (London: T&T Clark, 2004).

8. The Loved and Loving Life

1. Max Scheler, *Die Stellung des Menschen im Kosmos* (Munich 1946 [1927]), 56. See also Karl Marx, *Die Frühschiften*, ed. Siegfried Landshut (Stuttgart: Kröner, 1953), 275. "The human being as an objective, sensory being . . . is a suffering and a passionate being—suffering because he is aware that he suffers. The passion is the essential power of human nature, which strives energetically towards its objective."

2. Jürgen Moltmann, "Theology of Mystical Experience," in *Experiences of God*, trans. Margaret Kohl (London: SCM Press, 1980 [1979]). Cf. also Ernesto Cardenal, *Das Buch von der Liebe*, with a foreword by Thomas Merton, 4th ed. (Stuttgart: Europäische Bildungsgemeinschaft, 1976). For the whole subject, cf. also Konrad Stock, *Gottes wahre Liebe. Theologische Phänomenologie der Liebe* (Tübingen: Mohr Siebeck, 2000).

3. *Reden des Buddha*, ed. and with an introduction by Helmuth von Glasenapp (Stuttgart: Reclam, 1957).

4. Ibid., 40.

5. Ibid., 42.

6. Ibid., 42, 31.

7. See also Gerhard Marcel Martin's excellent article, "Liebe, Hass, Barmherzigkeit (Karuna). Ein Beitrag zum buddhistisch-christlichen Dialog," *Wege zum Menschen* 65 (2013): 19–32.

8. Aristotle, *Magna Moralia* II, 11. Thus also Confucius's "ethic of reciprocity." Hans O. H. Stange, *Die Weisheit des Konfuzius* (Frankfurt: Insel, 1964), 13.

9. Jürgen Moltmann, *Experiences in Theology*, trans. Margaret Kohl (Minneapolis: Fortress Press, 2000), ch. 2, §4.

10. Johann Wolfgang von Goethe, *Zahme Xenien* III.

11. The classic text is that of the Fourth Vatican Council of 1215: *"Inter creatorem et creaturam non potest tanta similitudo notari, quin inter eas major sit dissimilitudo notanda."* Heinrich Denzinger, *Enchiridion Symbolorum* (Freiburg: Herder, 1947), nr. 4 32; cf. Moltmann, *Experiences in Theology.*

12. Moltmann, *Experiences in Theology.*

13. Bernd Janowski, "Ich will in eurer Mitte wohnen. Struktur und Genese de nachexilischen Shekina Theologie," in *Gottes Gegenwart in Israel. Beiträge zur Theologie des Alten Testaments* (Neukirchen: Neukirchener, 1993), 119–27.

14. Arnold M. Goldberg, *Untersuchungen über die Vorstellung von der Schekhinah in der frühen rabbinischen Literatur—Talmud und Midrasch* (Berlin: de Gruyter, 1969); Franz Rosenzweig, "Die Irrfahrt der Schechina," in *Der Stern der Erlösung* III/3, 3d ed. (Heidelberg: Lambert Schneider, 1954), 192–94. For the comparison between *Shekinah* theology and incarnation theology, cf. Jürgen Moltmann, *Sun of Righteousness, Arise! God's Future for Humanity*, trans. Margaret Kohl (Minneapolis: Fortress Press, 2010 [2009]).

15. Joachim Jeremias, *Der Prophet Hosea*, Das Alte Testament Deutsch 24/1 (Göttingen: Vandenhoeck & Ruprecht, 1983).

16. Richard Bauckham, *Jesus and the God of Israel: God Crucified and Other Studies on the New Testament's Christology of Divine Identity* (Grand Rapids: Eerdmans, 2009). On the whole complex, cf. Hans-Joachim Kraus, *Systematische Theologie im Kontext biblischer Geschichte und Eschatologie* (Neukirchen: Neukirchener, 1983).

17. Klaus Scholtissek, *In ihm sein und bleiben. Die Sprache der Immanenz in den johanneischen Schriften*, Herders biblische Studien 21 (Freiburg: Herder, 2000).

18. G. A. Studdert Kennedy, "The Sorrow of God" (1929), in *After War, Is Faith Possible?* ed. Kerry Walters (Eugene, OR: Wipf & Stock, 2008), 107–112.

19. Lyle Dabney, *Die Kenosis des Geistes. Kontinuität zwischen Schöpfung und Erlösung* (Neukirchen: Neukirchener, 1989).

20. Michael Welker, *Gottes Offenbarung. Christologie, Teil II: Die Auferstehung* (Neukirchen: Neukirchener, 2012), 99–134.

21. Vicco von Bülow drew attention to this correction of Barth by Otto Weber in *Otto Weber (1902–1966). Reformierter Theologe und Kirchenpolitiker* (Göttingen: Vandenhoeck & Ruprecht, 1999), 329. It corresponds to my criticism in *The Trinity and the Kingdom: The Doctrine of God*, trans. Margaret Kohl (Minneapolis: Fortress Press, 1993 [Ger.: 1980/Eng.: 1981]) of Karl Barth's definition of God as "the one who loves in freedom" (Barth, *Kirchliche Dogmatik* I/1: Die Lehre vom Wort Gottes [*Zurich:* Evangelischer Verlag A. G. Zollikon, 1932, 1964], §28).

22. I have written about God and Christ mysticism in "The Theology of Mystical Experience," in *Experiences of God*.

23. On the perichoretic doctrine of the Trinity, cf. Moltmann, *The Trinity and the Kingdom*; on the trinitarian experience of God, the experience

of community, and the experience of space, cf. idem, *Sun of Righteousness, Arise!* On perichoretic thinking, cf. Ciril Sorc, *Entwürfe einer perichoretischen Theologie* (Münster: Lit, 2004); and Daniel Munteanu, "Dreieinigkeit als heimatlicher Raum unserer ewigen Vollendung," in Michael Welker and Miroslav Volf, eds., *Der lebendige Gott als Trinität. Festschrift für Jürgen Moltmann* (Gütersloh: Gütersloher, 2006), 257–78.

24. Axel Honneth, *Der Kampf um Anerkennung. Zur moralischen Grammatik sozialer Konflikte* (Frankfurt: Suhrkamp, 1994). Cf. also Joachim Bauer's psychosomatic investigations, *Prinzip Menschlichkeit. Warum wir von Natur aus kooperieren* (Hamburg: Hoffmann und Campe, 2006); and idem, *Das Gedächtnis des Körpers. Wie Beziehungen und Lebensstile unsere Gene steuern* (Munich: Piper Taschenbuch, 2004).

25. Jürgen Moltmann, "There is enough for everyone," in *The Source of Life: The Holy Spirit and the Theology of Life*, trans. Margaret Kohl (Minneapolis: Fortress Press, 1997).

26. Here I am following Christos Yannaras, *Person and Eros*, trans. Norman Russell (Brookline, Mass.: Holy Cross Orthodox Press, 2007 [1982]), a comparison of the ontology of the Greek Fathers and Western existential philosophy; with reference also to Zenon Tsikrikas, *Der Sohn des Menschen. Theodizee oder Theogonie des christlichen Gottes?* (Paderborn: Schoeningh, 2012). For Maximus Confessor and my previous interest in him, see Brock Bingaman, *All Things New: The Human Calling in Creation within Maximus the Confessor and Jürgen Moltmann's Trinitarian-Christocentric Visions* (Eugene, OR: Pickwick, 2013).

27. Basil, quoted by Yannaras, *Person and Eros*, 93.

28. Didymus, cited in ibid., 94.

29. Ibid., 122.

30. Jan C. Schmidt, "Physikalische Zugänge zur Schönheit," *Evangelium und Wissenschaft* 31 (2010): 2–17.

31. Yannaras, *Person and Eros*, 122n.152.

32. Ibid., 122–23. The English translation is based on Yannaras's German rendering of the Greek text.

9. A Spirituality of the Senses

1. This chapter is based on a lecture held during the Festivalfilosophia in Modena, Italy, on 17 September 2008.

2. Jürgen Moltmann, "Grundzüge mystischer Theologie bei Gerhard Tersteegen," *Evangelische Theologie* 16, no. 2 (1956): 205–224; idem, "Theology of Mystical Experience," in *Experiences of God*, trans. Margaret Kohl (London: SCM Press, 1980 [1979]), 55–80.

3. Jürgen Moltmann, "Gott und die Seele—Gott und die Sinne," in Bernd Janowski and Christoph Schwöbel, eds., *Gott—Seele—Welt. Beiträge zur Rede von der Seele* (Neukirchen: Neukirchen-Vluyn, 2013), 71–95.

4. Dietrich Bonhoeffer, letter to Eberhard Bethge, Tegel, 30 June and 1 July 1944, in John W. deGruchy, ed., *Letters and Papers from Prison*, trans. Isabel Best, et al., *Dietrich Bonhoeffer Works*, vol. 8 (Minneapolis: Fortress Press, 2009), 449.

5. Hans-Walter Wolff, *Anthropology of the Old Testament*, trans. Margaret Kohl (Philadelphia: Fortress Press, 1974).

6. Karl-Adolf Bauer, *Leiblichkeit—das Ende aller Werke Gottes. Die Bedeutung der Leiblichkeit bei Paulus.* Studien zum NT 4 (Gütersloh: Mohn, 1971).

7. Helmuth Plessner, *Conditio Humana. Einleitung zur Prophylaen-Weltgeschichte* (Pfullingen: Günther Neske, 1964).

8. See ch. 3, above.

9. Francis of Assisi, "Canticle of Brother Sun": "Blessed be thou, Lord, with all the creatures you have created, above all Sister Sun . . . blessed be thou Lord, through Brother Moon and stars . . . Blessed be thou, Lord, through Brother Wind, . . . through Sister Water . . . through Brother Fire . . . Through our sister Mother Earth . . ."

10. In this section I am taking over observations and insights from Ingrid Riedel, *Geschmack am Leben finden. Eine Entdeckungsreise mit allen Sinnen* (Freiburg: Herder, 2004).

11. Susanne Kahl-Passoth, *Nimmt das denn nie eine Ende? Mit der Trauer leben lernen* (Gütersloh: Gütersloher, 1992).

12. Jürgen Moltmann, *A Broad Place: An Autobiography*, trans. Margaret Kohl (Minneapolis: Fortress Press, 2008 [Ger.: 2006/Eng.: 2007]).

13. Wolf Biermann, *Preussischer Ikarus. Lieder/Balladen/Gedichte/Prosa* (Darmstadt: Kiepenheuer und Witsch, 1978), III:80.

14. Manfred Spitzer, *Digitale Demenz. Wie wir uns und unsere Kinder um den Verstand bringen* (Munich: Droemer, 2012).

15. Jürgen Moltmann, "What are we doing when we pray?," in *The Source of Life: The Holy Spirit and the Theology of Life*, trans. Margaret Kohl

(Minneapolis: Fortress Press, 1997 [Ger: 1991/Eng.: 1992]); ibid., *In the End—the Beginning: The Life of Hope*, trans. Margaret Kohl (Minneapolis: Fortress Press, 2004).

16. On the concept of "numbing," cf. Robert Jay Lifton, *The Life of the Self: Toward a New Psychology* (New York: Simon & Schuster, 1976); Geiko Müller-Fahrenholz, *Erwecke die Welt. Unser Glaube an Gottes Geist in dieser bedrohten Zeit* (Gütersloh: Gütersloher, 1993).

17. Johann Baptist Metz, *Mystik der offenen Augen. Wenn Spiritualität aufbricht* (Freiburg: Herder, 2011), 47ff.: "Wachen, aufwachen, die Augen öffnen . . ."

18. Heraclitus, fragment 89 in Wilhelm Capelle, *Die Vorsokratiker. Fragmente und Quellenberichte* (Berlin: Akademie Verlag, 1958), 132.

10. Hoping and Thinking

1. Jürgen Moltmann, *Theologie der Hoffnung. Untersuchungen zur Begründung und zu den Konsequenzen einer christlichen Eschatologie*, 14th ed. (Gütersloh: Gütersloher, 2005 [1964]). Translations have been made into English, Dutch, French, Spanish, Portuguese, Italian, Serbocroat, Japanese, Korean, and Chinese.

2. Ernst Bloch, *Das Prinzip Hoffnung* (Frankfurt: Suhrkamp, 1961).

3. Cf. Jürgen Moltmann, *The Coming of God: Christian Eschatology*, trans. Margaret Kohl (Minneapolis: Fortress Press, 1996 [1995]).

4. Joachim Fest, *Der zerstörte Traum. Vom Ende des utopischen Zeitalters* (Berlin: Siedler, 1991).

5. Francis Fukuyama, "The End of History?" in *The National Interest* 16 (1989): 3–18.

6. Ernst Bloch, *Geist der Utopie* (Munich: Duncker & Humblot, 1918, 1923).

7. Max Horkheimer, *Die Sehnsucht nach dem ganz anderen. Ein Interview mit Kommentar von H. Gumnior* (Hamburg: Furche, 1970), 61.

8. Ernst Bloch, *Thomas Münzer als Theologe der Revolution* (Frankfurt: Suhrkamp, 1976 [1921]), 94.

9. Fritz Gerlich, *Der Kommunismus als Lehre vom Tausendjährigen Reich* (Munich: Bruckmann, 1920). Here the secularization of the hope for the kingdom of God in the 18th and 19th century is exactly described, historically.

10. Moltmann, "The Kingdom of God—Historical Eschatology," in *The Coming of God*, 129–255. For the "forward-looking hope," see also Leonhard Ragaz, *Der Kampf um das Reich Gottes in Blumhardt, Vater und Sohn—und weiter* (Munich/Leipzig: Rotapfel, 1922).

11. Ernst Bloch, *Atheismus im Christentum. Zur Religion des Exodus und des Reiches* (Frankfurt: Suhrkamp, 1968), 17: "Decisive is a transscending without transcendence."

12. Michael Eckert, *Transzendieren und immanente Transzendenz. Die Transformation der traditionellen Zwei-Welten-Theorie von Transzendenz und Immanenz in Blochs Zwei-Welten-Theorie* (Freiburg: Wien, 1981); cf. also Henning Tegtmeyer, "Ernst Bloch und der philosophische Theismus," in Susanne Herrmann-Sinai and Henning Tegtmeyer, eds., *Metaphysik der Hoffnung. Ernst Bloch als Denker des Humanen,* Leipziger Schriften zur Philosophie 22 (Leipzig: Leipziger, 2012), 103–116.

13. Jürgen Moltmann, "Die Kategorie *Novum* in der christlichen Theologie," in Siegfried Unseld, ed., *Ernst Bloch zu ehren* (Frankfurt: Suhrkamp, 1965), 243–63.

14. G. W. F. Hegel, *Gundlinien der Philosophie des Rechts* (1821), Vorrede XXIV.

15. Reinhart Koselleck, *Vergangene Zukunft. Zur Semantiik geschichtlicher Zeiten* (Frankfurt: Suhrkamp, 1979).

16. Wolfgang Weidlich, "Transzendenz und Immanenz—oder Gott und die Welt. Können wir ihr Verhältnis verstehen?" in *Glauben und Denken. Jahrbuch der Karl-Heim-Gesellschaft* 22 (2009): 209: "The openness in the complexity, on the other hand, consists in the potential limitlessness of reality, of which only a very small part is realized. The best example is the evolution of life. Although a great diversity of living things exists, the diversity of possible but no longer, or not yet, realized forms of life is immensely much greater. That means that the realized reality is only a small part of the potential reality, what one might call its potential shell of reality. The relation between realized and potential reality is a sign of the way immanent reality is embedded in transcendence." Weidlich is a physicist.

17. Martin Heidegger, *Sein und Zeit*, 8th ed. (Tübingen: Niemeyer, 1957 [1926]).

18. Søren Kierkegaard, *Der Begriff der Angst* (1844).

19. Jürgen Moltmann, *Das Geheimnis der Vergangenheit* (Neukirchen: Neukirchener, 2012).

20. Immanuel Kant, *Kritik der reinen Vernunft*. Transzendental Analytik §24.

21. Barack Obama, *The Audacity of Hope: Thoughts on Reclaiming the American Dream* (New York: Random House, 2006).

22. Ernst Käsemann, *Exegetische Versuche und Besinnungen,* vol. 2 (Göttingen: Vandenhoeck & Ruprecht, 1964), 127, 128, 130. Karl Barth already used the term. See *"Kirche und Kultur"* (1926), in *Die Theologie und die Kirche* (Munich: Chr. Kaiser, 1928), 384: "With this, the eschatological proviso [*Vorbehalt*], it counters society . . ."

11. Life: A Never-Ending Festival

1. Friedrich Nietzsche, *Nachgelassene Fragmente Herbst 1887*, in *Sämtliche Werke. Kritische Studienausgabe* (Munich: de Gruyter, 1980), 12:553.

2. Athanasius, PG 28, 1061b. I am indebted to Dr. Petros Giatzakis for this reference.

3. For the present theological discussion about Christ's resurrection, cf. now Michael Welker's admirable study, *Gottes Offenbarung. Christologie* (Neukirchen: Neukirchener, 2012), 99–134.

4. Hugo Rahner, "Das himmlische Tanzspiel," in *Der spielende Mensch* (Einsiedeln: Johannes Verlag, 1972), 59–79.

5. Jürgen Moltmann, "Totentänze—Auferstehungstanz," in Jürgen Moltmann and Theo Sundermeier, *Totentänze. Tanz des Lebens* (Frankfurt: Lembeck, 2006). Sidney Carter's well-known song derives from an old American Shaker song, "I used to dance before the Lord"; text in ibid., 33.

6. *Johannes-Akten*, in Wilhelm Schneemelcher, ed., in *Neutestamentliche Apokryphen*, vol. 2 (Tübingen: Mohr Siebeck, 1964), 155.

7. See Dumitru Staniloae, *Orthodoxe Dogmatik*, vol. 2 (Gütersloh: Gütersloher, 1990), 123–29.

8. Here I am taking up again thoughts that I already expressed in *The Passion for Life: A Messianic Lifestyle*, trans. M. Douglas Meeks (Philadelphia: Fortress Press, 1978).

9. Jacqueline Bussie, *The Laughter of the Oppressed: Ethical Resistance in Wiesel, Morison, and Ende* (New York: Bloomsbury T&T Clark, 2007).

10. I maintained this thesis in *Theology of Play*, trans. Robert E. Neale (New York: Harper & Row, 1972).

11. Mihaly Csikszentmihalyi, *Flow—der Weg zum Glück* (Freiburg: Herder, 2010).

12. "Confucius," in *Die Weisheit des Konfuzius*, trans. and introduction by Hans O. H. Stange (Frankfurt: Insel, 1964), 13.

13. I have treated this in more detail in *Das Geheimnis der Vergangenheit. Erinnern—Vergessen—Entschuldigen—Vergeben—Loslassen—Anfangen* (Neukirchen: Neukirchener, 2012), 81–123. Cf. also J. Christoph Arnold, *Wer vergibt, heilt auch sich selbst* (Freiburg: Kreuz, 2010); Aaron Lazare, *On Apology* (New York: Oxford University Press, 2004); Geiko Müller-Fahrenholz, *Vergebung macht frei. Vorschläge für eine Theologie der Versöhnung* (Frankfurt: Lembeck, 1996).

14. Jürgen Moltmann, "What Are We Doing when We Pray?" ch. 11 in *The Source of Life: The Holy Spirit and the Theology of Life*, trans. Margaret Kohl (Minneapolis: Fortress Press, 1997). In what follows I am taking up these ideas once more and am developing them further.

15. Ernst Käsemann, *An die Römer.* Handbuch zum Neuen Testament 8a,(Tübingen: Mohr, 1973).

16. Karl Marx, *Die Frühschriften*, 208. The Pauline "sighings of creation" actually contributed to his concept of matter, when he talked about the "torment of matter," meaning by that "movement as the spirit of life"; cf. ibid., 330.

17. Daniel W. Hardy and David F. Ford, *Jubilate: Theology in Praise* (London: Darton, Longman & Todd, 1984).

18. F. J. J. Buytendijk, *Wesen und Sinn des Spiels* (Berlin: Wolff, 1934); cf. also Johan Huizinga, *Homo ludens. Vom Ursprung der Kultur im Spiel* (Hamburg: Rowohlt, 1956); Adolf Portmann, *Zoologie und das neue Bild des Menschen* (Hamburg: Rowohlt, 1951).

19. Quoted in Moltmann, *Theology of Play.*

20. Cf. Günter Thomas's excellent contribution, "Die Affizierbarkeit Gottes im Gebet," in Alexandra Grund, et al., eds., *Ich will dir danken unter den Völkern. Festschrift für Bernd Janowski* (Gütersloh: Gütersloher, 2013), 709–713, with references to Schleiermacher, Barth, and the more recent theological discussion about prayer.

CPSIA information can be obtained
at www.ICGtesting.com
Printed in the USA
BVHW030054230722
642818BV00018B/274